The People's Dictatorship

D1239519

In this up-to-date, succinct, and highly readable volume, Alan E. Steinweis presents a new synthesis of the origins, development, and downfall of Nazi Germany. After tracing the intellectual and cultural origins of Nazi ideology, the book recounts the rise and eventual victory of the Nazi movement against the background of the struggling Weimar Republic. The book details the rapid transformation of Germany into a dictatorship, focusing on the interplay of Nazi violence and the readiness of Germans to accommodate themselves to the new regime. Steinweis chronicles Nazi efforts to transform German society into a so-called People's Community, imbued with hyper-nationalism, an authoritarian spirit, Nazi racial doctrine, and antisemitism. The result was less a People's Community than what Steinweis calls a People's Dictatorship – a repressive regime that acted brutally toward the targets of its persecution, its internal opponents, and its foreign enemies even as it enjoyed support across much of German society.

Alan E. Steinweis is Professor of History and Raul Hilberg Distinguished Professor of Holocaust Studies, University of Vermont. He is the author of three previous books about Nazi Germany: *Art, Ideology, and Economics in Nazi Germany: The Reich Chambers of Music, Theater, and the Visual Arts* (1993); *Studying the Jew: Scholarly Antisemitism in Nazi Germany* (2006); and *Kristallnacht 1938* (2009). He has been a visiting fellow at the US Holocaust Memorial Museum and the University of Oxford, and has held visiting professorships at the Universities of Hanover, Heidelberg, Frankfurt, Munich, and Augsburg.

NEW APPROACHES TO EUROPEAN HISTORY

New Approaches to European History is an important textbook series, which provides concise but authoritative surveys of major themes and problems in European history since the Renaissance. Written at a level and length accessible to advanced school students and undergraduates, each book in the series addresses topics or themes that students of European history encounter daily: the series embraces both some of the more 'traditional' subjects of study and those cultural and social issues to which increasing numbers of school and college courses are devoted. A particular effort is made to consider the wider international implications of the subject under scrutiny.

To aid the student reader, scholarly apparatus and annotation is light, but each work has full supplementary bibliographies and notes for further reading: where appropriate, chronologies, maps, diagrams, and other illustrative material are also provided.

For a complete list of titles published in the series, please see:
www.cambridge.org/newapproaches

The People's Dictatorship

A History of Nazi Germany

Alan E. Steinweis

University of Vermont

Shaftesbury Road, Cambridge CB2 8EA, United Kingdom

One Liberty Plaza, 20th Floor, New York, NY 10006, USA

477 Williamstown Road, Port Melbourne, VIC 3207, Australia

314–321, 3rd Floor, Plot 3, Splendor Forum, Jasola District Centre,
New Delhi – 110025, India

103 Penang Road, #05–06/07, Visioncrest Commercial, Singapore 238467

Cambridge University Press is part of Cambridge University Press & Assessment,
a department of the University of Cambridge.

We share the University's mission to contribute to society through the pursuit of
education, learning and research at the highest international levels of excellence.

www.cambridge.org
Information on this title: www.cambridge.org/highereducation/isbn/9781107012363

DOI: 10.1017/9780511998140

© Alan E. Steinweis 2023

First published 2023

Printed in the United Kingdom by TJ Books Limited, Padstow, Cornwall

A catalogue record for this publication is available from the British Library.

Library of Congress Cataloging-in-Publication Data
Names: Steinweis, Alan E., author.
Title: The people's dictatorship : a history of Nazi Germany / Alan E. Steinweis.
Other titles: History of Nazi Germany
Description: Cambridge, United Kingdom ; New York, NY : Cambridge
University Press, [2023] | Series: New approaches to European history |
Includes bibliographical references and index.
Identifiers: LCCN 2022029803 | ISBN 9781107012363 (hardback) |
ISBN 9780511998140 (ebook)
Subjects: LCSH: Germany – Politics and government – 1918–1933. |
Germany – Politics and government – 1933–1945. | National socialism. |
Hitler, Adolf, 1889–1945.
Classification: LCC DD240 .S7616 2023 | DDC 943.085–dc23/eng/20220629
LC record available at https://lccn.loc.gov/2022029803

ISBN 978-1-107-01236-3 Hardback
ISBN 978-1-107-65284-2 Paperback

Additional resources for this publication at www.cambridge.org/steinweis.

In memory of Richard S. Levy and Jürgen Zarusky

Contents

Illustrations

Maps

Acknowledgements

I am grateful to multiple institutions and colleagues for supporting my work on this book. At the University of Vermont (UVM), the Department of History and the Miller Center for Holocaust Studies have provided an atmosphere very conducive to research, reflection, and writing. I have profited from the intellectual guidance of my UVM colleagues Jonathan Huener and Frank Nicosia in particular. A sabbatical from UVM released me from my teaching and service commitments for a year, enabling me to work on this project full time. I enjoyed an additional semester devoted entirely to this project while holding the Ina Levine Senior Invitational Scholar position at the United States Holocaust Memorial Museum in Washington, DC. I am very grateful for the assistance and advice received from the academic staff and librarians at the Museum's Center for Advanced Holocaust Studies. I completed much of the work on this book in the reading room of the Leibniz Institute for Contemporary History in Munich. It would be difficult to imagine a more hospitable venue for conducting research on a book of this kind. At Cambridge University Press, Michael Watson first proposed that I undertake this project, and Elizabeth Friend-Smith displayed great patience in helping me bring it to fruition. A reader commissioned by Cambridge provided a valuable critique of an earlier version of the manuscript, as did Peter Hayes and Geoffrey Giles, friends and colleagues of great erudition. I am grateful to Christopher Jackson for his meticulous copy-editing and to Lucy Edwards for coordinating the preparation of the final text, the figures, and the index. Timber Wright, my former student at UVM, designed and produced the three excellent maps.

I want to acknowledge the great intellectual debt I owe to my teachers Gerhard L. Weinberg, Konrad H. Jarausch, Carole Fink, and George H. Stein. My understanding of the history of Nazi Germany has benefitted greatly from my personal friendships with Annette Eberle, Winfried Süß, Christiane Kuller, and Dietmar Süß. Two additional close friends from whom I learned much and from whose examples I drew inspiration,

Jürgen Zarusky and Richard S. Levy, passed away as I was working toward the completion of this book. My greatest debt is to my wife and UVM colleague Susanna Schrafstetter, whose intellectual and emotional support have provided the foundation for my scholarly career over the past two decades.

Abbreviations

ADGB	Allgemeiner deutscher Gewerkschaftsbund (General German Trade Union Federation)
BdM	Bund deutscher Mädel (League of German Girls)
DAF	Deutsche Arbeitsfront (German Labor Front)
DAP	Deutsche Arbeiterpartei (German Workers' Party)
DDP	Deutsche Demokratische Partei (German Democratic Party)
DNVP	Deutschnationaler Volkspartei (German National People's Party)
DVP	Deutsche Volkspartei (German People's Party)
Gestapo	Geheime Staatspolizei (Secret State Police)
KdF	Kraft durch Freude (Strength through Joy)
KPD	Kommunistische Partei Deutschlands (Communist Party of Germany)
NSBO	Nationalsozialistische Betriebszellenorganisation (National Socialist Factory Cell Organization)
NSDAP	Nationalsozialistische Deutsche Arbeiterpartei (National Socialist German Workers' Party)
SA	Sturmabteilung (Storm Detachment)
SD	Sicherheitsdienst (Security Service)
SPD	Sozialdemokratische Partei Deutschlands (Social Democratic Party of Germany)
SS	Schutzstaffel (Protection Squadron)

Introduction

Nazi Germany continues to fascinate and horrify more than three-quarters of a century after its demise. There are many reasons for the sustained interest in the subject, but the basic reason is a simple one. Students and other readers of history want to understand how a nation known for its formidable accomplishments in science, technology, philosophy, art, music, and literature came under the control of a violent regime with an agenda of persecution and conquest. This question has generated an immense body of scholarship in multiple languages over many decades. The first studies appeared in the 1930s, when the Nazi regime was still in power and its end could not yet be foreseen. After 1945, as the Nazi regime receded into the past, attention did not diminish but rather increased. While a non-specialist might be tempted to think that research on the subject would have by now been exhausted, important new scholarship continues to appear on a regular basis, much of it produced by young German historians. While much of the recent work has focused on the Holocaust and other dimensions of Nazi persecution, other studies have rounded out our knowledge of how millions of ordinary Germans experienced Nazi rule as women, men, children, teenagers, soldiers, workers, committed Nazis, and members of the resistance.

Precisely because the history of Nazi Germany continues to be an active area of research, there is a periodic need for an up-to-date general history that synthesizes the latest findings and makes them accessible to students and lay readers. That is the purpose of the present volume. It offers an historical narrative that draws heavily on recent research, much of which has appeared only in German. But it also relies on older scholarship, which has by no means been rendered obsolete by the more recent research. For example, this book's analysis of the political and constitutional weaknesses of the Weimar Republic draws to a significant degree from 1960s-era scholarship even while historians have continued to produce important new work about that subject. Similarly, its examination of the social composition of the Nazi Party's membership and voters is based on the findings of social science–inspired quantitative studies that appeared in the 1980s. At the same time, its discussions of gender, sexuality, the small rituals of everyday life, and the German occupation of Eastern Europe depend on research of much more recent vintage. Few historical topics have been researched as closely as Nazi Germany, and the depth of understanding that has been reached is the cumulative achievement of scholars in multiple countries working over several generations.

Much recent scholarship about the Third Reich has been framed around the notion of the People's Community (*Volksgemeinschaft*). This concept, which antedated the Nazi era, but which the Nazi movement appropriated and bent to its purposes as both an ideological construct and a propaganda catchphrase, imagined the German nation as a racially exclusive, harmonious entity united under authoritarian leadership.[1] In refuting the claims of the regime's own propaganda that Nazism had succeeded in fostering this highly vaunted "community," some historians have pointed to the ample evidence of dissent within the German population, and to the elaborate apparatus of terror that was set in place after 1933 to deter criticism and punish non-compliance. It is nonetheless undeniable that the Nazi regime enjoyed a good deal of popular legitimacy even in circles where specific elements of policy were resented. This legitimacy was derived from the reassertion of Germany as a great power, the attainment of full employment, the establishment of political stability, the charisma of the leader, and, after 1939, the rallying effects of war. Among the most important and difficult tasks facing historians of Nazi Germany is the challenge of striking the proper balance between legitimacy and coercion. A central interpretive thrust of this book will be to recognize the popular legitimacy of Nazi rule in German society, but at the same time to acknowledge the complexity of contemporaneous German opinions and responses, which included persistent opposition in some quarters. This study will also endeavor to restore an emphasis on the Nazi regime's reliance on violence and intimidation for the maintenance of its rule inside Germany. Such an emphasis, which was common in the immediate post-1945 period, has diminished considerably as a result of the more recent "voluntarist turn" (to use Neil Gregor's term)[2] taken by historians. The complex interplay between legitimacy and coercion in the relationship between the Nazi regime and the German people is reflected in the main title of this book, *The People's Dictatorship*, a concept designed to capture the paradox of a repressive authoritarian regime with significant popular support. It possesses the additional advantage of not having been a Nazi slogan.

Rather than privileging high politics, social history, or any other single perspective, this book integrates multiple approaches to historical analysis into a single narrative. High politics is combined with social history, cultural history, and economic history. Hitler and other Nazi leaders feature prominently, but so do the "ordinary" Germans, whose reactions ranged across a broad spectrum of behaviors. In understanding the so-called Final Solution, for example, it is important to look not only at Hitler, who acted as the prime mover behind the mass murder, but also at the low-ranking Germans who carried out the killing.

Nazism was an agent and catalyst of radical transformation. In some respects (e.g., technological promotion) it was modern; in others (e.g., women's reproductive freedom) it was retrogressive. It was not merely an effort to tinker with a system that had collapsed or failed, or to restore power to traditional elites. It had racist–utopian aspirations. It was predicated on a biological and racist understanding of human nature that was regarded as the absolute truth by its adherents. The realization of the utopian vision, they also understood, could be attained only by means of territorial conquest and an apocalyptic confrontation with forces such as "World Jewry," Communism, and liberalism, which, they believed, were determined to destroy Germany.

Once in power, the Nazi movement employed the tools at its disposal – propaganda, mass mobilization, coercion, and terror – to impose its utopian vision on German society. The reality of "Nazi Germany" – the regime and the social order that pertained in Germany between January 1933 and May 1945 – was by no means identical with this utopian vision. It was instead the product of the clash of this vision with a tradition-bound society in which sympathy for Nazism, while considerable, was limited and uneven. Thus, Nazi society – or, more precisely formulated, German society under Nazi rule – was never static, but always in the process of becoming. Germany never became the People's Community envisaged by Nazi true believers (and projected in official propaganda). On the other hand, the degree of transformation in a few short years was indeed remarkable. This holds true also for the dramatic turnaround of Germany's international situation between 1933 and 1939. The Nazi regime did, in fact, revolutionize German society in important respects within a very short span of time. Despite internal opposition, the regime achieved considerable stability as a dictatorship backed by popular consensus and defended by a system of coercion and terror. In the end, this system was destroyed not by the Germans themselves but by the military force brought to bear by a broad coalition of nations.

This book narrates its story in ten chapters. Chapter 1 examines the ideology of Nazism – or National Socialism, as it was officially known – as the product of numerous cultural, intellectual, and sociological currents, in some cases, such as that of antisemitism, dating back centuries.

Chapter 2 describes the origins of the Nazi movement within the context of post–World War I Germany, analyzing its structure, tactics, and attractions to specific segments of German society. The political victory of Nazism in Germany in 1933 is explained against the background of the history of the Weimar Republic, the replacement of which by a Nazi regime was not inevitable. Chapter 3 explains how Adolf Hitler and his movement rapidly transformed the country into a one-party dictatorship and subjected German society to a process of political and ideological "coordination" in 1933 and 1934. Nazi ideas about economics, although usually subordinated to political and ideological priorities, deeply influenced the regime's approach to Germany's social problems. Chapter 4 shows how the regime implemented a system of managed capitalism, the goal of which was to preserve the private ownership of economic assets while imposing a truce between capital and labor. The Nazi regime attempted to tame the German working class through a carrot-and-stick approach, destroying the independent labor movement, on the one hand, while coopting workers with certain improvements, on the other. In the agricultural sector, the imposition of an "Ordered Market" limited the freedom of farmers but stabilized their incomes. Members of the German middle classes and German professionals also profited from the country's general economic recovery, which was induced in large part by rearmament.

Chapter 5, which assesses the experiences of Germans under Nazism through the late 1930s, is organized around specific segments of German society such as women, men, youth, and university students. This chapter also examines how policies targeted at women, men, and youth were shaped by Nazi conceptions of femininity and masculinity, and by a strongly gendered understanding of economic roles. Nazism found enthusiastic followers among all the aforementioned groups, most notably among highly impressionable children and youths. Even if many Germans never bought into the notion of a People's Community, the majority came to regard the Nazi regime as legitimate and effective. Chapter 6 analyzes the Nazi regime's apparatus of coercion, which ranged from institutions like the secret police and concentration camps to everyday rituals, such as the Hitler salute, which enforced and signaled conformity. Forms of dissent and resistance are discussed here as well. This chapter also deals in some depth with the Nazi regime's policies targeted at Jews and other so-called aliens, as well as with eugenically motivated mass sterilization of mentally disabled Germans. While the Nazi regime's policies of racial persecution are the subject of Chapter 6, it should be emphasized that antisemitism and other policies based on Nazi racism are themes interwoven through the entire text of the book.

Chapters 7 through 10 deal with Nazi Germany during World War II. In these chapters, the book integrates military developments, the German "home front," and German crimes in occupied Europe, including the mass murder of the Jews, into a single narrative. While considerable emphasis is given to the Holocaust, that crime is explained as part and parcel of the Nazi regime's attempt to colonize Europe. This program of conquest ultimately failed in the face of an alliance capable of mobilizing greater economic and military resources than Germany could. Chapter 7 begins by outlining Hitler's views on international affairs and his methods for pursuing his goals, moves on to a summary of the major diplomatic events of the late 1930s, and concludes by describing the key military developments of the initial phase of the war, through 1941, and the reactions to them in German society. Chapter 8 addresses the imperial system erected by Nazi Germany on the European continent west of the Soviet Union through June 1941, focusing on the German exploitation of foreign labor, the intensification and geographical expansion of anti-Jewish measures, and the mass murder of disabled Germans. Chapter 9 follows World War II into its next phase, detailing the German invasion of the Soviet Union in June 1941 and the campaign of annihilation, including the Final Solution, that followed. Chapter 10 describes life on the German "home front," particularly with regard to the mobilization for "Total War" in 1943 after the defeat at Stalingrad and to the impact of Allied bombing on everyday life and on German morale. This chapter also discusses several important instances of resistance to Nazi rule within German society during the war. Finally, Chapter 10 describes the end phase of the Nazi regime in 1944 and 1945. The extraordinary violence of this period took several forms: military invasion by foreign armies; the destruction of German cities from the air; and vengeful attacks by Germans on foreign laborers living in their midst, as well as on Germans who were seen as defeatist. The so-called Third Reich ended with an epidemic of suicides by Germans who could not imagine a future without Nazism.

For readers approaching the serious study of Nazism for the first time, one of the most important purposes this book can fulfill is to demythologize its subject. In popular culture, Nazism has become a shorthand expression for the apotheosis of evil, a theme for sensationalist fantasy fiction and cinema, and an often recklessly levelled political accusation.[3] Readers of this book might well have encountered the concept more frequently in one of these contexts than they have in their readings about the history of Germany and Europe during the first half of the twentieth century. Moreover, the subject, even when approached earnestly, is often framed as a story of a brainwashed nation or as an overly simplified morality tale, one in which a large and powerful country, reeling from defeat, high unemployment, and political instability, knowingly embraced the dark side in a kind of Faustian bargain. The reality, however, was far more complex. Many millions of Germans did not become blind followers of Nazism, and millions of those who did support Nazism did not understand themselves as making a moral compromise. Fanatical nationalism, antisemitism, and material self-interest undoubtedly accounted for a great deal of Nazism's support, but Germans were also influenced by fear of their own government, a sincere idealism for overcoming the social and class divisions of the past, and a sense of patriotism and social solidarity during wartime. We need to investigate what Nazism and war meant to Germans, and what personal predicaments they faced as they tried to sort through the choices available to them. None of this is intended to retroactively justify decisions and sentiments that we can now recognize as foolish, cowardly, or ethically questionable. The task before us is not to condemn, but to explain how and why so many Germans became implicated in a hubristic and ultimately destructive national project.

1   The Idea of Nazism

On November 9, 1923, a coalition of right-wing opponents of the Weimar Republic attempted to seize power in Munich, the capital city of the German state of Bavaria. Among the leaders of this attempted coup d'état (*Putsch* in German) was Adolf Hitler, the head of the National Socialist German Workers' Party (NSDAP) – the Nazi Party – a relatively small ultra-nationalist, racist, antisemitic movement dedicated to violent revolution. Their intention was, first, to consolidate power in Munich and then, from there, to inspire and lead a massive March on Berlin, patterned on Mussolini's March on Rome during the previous year. The ultimate goal was to overthrow the Weimar Republic, the parliamentary democracy that had replaced the German Empire at the end of World War I, and which was seen by its right-wing critics as having betrayed the interests of the German Fatherland. As is well known, this "Beer Hall Putsch" (known to Germans as the *Hitler-Putsch*) failed miserably. Hitler was arrested, prosecuted, and thrown into prison.

Few Germans or foreign observers imagined at the time that Hitler would later become a figure of world-historical importance, a dictator of almost incomprehensible ruthlessness, and the author of one of history's greatest mass murders. Born in 1889 in Austria, Hitler had fought in the Bavarian army in World War I and was drawn into right-wing politics in the turbulent atmosphere of post-war Munich. Founded in 1919, the Nazi Party was but one of a large number of right-radical organizations that had emerged in response to the immediate consequences of Germany's defeat in World War I. Hitler was not the founder of the Nazi Party, but he became its dominant figure soon after joining it. From that point onward, Hitler's political biography became inextricably intertwined with the development of Nazism as both a political movement and as an ideology.

While Fascist movements with similar aims were active and, in some cases, eventually rose to power in other countries, Nazism – or National Socialism, as it was, and continues to be, known in Germany – embodied a unique ideological and political synthesis. To understand Nazism as an historical phenomenon, we must isolate it from the mythologies, pop-cultural memes, and presentist political usages that often dominate popular perceptions of the subject. We must also remind ourselves that there was a good deal more to the history of Nazism than the racially motivated persecutions and mass atrocities collectively referred to as "the Holocaust," a subject that has justifiably received a tremendous amount of attention in recent years, but which has also overshadowed other issues of major historical importance. Racial antisemitism was a linchpin of Nazism, but by no means the entirety of its ideology and program.

The genealogy of the ideas at the core of Nazism reaches back into earlier centuries and extends well beyond the borders of modern Germany. Some historians have questioned whether Nazism actually possessed anything amounting to an ideology or a worldview, contrasting it with the various forms of Communism, the doctrinal aspects of which had been much more fully elaborated by its leadership and intelligentsia. Some of the early, Marxist-inspired scholarship on Nazism failed to take seriously the doctrines propagated by the Nazi Party and regime, regarding Nazism's ideological self-descriptions as smokescreens for its true purpose and intention, namely the maintenance of the capitalist order.[1] Similarly, some biographers of Hitler portrayed their subject as a traditional tyrant for whom ideology was unimportant or merely an instrument for the exercise of power.[2] But even if we accept the proposition that Nazism lacked the ideological coherence and intellectual depth of, say, Marxism-Leninism, historians have identified a cluster of ideas and a unique convergence of intellectual streams that defined Nazism and set it apart from contemporaneous political movements.

Nazism pointedly and proudly rejected values that tend to be celebrated in the liberal-democratic West of our own day. For some readers of this book – students, for example, at colleges and universities – a significant leap of imagination might be required in order to comprehend Nazism's self-image. Nazism regarded human equality not merely as an unattainable chimera, but as a misguided aspiration and a violation of a natural order in which culture and behavior are reducible almost entirely to heredity. It boasted of the superiority of some human groups over others, and openly espoused hatred toward one particular minority group. It romanticized violence, denigrating the weak and the disabled. It celebrated authoritarian leadership as the instinctive and authentic system of government, disparaging liberalism and democracy as artificial practices that introduce weakness, chaos, and degeneracy into a society.

A Racial View of Humanity

At the very core of the Nazi worldview lay the concept of race, a word that was employed literally, in its biological sense, and not merely as a metaphor for population groups defined in ethnic or national terms. (The German word *Rasse* has historically been applied to supposed human races, but also means "breed" when applied to dogs, cats, and horses.) Hitler's earliest political speeches and writings from 1919 and 1920 are infused with the idea of human races as defined by "blood" and heredity. The official program of the Nazi Party, issued in February 1920, stipulated that "only those of German blood, whatever their creed, may be members of the [German] nation." In the first volume of his political autobiography, *Mein Kampf*, published in 1925 (see Figure 1.1), Hitler laid out his racist understanding of history and human affairs in a chapter titled "Volk and Race." In the political rhetoric of Nazism, these two terms were often employed interchangeably (even though the more intellectually serious Nazi racial theorists insisted on a distinction between the two, according to which a Volk consisted of a mixture of races).[3] The German cognate for the English "folk," and idiomatic equivalent of the English collective singular noun "the people," Volk had a rich etymology that made it especially useful for Nazism. The term came into widespread use at the beginning of the nineteenth century, when the German lands, still politically fragmented, struggled to liberate themselves from Napoleonic occupation. The German Wars of Liberation gave rise to a romantic nationalism celebrating the cultural and spiritual unity of the "German people" (*das deutsche Volk*). The term, understood in this sense, remained a central feature of the vocabulary of German nationalism for many decades, and only late in the nineteenth century began to take on a racial connotation among some Germans. After World War I, the radical nationalist anti-republican right came to be known as the *völkisch* movement, fusing populist romantic nationalism with modern biological racism. While Volk was defined in racial terms by Nazism, it could also be employed rhetorically in a broader sense, appealing to Germans with a more traditional notion of German nationhood. Nazi rhetoric appropriated the concept of the People's Community (*Volksgemeinschaft*), which democratic parties in Germany had employed as a call to greater social solidarity, recasting it as a slogan for a racially pure, culturally homogeneous, and politically harmonious nation under strong authoritarian leadership. Although attention has rightly tended to focus on Nazism as an ideology of exclusion, the *völkisch* idea also championed, at least rhetorically, the value of a community of mutual obligation and solidarity among racially pure Germans.[4]

Figure 1.1 The cover of volume 2 of *Mein Kampf* (Photo12/Universal Images Group via Getty Images).

The racial element of Nazism may be seen as the apotheosis of one particular stream of intellectual development dating back to the eighteenth century in Europe. One consequence of the spread of Enlightenment rationalism was a reconceptualization of the causes of human inequality. In an era when theological notions such as the "Divine Right of Kings" were rendered quaint by the shift to rationalism and a scientific approach to comprehending the world, cultural differences among human groups were increasingly associated with their observable anatomical characteristics, such as the color of the skin and the shape of the head. Humans were described, measured, and categorized as part of the natural world, and their cultural attributes were attributed to their innate biological nature. These early methods of physical anthropology were deployed to validate notions of white European superiority over non-white peoples and to justify colonial rule. Historians often cite the example of Peter Camper, a Dutch anatomist of the eighteenth century, who used his technique for measuring head shapes, the so-called facial angle, to posit the biological proximity of Black Africans to orangutans. Such methodologies seem absurd in the age of modern genome research, yet they were regarded as serious science in their day.

Racial thinking developed in nineteenth-century Europe very much as a transnational phenomenon. The French aristocrat Arthur de Gobineau is often regarded as the "father of modern racial theory" on the basis of his typology of human races, published during the 1850s. Building on European stereotypes about others and themselves, Gobineau divided humanity into races defined by skin color, ascribing general characteristics to each group. In contrast to Africans, whom he characterized as physically superior but of low intelligence, and to Asians, whom he described as industrious but imitative, Europeans were depicted as noble creators of culture. Gobineau attributed the greatest achievements of European civilization to the so-called Aryans, by which he did not mean Germans but rather the ancestors of the European nobility of his own day. The power and prerogatives of the nobility had been under threat in France, and many other places in Europe, since the French Revolution of 1789, and thus Gobineau's racial theory was an attempt to justify not only European rule over other regions of the globe but also a domestic system of inequality-by-caste that was being dismantled before his eyes.[5]

The Emergence of Racial Antisemitism

Gobineau had relatively little to say about Jews, but during the second half of the nineteenth century, racist theory merged increasingly with anti-Jewish prejudice. Racial antisemitism arose in response to the legal emancipation of the Jews and their gradual acceptance into the mainstream of society. Non-Jewish champions of emancipation had argued that the removal of legal and economic restrictions would lead to a normalization of the Jews. Some critics of emancipation argued that the essential otherness of the Jews made such normalization impossible. One of the most prominent figures who promoted this argument was the celebrated German composer Richard Wagner. In his essay "Judaism in Music," first published pseudonymously in 1850 and then again in 1869 under the author's real name, Wagner attacked Jewish composers for the supposed foreignness of their music. Much as they intended their music to sound European, they could not but contaminate their compositions with "foreign" and "repulsive" sounds derived from Jewish speech patterns. Wagner did not specifically identify the Jews as a distinct race, but the strong essentialism of his argument prefigured the more explicitly racist positions of later theorists. One of these was Wilhelm Marr, a German anti-Jewish publicist and agitator who was especially active during the 1860s and 1870s. Historians credit Marr with coining the term "antisemitism," by which he intended to underscore the non-European racial origin of Jews.[6]

Germanic Aryan superiority and a demonic characterization of the Jews were two central tenets of the racial theory expounded at the end of the nineteenth century by Houston Stewart Chamberlain, an Englishman with close personal ties to Germany. Chamberlain's two-volume work, *The Foundations of the Nineteenth Century*, which appeared in 1899, summarized the history of Europe as an epic struggle between the culture-creating Germanic Aryans and the parasitic, culture-destroying Jews. Chamberlain regarded the emancipation of the Jews in Western and Central Europe, one of the signal achievements of liberalism, as a fatal error of the nineteenth century, one that had enabled Jews to achieve positions of power, from which they promoted various forms of degeneration. Published originally in German, *Foundations* was subsequently translated into several languages and republished numerous times in Germany and Britain. It was well received in political and journalistic circles in Germany, Britain, and Russia. Emperor Wilhelm II of Germany was purported to have read and expressed approval of the book.[7]

Chamberlain was by no means the only author promoting such views in turn-of-the-century Germany. A wide-ranging discourse concerned itself with questions of racial degeneration and the alleged destructive influence of the Jews. In contrast to Chamberlain, who believed in the ultimate triumph of the Aryan race, Julius Langbehn expressed pessimism about the future. But they, and many others, argued from the same basic premises about race, Aryans, and Jews. Nor were such views limited to a small number of isolated individuals. They were embraced by organizations and lobby groups on the nationalist right, such as the Pan-German League, whose advocacy of the unification of all German-speaking peoples took on an increasingly racist and antisemitic flavor in the years before World War I. To be sure, organized political antisemitism attracted only limited support in Imperial Germany, when measured, for example, by the vote received by antisemitic political parties during the two decades preceding World War I.[8] But military defeat in 1918 and the turbulence of the Weimar era helped bring the descendants of this intellectual and political tradition to power in 1933.

When compared with later statements and writings about Jews and race by Nazi-era race theorists, such as Hans F. K. Günther, and by Hitler himself, the biologism of Chamberlain's argument was rather vague. But Chamberlain nevertheless remains significant as an encapsulation of where European antisemitism, or at least one particular strain of it, had arrived on the eve of the twentieth century. Modern antisemitism can be thought of as a complex structure built from the accretion of historical layers. The oldest of these layers is the anti-Judaism that arose as early Christianity endeavored to separate itself from the religious tradition that had spawned it. Throughout the following centuries, even as antipathy toward Jews in Christian Europe took on additional social and economic layers, aversion to Judaism as an obsolete religion, and resentment toward Jews on the basis of their ostensible collective responsibility for the suffering and crucifixion of Christ, persisted in European society. When Jews were subjected to "disabilities" in medieval Europe – prohibited from certain occupations, held liable for special taxation, compelled to live in ghettoes stigmatized by special clothing – religious prejudice became compounded by social and cultural separateness. Bans against Jewish participation in the craft trades and in agriculture – the so-called "productive" occupations – facilitated the concentration of Jews into peddling and moneylending, activities that were often perceived as exploitative of the honest labor of others. Multi-generational experience in these occupations positioned Jews to benefit from the transition to modern capitalism, but left them even more vulnerable to accusations of selfishness and exploitation at times of economic difficulty.

From the middle of the nineteenth century into the early part of the twentieth, Jewish bankers and businessmen, widely perceived as the "winners" of modern capitalism, were often blamed when artisans lost their jobs to modern industry or when farmers ran out of credit. Economic populism targeted against Jews as agents of capitalism was a common feature of Central European politics in the late nineteenth century. It was promoted in Germany by Adolf Stoecker, an influential Lutheran pastor, leader of the Christian Social Party, and, for a while, chaplain to the court of the German emperor. In the central German region of Hesse, a politically powerful peasant movement agitated against Jewish cattle traders and grain dealers. In Austria, Karl Lueger, the mayor of Vienna, exploited anti-Jewish economic resentment to gain and hold power. Such economically motivated resentment of Jews did not replace older forms of anti-Jewish sentiment, such as theological anti-Judaism, but accreted atop them, adding a modern layer to a centuries-old intellectual structure of religious prejudice. During the Nazi era, anti-Jewish policy was predicated on a racial, rather than religious or cultural, definition of Jews. Nevertheless, the propaganda produced by the regime to justify its anti-Jewish measures deployed numerous stereotypes and accusations drawn not from modern racism but rather from older traditions of religious, cultural, and economic antisemitism.[9]

Further complicating the situation at the end of the nineteenth century and the beginning of the twentieth was the emergence of Jews, or at least persons of Jewish heritage, in highly visible positions in the labor movement and in Marxist political parties. Jews were simultaneously prominent both as capitalists and as critics of capitalism, and the epithet "Judeo-Bolshevism" arose as a popular meme in antisemitic circles (see Figure 1.2). This situation, a contradiction on its surface, can be explained as the product of the complex historical experience of a religious and ethnic community possessing "outsider" status. But those who were predisposed to be less charitable to Jews saw a different dynamic at work. Jews, in their view, employed capitalism and Marxism in concert as a pincer, generating economic exploitation and suffering on one side and exploiting the desperation of the working class on the other. Jewish duplicity on such a vast scale seemed credible only to those who comprehended the Jews as a monolithic community engaged in systematic parasitic behavior at the expense of those around them.[10]

The historical significance of the reconceptualization of Jews from a religious or ethnic community to a race should not be underestimated. Europeans had long been discussing possible solutions to the "Jewish Question," a shorthand referring to the problems posed by Jewish otherness. It had long been understood that problems arising from religious difference could be solved through conversion. At least theoretically, a Jew could convert to Christianity and be quickly accepted into the Christian majority. This practice was widespread throughout the Middle Ages. In Spain, a major center of Jewish culture and learning over many centuries, Jews were converted *en masse*, and those who refused were expelled from the country in the fifteenth century. Other manifestations of Jewish otherness, including the unusual occupational structure of the Jewish population, could be addressed by assimilation, a process that would

Figure 1.2 Poster for the antisemitic exhibition *The Eternal Jew*, 1938 (Imagno/Getty Images).

occur over generations. Through much of the nineteenth century, the Russian Empire pursued a policy of coerced assimilation on its sizable Jewish population. Whether conversion or assimilation, the operating assumption was that Jewish behavior was malleable and could be modified. This assumption no longer applied once Jews had been redefined as a race. When the sources of human behavior are deemed to be innate and biological rather than environmental, adjustments to behavior do not alter the inner essence of the person. A Jew would remain a Jew no matter what. This explains why Nazi Germany, both within its own borders and, after 1939, in German-dominated Europe, never entertained the possibility of assimilating the Jews, but instead resolved to remove them physically – one way or another.

Social Darwinism, *Lebensraum*, and Eugenics

If racism and antisemitism were two essential components of the Nazi worldview, a third was Social Darwinism. Taking their cue from the concept of natural selection that lay at the heart of Darwin's theory of evolution, the Social Darwinists depicted the human world as a grand arena of struggle for survival. Like modern racism (with which it was not identical, but with which it would eventually merge), Social Darwinism served as a non-religious, supposedly scientific justification both for social inequality in Europe and for European overseas colonialism. It purported to refute ideas of egalitarianism and charity, be they based in the Christian tradition or in Marxian socialism. Social Darwinists held that inequalities of wealth and power belonged to the natural order of things. In a world of limited resources and space, the strong and talented take what is rightfully theirs, surviving, prospering, and reproducing at the expense of the weak.[11]

The Nazi synthesis of racism, antisemitism, and Social Darwinism is conspicuous in Hitler's writings and speeches of the 1920s. Humanity, he maintained, consisted of races – and not simply nations – engaged in a constant struggle for living space, power, and resources. Among these races, the Germans (sometimes referred to as Aryan) had played an especially positive role in the building of European civilization. On the other hand, the Jewish race had been a destructive force. Lacking their own territory and army, and constituting an alien presence in Europe, the Jews had adapted themselves to the role of parasite, nourishing themselves at the expense of the races among whom they reside as minorities. Clever, ruthless, and cunning by their nature, Jews are adept at seizing control of societies from within, establishing themselves in decisive positions in the economy, culture, the medical and legal professions, and journalism. Whether as capitalists, Marxists, liberals, democrats, or exponents of artistic modernism, Jews exploit their influence to produce economic distress, sow political discord, and promote cultural decadence in their host societies. Germany's defeat in World War I, the draconian peace terms imposed on it, and the alien system of government foisted onto it in the form of the Weimar Republic – all of these were attributable to the machinations of "Jewry." For the sake of its future survival in a world of competing races, Germany would have to purify itself from Jewish contamination.

The Social Darwinist element of Nazi thinking also determined basic assumptions about international relations and military affairs. When the world is imagined as an arena of struggle among races, comity among nations cannot be regarded as a desirable or even attainable goal, except for reasons of short-term expediency. The natural relationship between large, powerful states and their smaller neighbors is not one of mutually beneficial peaceful co-existence, but one of domination. Hitler articulated this view of international relations quite categorically in his second book, written in 1928, but which remained unpublished during his lifetime. The work, which focused on international affairs, was infused by notions of struggle and survival among nations. Peace, Hitler explained, was not a laudable goal in and of itself, but was desirable when it preserved the power of a country. Once this was no longer the case, war represented a legitimate alternative. "Never-ending war" could have catastrophic consequences for the nation's best "blood lines" (a lesson supposedly learned during World War I). On the other hand, a long-lasting peace would make a people soft and lazy, undermining its will to struggle and survive. War, therefore, is not only a useful tool for the pursuit of concrete national goals but is also fundamentally a psychologically healthy endeavor for the race.

The impulse to acquire additional "living space" – *Lebensraum* – for the German Volk arose inevitably from the logic of a worldview based on Social Darwinism. Races required space to proliferate, to produce the food necessary to feed themselves, and to extract the natural resources needed for economic prosperity and military strength. As a result of the Treaty of Versailles, Germany had been forced to cede territory to France and Poland, but Hitler, in his second book, emphasized the long-term importance of expanding German control over far greater reaches of land than those that had been lost in the war. He imagined a future German racial colonization of the Slavic lands of Eastern Europe, with its vast expanses of arable land, similar in concept to what European (and partly German) settlers had achieved on the North American continent during the nineteenth century. And he understood that this grand imperial ambition could not be achieved peacefully (which was one of the reasons he decided against publishing his second book, in which his expansionistic intentions were laid bare). Such a vision of German colonial conquest in Eastern Europe was by no means original to Hitler. It drew inspiration from a long tradition of fantasies about a German "Drive to the

East" – *Drang nach Osten* – extending from the Middle Ages to the nine-teenth century. After World War I, the idea of eastward expansion was granted intellectual legitimation by theorists of the new discipline of geo-politics. The most prominent such figure in the 1920s, Karl Haushofer, was a professor at the University of Munich. In response to the disaster of Germany's defeat in the war, Haushofer advocated an expansion of German *Lebensraum*, which would enable the country to enhance its mili-tary security and to achieve economic self-sufficiency (so-called autarky). Haushofer exerted direct influence over the development of Nazi thinking about such questions through his former student, Rudolf Hess, one of Hitler's chief assistants and closest confidants in the Nazi Party.[12]

Like *Lebensraum*, eugenics was also an idea inherent in the Social Dar-winist and racist world of Nazi thinking. Having originated as an interna-tional movement in the late nineteenth century, eugenics aimed to improve the genetic composition of human population groups. Many of its early supporters were political progressives who hoped to improve the human condition through an applied science of heredity. Through a combination of "positive" measures – breeding – as well as "negative" ones – steriliza-tion – a society could impose quality controls on the practice of human reproduction, in the process reducing or eliminating poverty, illiteracy, criminality, and other behaviors that were believed to result from hereditary factors. During the first three decades of the twentieth century, a significant number of American states and several Northern European countries insti-tuted laws providing for the compulsory sterilization of persons who were regarded as unfit for reproduction. Germany was not among these coun-tries, but eugenics attracted a significant following in the Weimar Republic, not least in the medical and scientific communities. Some praised it as a method for reducing disease and social pathologies, while others empha-sized "racial hygiene" as a tool for strengthening the nation. Members of the Nazi Party were drawn to eugenics in the early 1920s, when, in the immediate aftermath of World War I, Germany suffered from shortages of essential supplies, and much thought was given to long-term strategies for national renewal. Eugenics was endorsed by Hitler in the first volume of *Mein Kampf*, published in 1925, and was embraced widely within the party before it came to power. One of the first major pieces of legislation that would be promulgated by the newly established Nazi dictatorship in 1933 was the eugenic sterilization law of July 14 of that year.[13]

The obsession with questions of human reproduction reflected in Nazism's embrace of eugenics also had implications for Nazism's views on sexuality. Heteronormativity had been anchored in German law since 1871, and Nazism was by no means unique in its negative attitude toward homosexuality. Traditionally, however, opposition to homosexuality had been justified on religious or moral objections, or on a vague sense of normal vs. abnormal behavior. Nazism's racialized understanding of humanity magnified the supposed dangers posed to the German Volk by homosexuality. Ideally, sex would occur among heterosexual Aryan couples and would result in the production of healthy, racially pure offspring. Homosexuality was believed to impede this goal. Nazi propaganda was fiercely critical of Weimar-era sexual research that intended to destigmatize homosexuality, emphasizing the Jewishness of Magnus Hirschfeld, one of the leading scholars in this field. The heteronormative logic of Nazi thinking was reinforced by strongly held notions of virile masculinity. Stereotypes of effeminate gay men fed into concerns about the nation's military prowess. The irony here is that homosexuality was common among the members of the Nazi Party's paramilitary organization, the SA (short for Sturmabteilung, or Storm Detachment). This widely known fact, and the hypocrisy that it underscored, was a source of considerable embarrassment to Hitler for many years until his violent purge of the SA in 1934.[14]

Nazism as a Revolt against Liberal Democracy

Eugenics was regarded as *völkisch* in that it would cleanse the German race of impurities while reducing the financial burden of caring for unproductive members of society. In this regard, the biologism of Nazism converged with another one of its essential features, its illiberalism. The great German scholar Karl Dietrich Bracher has characterized Nazism as (among other things) a "revolt against liberal democracy."[15] This feature was present in Nazism from the time of its creation, and was not simply a reaction to the perceived messiness of parliamentary democracy as practiced in Germany during the 1920s. Looking back at the development of liberal democracies in Europe through the creation of the Weimar Republic, Nazism rejected a system of government that had facilitated the emancipation of the Jews, tolerated exploitative forms of capitalism, and permitted the rise of Marxist radicalism, all of which, it was alleged, had undermined the unity and vitality of the German Volk. Nazism, in contrast, intended to elevate the welfare of the society over the liberty of the individual. A common expression during the Nazi era was *Gemeinnutz geht vor Eigennutz* – "the common interest comes before self-interest" – a slogan drawn directly from point 24 of the Nazi Party program of 1920. Translating this principle into political practice would require the imposition of an authoritarian system of government, the rolling back of civil liberties, and the imposition of *dirigiste* controls over the national economy. The party program of 1920 demanded "a strong central state power for the Reich," and over time the "Leader Principle" (*Führerprinzip*) emerged as a central tenet of Nazism. The leader, whose authority should be absolute, should rise organically from the Volk, rather than inherit power from a degenerate monarchy or be dependent on bickering parliamentary party brokers. This charismatic notion of leadership hearkened back to romantic "Great Man" theories of the late nineteenth century, which had arisen in opposition to the perceived mediocrity or paralysis of the parliamentarianism that was ascendant at the time.

On the economic front, Nazism's revolt against liberalism was anchored in a widely held critique of modern capitalism, which had created great wealth but had also led to the displacement of many members of the "old" middle class of artisans and shopkeepers. Modern industry had rendered much of artisanal production obsolete, and the rise of department stores had undermined the viability of the small-scale retail sector. Nazism did not attack capitalism per se, but rather specific manifestations of the system, such as "finance capital," which, it was claimed, worked to the detriment of most members of society. Liberal economic policies had proved incapable of protecting ordinary Germans from the predations of financiers and big businesses. The fact that many of the German department stores had been founded by Jewish merchants, and that the activity of banking was widely (although no longer correctly) associated with Jews provided a point of intersection between Nazi illiberalism and Nazi antisemitism.

The label "National Socialism" raises the obvious question of whether Nazism can in any way be considered to have been socialist. "I am a socialist," Hitler wrote in his second book. "I see before me no class or rank, but rather a community of people who are connected by blood, united by language, and subject to the same collective fate."[16] Nazism was, quite obviously, not socialist in any Marxist sense of the word, but it had a specific purpose for appropriating the term for its own ends. It wished to emphasize that it possessed a social conscience and a sense of fairness, the claim to which it refused to cede to the Marxist parties. The "socialist" self-styling was designed to communicate a critical stance toward certain aspects of capitalism, and to express solidarity with nationalistically inclined working- and middle-class Germans who possessed legitimate economic grievances, but who were repelled by the radicalism and internationalism of the Marxist parties. The party program of February 1920 (adopted immediately before the phrase "National Socialist" was added to the existing name "German Workers' Party") contained several demands that were intended to address the economic concerns of ordinary Germans. These included a requirement that "the state shall make it its primary duty to provide a livelihood for its citizens," "the abolition of incomes unearned by work," "the breaking of the slavery of interest," the "ruthless confiscation of all war profits," "the nationalization of all businesses that have been formed into corporations," "profit sharing in large industrial enterprises," the "communalizing of big department stores," the "prohibition of all speculation in land," and the "extensive development of insurance for old age." The economic populism reflected in this wish-list of measures remained a fixture of Nazi rhetoric and was seriously embraced by a faction of the movement that coalesced around the brothers Gregor and Otto Strasser during the 1920s, although very little of it actually materialized as concrete policy after 1933, when Hitler and his party made their peace with German big business. Nazi economic populism, whether in rhetoric or practice, was always racially exclusive, its benefits restricted to Aryans in good standing.

One of the economic demands contained in the 1920 party program might seem somewhat obscure in retrospect. The party called for "the formation of corporations based on estate and occupation for the purpose of carrying out the general legislation passed by the Reich." The vision of a society composed not of individuals but of occupational groups was the essence of corporatism, an alternative model to liberal individualism that had been gaining currency since the late nineteenth century. Its advocates pointed to precedents from the Middle Ages, when society had functioned as a collection of "estates." A modern society organized in a "neo-corporatist" fashion, under a strong central authority, would purportedly function more harmoniously than the modern liberal state, in which individuals were free to pursue their own selfish interests. A neo-corporatist reconstruction of society was a feature common to the ideologies of both Nazism and Italian Fascism, reflecting a common desire to address the challenges posed by modern capitalism by reconfiguring the relationship between state and society. This was not socialism, as that term is normally understood, but rather a "Third Way" between the liberal, capitalist order, which was believed to have failed, and Soviet Communism, which was deemed unacceptable for a host of reasons.

It is important to emphasize the distinction between ideological doctrine and political appeal. Hitler and his movement rose to power largely on their ability to exploit the anxieties and hopes of Germans in the very specific political and economic circumstances of the Weimar Republic. Germans who joined or voted for the Nazi Party before 1933 did not necessarily understand themselves to be embracing an ideology in its entirety. Some were attracted to specific elements of the ideology but not to others. Many were not ideological at all, but were attracted by the dynamism of the movement, the charisma of its leader, and emotional appeals to fears and resentments that were widespread in German society. Still others supported Nazism for pragmatic reasons of professional or economic self-interest. Although Hitler and his party, once in charge of the country, pursued long-term goals that were anchored in a worldview that they had long openly espoused, ideological doctrine had been but one among many factors that had brought them into power.

2   The Triumph of Nazism

In the Reichstag election of May 1928, the Nazi Party's share of the national vote was 2.6 percent. No fewer than eight political parties fared better. The NSDAP was not represented in a single regional government in Germany. At the time of the election, the Nazi Party claimed fewer than 100,000 members, not an insignificant number, but by no means representative of a mass movement in a country of 60 million people. Less than five years later, in January 1933, when Adolf Hitler was appointed to lead the Reich government, the party possessed the largest delegation in the Reichstag and counted about three-quarters of a million members. Within a few months after his appointment to the chancellorship, Hitler had outmaneuvered his conservative nationalist coalition partners, had dissolved all political parties except his own, and had exploited emergency decrees to put an end to civil rights and due process in Germany. The speed with which these events unfolded appears breathtaking in retrospect. In the space of five years, a seemingly stable liberal democracy was dismantled and replaced by a one-party dictatorship.

The demise of Weimar democracy and the rise and ultimate triumph of the Nazi movement were closely interrelated historical developments, but they nevertheless pose distinct sets of questions. In a circular dynamic, the political and economic problems of the Weimar Republic created a political opportunity for the NSDAP, while attacks from the NSDAP contributed to the delegitimation and collapse of the Republic. But the actions of the NSDAP were but one factor among many that contributed to the destruction of Weimar, and a Nazi dictatorship was by no means the only possible outcome of the failure of German democracy. From the time of its creation, the Weimar Republic suffered from a persistent crisis of legitimacy that extended far beyond Nazi circles. A series of bad breaks and unfortunate political decisions rendered the parliamentary democracy of Weimar unworkable starting in 1930, leaving an opening for some other system to replace it. Hitler's appointment to the chancellorship under these circumstances, and the subsequent creation of a Nazi dictatorship, were the result of the NSDAP's ability to energize and mobilize its followers, as well as of the fragmentation of the Nazis' opponents across the political spectrum.

The transition from Weimar democracy to the Nazi dictatorship was a dominant theme in German historical scholarship for decades after 1945. The subject was regarded as especially relevant during the consolidation period of the newly established democratic state of West Germany (Federal Republic of Germany), which needed to defend its legitimacy in the face of challenges from Communist East Germany (German Democratic Republic) and from right-wing revanchists domestically. The slogan "Bonn is not Weimar" was often invoked to underscore the differences between the Federal Republic of 1949 and the Weimar Republic of 1918. The success of the former required research into the causes of the failure of the latter. Attention to the history of Weimar waned for a time, in part because it has been thoroughly researched, in part because German democracy had proved itself enduring, and in part because other subjects, such as the Holocaust, or German society under Nazi rule, which had remained relatively under-researched, had moved into the forefront. But Weimar has once again become a very active area of research in recent years. Some historians have stressed the importance of understanding Weimar on its own terms as a distinctive period of German history, marked by its own possibilities and contested visions of the future, rather than simply as an interregnum between the German Empire and the Third Reich.[1] Historians have nevertheless also continued to focus on the reasons for the failure of democracy in one of Europe's largest and most powerful nations, and on how a dictatorship was created in its place.[2]

Problems of the Weimar Republic

Analyzing the failure of Weimar must consider both long-term and short-term historical factors that contributed to the undermining of German democracy. A question of fundamental importance for historians has been whether to lay the emphasis of their explanations on the long-term factors, extending back into the nineteenth century, or on the short-term factors, beginning with the German defeat in World War I. The emphasis on long-term factors is usually associated with the idea of the German *Sonderweg*, or "special path," according to which Germany's historical development in the nineteenth century deviated from that of the countries that eventually emerged as liberal democracies, such as Britain, France, and the United States. This historical interpretation points to several key turning points on the road to liberal democracy where Germany failed to turn. The *Sonderweg* thesis was an expression of liberal modernization theory during the Cold War, which posited the existence of a "normal" trajectory of historical development from nineteenth-century liberalism through twentieth-century liberal democracy. The societies that had failed to follow this path had become the totalitarian dictatorships of the twentieth century, whether Nazi or Fascist dictatorships of the right or Communist dictatorships of the left.

Proponents of the *Sonderweg* thesis emphasized the importance of the years 1848, 1871, and 1918. When a tide of liberal and nationalist revolutions spread across Europe in 1848, the attempt to create a unified German national state along liberal lines was crushed by the military forces of the German monarchies, retarding the development of German liberalism at a time when it was making progress in France and Britain. A second fateful blow was dealt to German liberalism when the German lands were unified into the German Empire under the leadership of Otto von Bismarck in 1871. Bismarck superimposed onto the newly founded empire the authoritarian structures of Prussia, the largest and most conservative of the German states, of which he was the minister president. Most notably, the center of political power in the German Empire was the hereditary emperor (also the king of Prussia) and his hand-picked chancellor. A national parliament, the Reichstag, elected through universal male suffrage, possessed very limited real political authority. This system functioned in marked contrast to genuine parliamentary democracies, where the prime minister and other members of the governing cabinet derive their power from an elected parliament rather than from a hereditary monarch. The Prussian feudal elite, a distinctly pre-modern caste, exercised considerable influence through its dominant role in the army and other institutions. In 1918, when the empire was swept away by revolution and replaced by the Weimar Republic, much of this elite remained in positions of authority, serving a state for which it had little regard.

The system of government in the German Empire encouraged non-democratic forms of political behavior among German political parties. Precisely because the Reichstag was not constitutionally empowered to form governments, the parties had no incentive to develop the traditions of compromise required for building majorities or hammering out governing coalitions. Instead, they tended to remain true to their ideological positions or loyal to the narrow economic or religious interests of their voters, a mode of behavior that did not serve Germany well after the Weimar Constitution of 1919 put a genuine parliamentary democracy in place. Making matters worse was the discrepancy between the German Empire's authoritarianism – its failed modernization – on the political front and its rapid transformation after 1871 into an industrial and technological powerhouse. The dramatic economic modernization of the country generated social dislocation and cultural alienation on a massive scale, while the political system proved incapable of addressing the grievances of the newly emergent industrial working class, shopkeepers, artisans, and others whose lives and livelihoods were buffeted by the spread of modern industrial capitalism. This environment gave sustenance to the nascent populist ideologies, of both the left and the right, that would later tear the Weimar Republic apart.[3]

This interpretation, in a multitude of forms, prevailed in the historiography of modern Germany from the 1950s into the 1980s, when it was subjected to criticism by a number of scholars who attacked it on a variety of fronts. They questioned whether there was really a single path toward the achievement of liberal democracy, whether Britain, France, and the United States had really been models of liberal democratic development, and whether the feudal elites had really played as dominant a role in the German Empire as the supporters of the *Sonderweg* thesis had maintained. They located the source of German authoritarianism in the modern, capitalist middle class rather than in the feudal elite, and, when addressing the failure of the Weimar Republic, focused on causes that were more chronologically proximate, particularly the defeat in World War I and the circumstances of post-war peacemaking.[4] Some scholars embraced this critique and jettisoned the *Sonderweg* thesis altogether, while others accepted many of the critical arguments but continued to insist that long-term continuities in German history were at least partially responsible for the failure of Weimar and the rise of Nazism.[5]

Setting aside the *Sonderweg* debate, and the ultimately unanswerable question of whether the Weimar Republic was doomed from the start, there is no denying that the Republic was the product of a very difficult birth. It was the product of war, defeat, and revolution. The German war effort had been directed by two generals, Paul von Hindenburg and Erich Ludendorff, who executed their semi-dictatorial powers on the authority of the hereditary monarch Kaiser Wilhelm II. As the conflict wore on, demanding ever-greater sacrifices from the German people, the Social Democrats and other reform-minded parties in the Reichstag asserted themselves, eventually winning some concessions in the way of democratization. In September 1918, when the military high command recognized that defeat had been made inevitable by the arrival of large numbers of fresh American troops on the Western front, Hindenburg and Ludendorff advised the government to pursue an armistice with Germany's enemies in the West. As the understanding spread that four agonizing years of war and millions of casualties would all have been for naught, popular frustration boiled over in November in the form of mutinies among sailors and soldiers and revolts among workers. The uprising resulted, all within a few days, in the appointment of Friedrich Ebert, the leader of the Social Democrats (the largest party in the Reichstag), to the chancellorship, then to the abdication of Kaiser Wilhelm II, then to the declaration of a republic, and finally to the new government's signature on an armistice.[6]

Thus, the war had been fought and lost by the old regime, under the command of Hindenburg and Ludendorff acting on behalf of the Kaiser, but it was the government of the new democratic republic, led by Social Democrats, that was left with the task of suing for peace and dealing with the consequences of defeat. This sequence of events played into the hands of Germans who promoted the myth of the "stab in the back" (*Dolchstosslegende*), according to which Germany, rather than having been defeated on the battlefield, was betrayed from within by the political left. Desiring to shift the responsibility for defeat away from the military over which they themselves had presided, Generals Hindenburg and Ludendorff participated actively in the dissemination of this myth. The "stab in the back" scenario conformed to the way in which many Germans had perceived the events of the war. While German troops had occupied much of the Polish part of the Russian Empire and had dug into their trenches in France and Belgium, Germany itself had not been invaded. The inevitability of defeat in the West, which had been clear to the high command, was not widely understood in German society. The collapse of the military effort in November 1918 seemed to come out of nowhere, and even on the day of the armistice, there were no foreign troops on German territory. Many Germans who had served in uniform, or otherwise made sacrifices for the war effort, found psychological solace in the idea that victory would have been theirs had it not been for the traitors in their midst. Included among the so-called "November criminals" were not only the Social Democrats, Communists, and trade unionists who had inspired the mutinies and strikes of November 1918, but also the Jews. Ignoring the fact that about 12,000 German Jews had laid down their lives for their German Fatherland during the war, that many more had lost limbs and suffered injuries, and that Jews such as the industrialist Walther Rathenau and the chemist Fritz Haber had made indispensable contributions to the German war effort, the proponents of the "stab in the back" myth pointed to the actions of a small number of Jewish liberals and leftists who had criticized the wartime conduct of the German government. As Germany, a country with a proud military tradition, struggled to come to terms with its defeat, Jews were thrust into their traditional role as scapegoat.

The sense of national betrayal on the German right was deepened by the Treaty of Versailles, which was signed by Germany and its former enemies in June 1919. The center-left coalition government, led by Social Democrats, shared in the widespread German condemnation of the peace terms, but succumbed to pressure from the British and the French. This action was seen on the German right as a validation of its narrative about Germany being served up to its enemies by traitors on the left. More generally, the fledgling Republic's association with Versailles became a major impediment to achieving legitimacy in the eyes of the German people.

Versailles was in certain respects severe, but it was not the fatal blow to the life of the German nation that it was presented to be by its right-wing critics. The punitive features of the treaty were justified by the so-called War Guilt Clause, which placed the sole responsibility for the outbreak of the conflict on the Germans. Most Germans were offended by this accusation, notwithstanding later historical scholarship that argued plausibly in favor of this interpretation of the origins of the war. The treaty limited Germany's army to a force of 100,000 troops, woefully inadequate for international combat, but deemed sufficient for maintaining domestic security. Germany was compelled to surrender territory on its western and eastern borders, but these regions had not always belonged to Germany and were substantially Polish or French in their ethnic composition. The four small African colonies stripped from Germany had possessed psychological importance to Germans in an age of European colonialism, but had hardly been crucial for German security or prosperity; in fact, they represented a financial burden from which the country was now involuntarily relieved. The reparations liability of 132 billion marks imposed by Versailles provoked outrage among Germans and among international experts, like the celebrated economist John Maynard Keynes, who predicted that the financial burden would be impossible to carry and would endanger the consolidation of Weimar democracy. Economic historians have debated whether Germany would have been capable of meeting this financial commitment, but the political will to do so was absent from the beginning.[7] Among the outraged Germans there were few who seemed to remember the considerable reparations bill imposed by the German Empire on France after the Franco-Prussian War of 1870–71. Moreover, the extremely punitive settlement imposed by Germany on Russia in the Treaty of Brest-Litovsk in March 1918, after the new Communist regime had decided to withdraw Russia from the conflict, hardly set a standard for generosity. The rationale for reparations after World War I was the need to finance the physical repairs that France and Belgium would need to undertake in areas that suffered damage during German military occupation. Reparations were intended to shift the cost of this work onto the Germans, whose territory suffered almost no physical damage during the war. As Germany ended up paying only about one-sixth of the projected amount before the reparation debts were cancelled in 1932, the cost of the repairs was, in the end, actually transferred back onto the nations that had suffered the damage between 1914 and 1918.

The parliamentary democracy envisaged by the architects of the Weimar Republic faced domestic opponents at both ends of the political spectrum. On the far left, the Communist Party of Germany (KPD), which was founded in early 1919, supported a system based on the model of the Soviet Union, which had just come into existence one year previously. The German Communists regarded Weimar as a bourgeois capitalist regime, and considered the Social Democrats, who represented the evolutionary wing of German Marxism, as traitors to the working class. The left in Weimar was deeply divided. Whereas the Social Democrats played an instrumental role in the creation and defense of the Republic, the Communists were hostile to the Republic from beginning to end. In 1919, in the so-called Spartacist Uprising, Communists mounted an ill-fated revolt against the recently established, Social Democratic-led national provisional government. The chancellor, Friedrich Ebert, recruited the assistance of the army and the Free Corps – right-wing paramilitary units composed of decommissioned soldiers – to quash the rebellion, a foreshadowing of the destructive role that paramilitary politics were to play during the life of the Republic. In the final phase of the Weimar Republic, after 1929, the KPD, following the line of the Communist International, characterized the Social Democrats as "Social Fascists" as a way of emphasizing their collaboration with capitalism.

On the far right, the *völkisch* movement, of which the Nazi Party was but one element, mobilized disgruntled war veterans and a constituency drawn from the lower middle classes behind a populist, nationalist, and antisemitic agenda aimed at overthrowing the Weimar Republic, annulling Versailles, and crushing the political left. This objective led to attempts to overthrow the national government by force. In March 1920, in the Kapp Putsch, an uprising by detachments of the Free Corps was repelled by a massive general strike organized by the trade unions. The Beer Hall Putsch of November 1923 was also a failure, but it exemplified the determination of the extreme right during the early phase of the Weimar Republic to topple the government through violence rather than at the ballot box. Only after the putsch did the Nazi Party begin to participate in electoral politics.

The center of the Weimar-era German political spectrum was occupied by several parties: the liberal German Democratic Party (DDP); the German People's Party (DVP), which represented the outlook and interests of big business; the German Center Party (Zentrum), which had originated as the confessional party of the German Catholic minority in the German Empire, and which, during the Weimar Republic, participated in every German governing coalition between February 1919 and December 1932; and the German National People's Party (DNVP), which represented the perspective of the old Prussian agrarian aristocracy, elements of big business, and the officer corps of the military, but attracted broad support from Germans of a conservative nationalist bent. The DNVP participated in a couple of Weimar-era governments, but factions that remained fundamentally hostile to the democratic Republic seized control of the party after 1928. When Hitler was appointed to the chancellorship in January 1933, it was as the head of a coalition between his own party and the DNVP.[8]

This political party system reflected the economic, ideological, and confessional structure of a society that was divided into four main camps: socialists, liberals, Catholics, and conservatives. Even though the ideological extremes received limited support before 1930, the fragmented Weimar party system did not lend itself to stability. With no single party ever coming close to commanding a parliamentary majority, governments had to depend on coalitions formed by three, four, or sometimes five parties. This situation resulted in frequent reshuffling and a vacillation between center-left and center-right coalition governments. Between February 1919 and January 1933, Germany had twenty-one different governments, with an average lifespan of eight and a half months. The longest-serving government lasted only twenty-one months. The inability to form enduring coalitions was attributable at least in part to the legacy of ideologically and programmatically parochial political parties inherited from the German Empire. The revolving door of governments did not inspire confidence in parliamentary democracy. Many Germans remembered that the authoritarian German Empire had been ruled by only three emperors, and governed by five chancellors, between 1871 and 1917.

Only in the office of the Reich president, subject to direct, popular election, did the Weimar Republic enjoy a modicum of stability. The first president, the Social Democrat Friedrich Ebert, held the office from his election in 1919 to his death in office in 1925. He was succeeded in 1925 by Paul von Hindenburg, who was officially non-partisan, but whose socialization and personal network were firmly rooted in the army and the Prussian aristocracy that dominated it. Regarded by many as a national hero, Hindenburg had attained cult-like status as the result of his role as the victor of the World War I Battle of Tannenberg.[9] In the Weimar system, which elevated the primacy of the parliament, the president was supposed to remain detached from the governance of the country except in times of national crisis, in which case he could invoke Article 48, the emergency clause of the constitution. Ebert made use of his emergency powers when defending the Republic against left-wing revolutions and right-wing putsches in the early 1920s. For his part, Hindenburg used Article 48 to transform Germany from a parliamentary to a presidential system starting in 1930, a measure that, in the end, contributed to the death of the Weimar Republic rather than to its preservation.

The Nazi Party from Its Founding through the Beer Hall Putsch

The Nazi Party began its life as the German Workers' Party (DAP), one organization among many on the anti-Weimar, *völkisch* right in the immediate post–World War I period. The DAP was founded and based in the Bavarian capital city of Munich. The political atmosphere in Bavaria had been extremely polarized since the end of the war. As a result of the revolution of November 1918, the Bavarian government came under the control of the left-wing socialist Kurt Eisner. After his defeat in a Bavarian parliamentary election by more moderate Social Democrats in January 1919, Eisner, who was of Jewish origin, was assassinated by a right-wing nationalist. In April, Communists launched a new revolution in Munich and declared the creation of a Soviet Republic in Bavaria. A few weeks later, units of the army and the Free Corps crushed the revolutionary government. These events led Bavaria to extend tolerance to the extreme right, which was seen as a counterweight to the threat from the radical left. The ironic and unintended consequence of revolutionary socialism in Bavaria was to help transform the region into an incubator of the *völkisch* movement.

The DAP was founded at the beginning of 1919 by Anton Drexler, a toolmaker at the Bavarian railroad, and Karl Harrer, a sports journalist. They envisaged it as an anti-Marxist party for nationalistically inclined workers, and many of the earliest members were, in fact, railroad workers. The DAP had close personal ties to the Thule Society, a secretive racist and antisemitic organization that had also been founded in post-war Munich. Although Hitler later tried to convey the impression that the NSDAP, as it became known, had been an insignificant entity until he took it over and transformed it into a formidable party, it was in fact already a well-established presence on the *völkisch* scene in Munich before he joined it in September 1919.

Hitler had been born in 1889 on the Austrian side of the border with Bavaria. He spent his youth in the Austrian city of Linz and then in the Austro-Hungarian imperial capital city of Vienna, where he lived the depressing life of a struggling artist and wannabe bohemian. He moved across the border into Germany in 1913, taking up residence in Munich. He joined the Bavarian army upon the outbreak of World War I in 1914. There are few reliable historical sources for Hitler's life before he took up politics in 1919. His political autobiography, *Mein Kampf*, published in the mid 1920s, was a self-serving work of political propaganda, full of self-pity as well as exaggerated and fabricated claims about his own suffering and heroism. It is important not to take this text at face value. For example, in *Mein Kampf* Hitler wrote that he had adopted the ideology of racial antisemitism while living in Vienna, where he had come into contact with Eastern European Jews and other peoples from the ethnically highly diverse Austro-Hungarian Empire. But his acquaintances from that time did not recall a doctrinaire racist antisemite and noted that Hitler had had cordial relationships with Jewish acquaintances, including two merchants who sold his paintings. Such behavior is not necessarily inconsistent with holding anti-Jewish views, but it seems likely that Hitler's antisemitism at that time involved the ethnic and economic prejudices against Jews that were then common in Vienna rather than any systematic racial theory of human affairs.[10]

Although Hitler served in the Bavarian army with some distinction, he did not rise beyond the rank of corporal. His participation in the war ended when he fell victim to a gas attack in the spring of 1918. He spent the remaining months of the war in a hospital. Jewish soldiers who knew him in the army did not notice any conspicuous antisemitism on his part. The officer who recommended him for an Iron Cross was Jewish. It is likely that only in the immediate post-war months did Hitler's antisemitism move to the center of his consciousness and worldview, spurred by defeat, revolution, the "stab in the back" myth, the Versailles treaty, and the ongoing threat of left-wing revolutions in the highly polarized atmosphere of post-war Munich. Hitler's adoption of a worldview centered on the evil machinations of the Jews was by no means unusual in Germany at that time.[11]

After the war, Hitler returned to Munich, where he was assigned political training duties at a local army regiment, a position in which he honed his speaking skills. His commanding officer, Karl Mayr, cultivated close connections with the local organizations and parties of the newly emergent *völkisch* right. In September 1919, Mayr instructed Hitler to take up contact with one of these groups, the DAP. It has often been asserted that Hitler's task was simply to monitor the activities of the party, but it is more likely that Mayr intended for Hitler to actually assist it. In any case, Hitler quickly joined the party, which became the main focus of his life after leaving the army in March 1920.

Hitler made a powerful impression on his party colleagues on the basis of his oratorical skills, rapidly becoming the party's most sought-after speaker. Many of his early speeches for the DAP were virulently antisemitic. Whatever the nature and depth of his antisemitic feelings might have been in Vienna in the years before World War I, racist antisemitism was now openly at the core of his worldview. Hitler's ability to deliver long, emotionally satisfying speeches to his listeners thus emerged early on as a key to his political success. He understood, both intellectually and intuitively, the issues and emotions that motivated his audiences, delivering the messages they wanted to hear in a speaking style that impressed them as authentic and that impelled them to action. He had a knack for appealing to the grievances, resentments, and prejudices of his listeners, and for channeling their anger at a particular set of designated villains, the Jews and the "November criminals" of the left. While he undoubtedly possessed a natural talent for this style of inflammatory rhetoric, he also contemplated and practiced the art of public speaking. The relationship between Hitler and his followers was "charismatic" in the sense used by the great German sociologist Max Weber. Charisma, in Weber's definition, is not a quality that resides objectively in an individual, but rather a bond that develops between a leader and his acolytes in a very specific set of historical and cultural circumstances.[12] In Hitler's case, speeches consisting of emotional screeds about national renewal and enemies of the Volk were crucial to the creation and maintenance of this charismatic bond. As the Nazi movement developed, the mystique of Hitler as the heroic, manly savior of his nation was also conveyed through images in photographs, propaganda posters, and films. To those who shared the charismatic bond, Hitler was both a brilliant orator and a remarkable leader. To those outside that circle, both then and now, the impression might well be that of a raving fanatic.

In February 1920, the DAP issued its official program, a document heavily influenced by Hitler. Shortly thereafter, the party adopted the label of "National Socialist" and rechristened itself the NSDAP. In 1921, on the basis of his position as the party's propaganda director and most popular speaker, Hitler successfully maneuvered to seize control of the party from its two founders, Drexler and Harrer. From this point onward, the history of the Nazi Party became inextricably linked with Hitler himself. Hitler established unquestioned authority over the party. The "Führer Cult" around Hitler, which became a defining feature of the party, was consciously manufactured starting in 1922. The dramatic success of Mussolini's March on Rome in October of that year further confirmed the faith of Nazi Party members in the political potentialities of intrepid, iron-fisted leadership.[13]

Much of the NSDAP's activity involved rallies and speeches in beer halls, emphasizing hostility to the Republic, Jews, and Marxists. The party continued to reach out to members of the German working class during this early phase, with disappointing results. While the NSDAP enjoyed some degree of success in attracting skilled workers, who in terms of income and outlook bore similarities to members of the lower middle class, the party was less effective in recruiting from the much larger population of unskilled workers. The political loyalties of this latter segment of German society tended to remain with the Social Democratic and Communist Parties. Some unskilled workers did gravitate to the Nazi Party between 1920 and 1923, but they were dramatically unrepresented there when compared with their percentage in the population as a whole. In contrast, the Nazi Party attracted members from the lower middle class in disproportionately high numbers. These party joiners included artisans, shopkeepers, business employees and civil servants at the lower ranks, and farmers. The recent historical experiences of Germans in these occupational categories were diverse, but one important shared sentiment was class anxiety – a fear of proletarianization – in the face of large-scale capitalism. The NSDAP's antisemitic message, which emphasized the Jewish connection to both capitalism and Communism, resonated among many such Germans. Thus, despite serious early efforts to mobilize the German working class behind Nazism, the middle class remained the core of the NSDAP's membership until the party's assumption of power in 1933.[14]

By early 1923, under Hitler's leadership, the NSDAP had grown to encompass around 8,000 members. These did not include the thousands of members of the party's paramilitary auxiliary, the SA, which possessed its own organizational structure. The party was organized locally into about 100 local chapters, the highest concentration being in Bavaria. (The state of Prussia, Germany's largest, had banned the party in November 1922.) The party financed itself from member contributions, also receiving substantial donations from a number of wealthy supporters. Hitler was embraced by several prominent members of Munich society, such as the art publisher Ernst Hanfstaengl and World War I aviation hero Hermann Göring, which helped bring respectability to him and his movement. The party published a newspaper, the *Völkischer Beobachter* (*Völkisch Observer*), which appeared daily as of February 1923. The structure of the party was loose. Influence within the organization depended more on personal proximity to the charismatic leader than to the authority attached to any particular office.[15]

The Weimar Republic faced a series of major crises in 1923. When Germany fell behind on its reparations payments, France and Belgium occupied the Ruhr industrial region, intending to forcibly extract the wealth that Germany had failed to turn over on its own. The German government responded by calling on the workers in the Ruhr to strike; if they did not produce, there would be nothing for the occupier to take. This strategy was referred to as "passive resistance." But the German government also committed to paying these workers. Meeting this new economic burden required the printing of additional currency at precisely the moment that the country's economic production underwent a serious decline. Germany had already been suffering from serious currency inflation since the end of the war, but the strategy for dealing with the Ruhr occupation triggered a hyperinflation. The speed with which the value of the mark declined created major disruptions in the functioning of businesses and in the everyday lives of Germans, who faced the pressure of having to spend their cash daily, before it lost its value. By late November 1923, the exchange rate of the mark vis-à-vis the US dollar was 4.2 trillion to one. Germans who possessed assets valued in marks, such as savings accounts or retirement pensions, saw this wealth disappear. The middle class was hit hardest by these losses, as members of the working class had little or nothing in the bank, while the upper classes owned land, houses, and forms of personal property that retained their value.

As the year 1923 wore on, Germany was gripped by a crisis atmosphere while the Ruhr occupation continued and the inflation worsened. These developments undermined confidence in the national government and led to unrest and planning of left-wing revolutions and right-wing coups d'état. They also fueled a dramatic growth of the Nazi Party, which began the year 1923 with 8,000 members but claimed 55,000 by the beginning of November. The new members, drawn disproportionately from the German middle class,[16] had transformed the NSDAP into a major political force, especially in Bavaria. In early November, as the staggering inflation persisted, Hitler decided to make his play for national power.

Emboldened by support from Erich Ludendorff, the World War I general and a prominent promoter of the "stab in the back" legend, Hitler intended to seize power through a putsch in Munich and, from there, lead a March on Berlin, modeled on Mussolini's March on Rome of the previous year. The successful putsch would install a dictatorship in Berlin. On the evening of November 8, the head of the Bavarian government, Gustav von Kahr, was holding an anti-republican, anti-Marxist speech in the Bürgerbräukeller, a large beer hall in Munich, to mark the following day's anniversary of the revolution of 1918. Hitler entered the hall with some members of his entourage and announced the overthrow of the Bavarian government. Von Kahr was a right-wing monarchist who despised the Republic, but he preferred the restoration of the Bavarian monarchy over a *völkisch* dictatorship. In the beer hall, however, Hitler intimidated him into expressing his support for the putsch. In the following hours, members of the SA and other Nazis spread out through Munich to arrest members of the city and Bavarian governments. But von Kahr turned against Hitler as soon as the chance presented itself, ordering the police and army to crush the putsch, which they did quickly and easily. Thirteen Nazis were killed. Hitler was injured, and, after a futile attempt to hide at the home of a devoted follower outside of Munich, he was arrested two days later.[17]

In the wake of the failed putsch, the Nazi Party was banned. At his trial, Hitler engaged in propaganda for his cause with the court's indulgence. Convicted of attempting to overthrow the government, he received the minimum sentence of five years with the possibility of early release on probation. Legally, he ought to have faced not only imprisonment but also, on account of his Austrian citizenship, expulsion from Germany. This leniency reflected the anti-republican sympathies of many officials in the German judicial system. Incarcerated rather comfortably in the prison at Landsberg, he wrote *Mein Kampf* with the help of visiting supporters and party comrades. He was released in December 1924, having spent less than a year in prison.

The putsch had been an impulsive, poorly planned, and amateurishly executed operation. It had been foolish to proceed without a firm guarantee of cooperation from the army and the police. This failure of the putsch led Hitler to draw two important lessons for his political future. First, he would jettison the revolutionary strategy, which had failed so spectacularly, and henceforth seek power through electoral means. Second, he would avoid, whenever possible, becoming dependent on allies or confederates whom he could not control. He did not forget who had betrayed him in November 1923. Over a decade later, during the "Night of the Long Knives" of June 1934, Hitler had Gustav von Kahr arrested and sent to the Dachau concentration camp, where he was murdered.

Weimar: The Illusion of Stability

While Hitler sat in Landsberg prison committing his racist, antisemitic vision of the world to paper in the form of *Mein Kampf*, the creative and pragmatic statesman Gustav Stresemann, leader of the German People's Party (DVP) and Germany's foreign minister, began the difficult work necessary for stabilizing the Weimar Republic. After inflation was brought under control by a reform of the German currency, Stresemann took a number of important steps to improve Germany's international position. He negotiated a revision of the schedule for

Germany's reparations payments, which, together with arrangement for American financing, was embodied in the Dawes Plan of 1924. Under Stresemann's leadership, the occupation of the Ruhr was ended, and a series of treaties signed in the Swiss town of Locarno in 1925 normalized Germany's relations with its neighbors. Germany joined the League of Nations in 1926, the same year in which Stresemann was awarded the Nobel Peace Prize. Even though difficult questions, such as Germany's disputed border with Poland, remained unresolved, the "Spirit of Locarno" generated optimism for a peaceful future for Germany in Europe during the second half of the 1920s.[18]

Germany's integration into the international system was accompanied by economic and political stability at home. Inflation having been conquered, unemployment was now kept in check, and an expanded system of unemployment insurance, passed with an overwhelming majority in the Reichstag in 1927, provided for workers who had lost their jobs. Although cabinets continued to be reshuffled on a regular basis, there was a good deal of continuity in the national government. Only three different men served as chancellor between November 1923 and March 1930, and Stresemann served continuously as foreign minister from 1923 until his death in 1929. After the 1924 Reichstag election produced a series of center-right cabinets, the election of 1928 resulted in a Grand Coalition, led by the Social Democrats and including the centrist parties. The anti-Weimar parties of the extreme left and right – the Communists and the Nazis – controlled only 54 seats out of a total of 491 after the 1928 election.

The rapidity with which this seemingly successful parliamentary democracy disintegrated after the onset of the Great Depression suggests that the stability of the years 1924 to 1930 had been deceptive. Other democracies, such as the United States, Britain, and France, were also hit hard by the Depression, but did not devolve into dictatorships because the majority of the citizens of those countries did not interpret the Depression as a symptom of a failed political system. The decline and fall of German democracy between 1930 and 1933 has led one influential historian of the Weimar Republic to characterize the stability of the preceding half-decade as an "illusion."[19] The legitimacy of the Republic was tenuous or absent in substantial segments of the population. There were so-called Republicans of Reason (*Vernunftrepublikaner*), who, while accepting Weimar as an inescapable reality, never embraced it enthusiastically. There were committed enemies of the Republic on the far left, in the Communist Party, which received 10.6 percent of the vote in the 1928 Reichstag election. Hostility to Weimar was even broader on the right. Although the Nazis received only 2.8 percent of the vote in the 1928 election, the conservative nationalists of the DNVP received 14.2 percent, and many DNVP supporters harbored deep hostility to Weimar. So even when times were good, over a quarter of the electorate harbored fundamental doubts about the Republic. In retrospect, we can understand how Weimar was likely to have great trouble surviving the kind of major crisis that came in the form of the Great Depression.

Hatred of Marxism, antisemitism, and bitterness over the alleged "stab in the back" and Versailles can only partially explain the antipathy toward Weimar on the German right. A powerful politics of cultural resentment was also at work. The collapse of the German Empire and the birth of the new republic inaugurated a period of dramatic social and artistic experimentation. Women received the right to vote, and a women's movement lobbied for expanded professional opportunities, birth control, and the right to abortion. A gay and lesbian subculture developed in Berlin and other cities, while scholars in the field of sex research endeavored to change negative perceptions of homosexuality. In architecture, the Bauhaus movement and other champions of modernism promoted an international style, questioning widely accepted assumptions about the traditional aesthetics and function of buildings. In music, atonality, which had originated in the years before World War I, challenged the dominant principles of composition, while jazz introduced rhythms and a sensibility associated with the culture of African Americans. In the visual arts, expressionism, which had also begun before 1914, upended traditional notions of representation in painting and heavily influenced the relatively new medium of film. Not a small number of Germans found these developments disorienting or threatening, and their disapproval fueled a right-wing backlash. The experimental and progressive elements of Weimar culture were denounced as degenerate, alien, and the products of Marxists and Jews.[20]

For a small group of right-wing intellectuals, associated with what is loosely termed the Conservative Revolution, the objection to Weimar culture ran deeper. Infected by anti-modernism and a deep cultural pessimism, they hated both the materialistic emphasis of Marxism and the flabbiness of bourgeois society. They condemned the morally corrupting influence of urban life and glorified the authenticity of the rural salt of the earth. Nostalgic for the sense of purpose bestowed by World War I, they embraced a Social Darwinist view of the world. Unlike genuine reactionaries, who desired to restore the institution of monarchy, these nationalists imagined an authoritarianism rooted in popular legitimacy. Two of these figures were authors with wide readerships. Ernst Jünger romanticized war as a means for transcending the class divisions within society, while Oswald Spengler called on Germans to reject Western constitutionalism and materialism and embrace instead an organic form of authoritarian, nationalist socialism. While these two writers, among many others, disparaged the Weimar Republic and helped to undermine its legitimacy, they did not embrace Nazism. The diversity of opinion in the German right during the Weimar Republic should not be obscured by the monopoly over opinion achieved by the Nazis after 1933.[21]

The Rebuilding of the Nazi Movement, 1924–30

After his release from Landsberg prison in December 1924, Hitler began the painstaking task of rebuilding the NSDAP. Having pledged to play by the rules of electoral politics, he would have to create a party organization suited to attracting not only members but also voters. A key to success would be the creation of an effective propaganda operation and the training of a cadre of speakers and activists capable of taking the messages of the NSDAP into urban neighborhoods and rural towns and villages.

He was distracted from this task, however, by the emergence of factionalism in the NSDAP, which arose from a dispute about the basic orientation of the party toward economic questions. A group of Nazi officials around Gregor Strasser, the regional leader (Gauleiter) of Lower Bavaria, hoped to amend the party program so as to make it more attractive to members of the industrial working class. Strasser and several Gauleiters based in industrial regions in northern and western Germany formed a "Working Group" to discuss possibilities for reorienting the party in this direction. Among the possibilities they discussed were the expropriation of property from the former German royal families and a German alliance with the Soviet Union aimed against the "Jewish-Capitalist" West.[22] Hitler rightly perceived the Working Group as a threat to the supremacy of the Munich headquarters of the party and to his status as unchallenged Führer of the Nazi movement. Any changes to the party program would have to emanate from him. Hitler brought Strasser and the others into line by means of a forceful speech at a meeting of party leaders in Bamberg in February 1926. Although Hitler was able to reassert his absolute authority over the party, Gregor Strasser would remain a thorn in his side until June 1934, when he was murdered on Hitler's order during the Night of the Long Knives.

In the late 1920s, much of the energy of Hitler and his lieutenants focused on building a party cadre. Only in retrospect, in light of the rapid expansion of the party after the onset of the Depression, did the importance of this foundational work become apparent.[23] The party built a national infrastructure based on regions (Gaue), which mirrored the country's electoral jurisdictions. The Nazi Gaue were later subdivided into districts and locals as the party grew. The regional party offices organized rallies and speeches. As only one Reichstag election took place between December 1924 and September 1930, relatively little effort was devoted to election campaigning. One strategy that would ultimately prove worthwhile was the establishment of party auxiliary organizations focused on specific occupation and social groups. A National Socialist German Student League was created in 1926 to mobilize university students behind the cause.[24] The year 1928 saw the creation of the National Socialist Factory Cell Organization (Nationalsozialistische Betriebszellenorganisation, or NSBO), which sought to extend the appeal of Nazism among working-class Germans.[25] The Combat League for German Culture, founded in 1928, intended to attract Germans repelled by the modernist manifestations of Weimar culture.[26] A National Socialist German Physicians' League took form in 1929.[27] More such auxiliaries, including a National Socialist Women's League, were put in place in the early 1930s.[28]

Despite receiving only 2.6 percent of the vote in the May 1928 election, the party experienced steady growth in the final years of the 1920s. Membership reached about 100,000 by the end of 1929. NSDAP rallies attracted large numbers of committed, enthusiastic supporters.[29] The party effectively exploited German anger engendered in 1929 by the Young Plan, an international effort to readjust German reparations payments. A campaign against German acceptance of the plan was organized by the German industrialist Alfred Hugenberg, who had taken over the DNVP in 1928 and then steered it hard to the right. The alliance with the DNVP enhanced the prestige of Hitler and the NSDAP in elite conservative and nationalist circles.

Although the German unemployment rate had been creeping upwards since the beginning of 1929, the crash of the New York Stock Exchange on October 24 of that year – Black Tuesday – heralded the onset of the Great Depression. The negative effects were felt quickly in the German economy, which was especially dependent on foreign credit that was now evaporating. Unemployment among German trade union members, which had been hovering at around 10 percent, almost doubled by the end of 1929. It remained at slightly over 20 percent for much of 1930, before rising to 31.7 percent at the close of the year. This rate rose again to an average of 34.3 percent in 1931 and to an astonishing 43.8 percent in 1932.[30]

The fragility of Weimar democracy was exposed by the economic crisis. In March 1930, the center-left Grand Coalition that had governed Germany since 1928 was ripped apart by the challenge of unemployment. The SPD, sensitive to the needs of workers, and the DVP, looking out for the interests of German business, could not overcome their differences and compromise on a formula for injecting more money into the overburdened system of unemployment insurance. A new center-right cabinet was formed under the chancellorship of Heinrich Brüning of the Catholic German Center Party. Brüning had an ambitious economic program that included measures to combat unemployment and the negotiation of yet another reduction in German reparations payments. He hoped to garner parliamentary majorities for his plan, but he was also prepared to rely, if necessary, on presidential emergency authority in the form of Article 48 of the Weimar Constitution. Paul von Hindenburg, the 82-year-old president of the Republic, supported this scheme, acting on the advice of one of his close confidants, General Kurt von Schleicher, chief of the ministerial office in the Ministry of Defense. Their intention was to stabilize the Republic by transforming it from a parliamentary system into a presidential one. Article 48 had not been intended for this purpose, but rather for that of defending parliamentary democracy by means of a temporary transfer of authority to the president in times of crisis. In the early 1920s, President Friedrich Ebert had invoked Article 48 in that spirit. But now, in 1930, the Prussian military aristocrats Paul von Hindenburg and Kurt von Schleicher, and the conservative Catholic Heinrich Brüning were prepared to experiment with Article 48 as a way to normalize the shift of power from the parliament to the executive. Their maneuver represented a serious blow to Weimar democracy.

In July 1930, Brüning invoked Article 48 to implement financial measures for which he had been unable to assemble a majority in the Reichstag. When a broad coalition of parties voted to rescind the Article 48 decree, credibly arguing that no national emergency existed, Brüning dissolved the parliament, scheduling a new election for September. He hoped that the new Reichstag sent to Berlin by the voters would be more amenable to his agenda. Until a new Reichstag was in place, Brüning would govern the country on presidential authority.

The decision to call a Reichstag election was a miscalculation of historic proportions. The new parliament was far more polarized than the previous one, rendering workable majorities even less likely, and therefore making continued reliance on Article 48 all but inevitable. The Communists' share of the vote increased from 10.6 percent in 1928 to 13.1, while the Nazis boosted their share from 2.6 to 18.3 percent, translating into an increase in Nazi Reichstag deputies from 12 to 107. Much of the new support for the NSDAP came from voters who abandoned the parties of the conservative nationalist right, the DNVP and the DVP. The Nazis also received support from first-time voters. The surge of the NSDAP resulted from the festering economic crisis and the apparent incompetence of the Weimar political system.

Nazism as a Mass Movement, 1930–32

The strong electoral showing for the Nazis in September 1930 did not come out of nowhere. Rallies featuring speeches by Hitler and other party leaders had been attracting massive crowds, and the number of party members had been rising steadily. A milestone in the development of the party had been reached in January 1930, when it entered a coalition government in the German state of Thuringia. The robust performance in the September 1930 election lent momentum to the party into 1931, encouraging new members to stream in at a dramatically accelerated pace, and transforming Nazism into a genuine mass movement. In May 1931, the NSDAP received 37.2 percent of the vote in the small northwestern province of Oldenburg. In July, Nazi activists took control of the national umbrella organization of German university students, the German Student Union. In November, the NSDAP won 37 percent of the vote in the populous state of Hesse.

Quantitative studies of both the membership of the Nazi Party and the voters who supported it have produced a detailed picture of the movement in the years immediately preceding its assumption of power. The movement had a middle-class core but also drew significant support from Germans of other social classes. Members of the lower middle class flocked to the NSDAP in numbers greater than their representation in the population, but by the early 1930s the party was also attracting members from elite circles, in addition to substantial numbers of working-class Germans. Even though most workers still tended to support the parties of the political left, Nazi outreach to workers helped build a party that extended across the boundaries of class (see Figure 2.1).[31]

The class structure of the NSDAP membership and electorate was reflected in the geographic distribution of its support. Before 1933, the party enjoyed greater success in the countryside and in small cities and towns than in the large cities. The working class was scarcer in these areas, and the Nazi critique of modern culture and of the supposed degeneracy of urban life was also a factor here. Some rural regions harbored a deep tradition of peasant antisemitism, derived in part from conflicts with Jewish grain and cattle dealers. The Nazis were substantially stronger in the Protestant countryside than in rural regions that were predominantly Catholic, owing to the long-standing loyalty of many Catholic voters to the German Center Party.

One hallmark of the Nazi Party's membership was its youth, a characteristic it shared with the Communist Party. The action-oriented image of the party, conveyed by parades, rallies, and animated speeches, appealed to young people who were put off by the more stolid self-presentation of the older, more established parties. The leadership of the NSDAP itself

Figure 2.1 Nazi election poster promising "jobs, freedom, and bread" to the working class, 1932 (Fine Art Images/Heritage Images via Getty Images).

was relatively young. Hitler turned only 41 in 1930, and many of the top party officials were still in their thirties. The appeal of radical politics proved especially strong among the generation of Germans born before

World War I but too young to fight. Their shared experience of wartime deprivation, defeat, hyperinflation, and mass unemployment engendered doubts about the ability of the traditional parties and the Weimar system to address the problems facing the country. Many among the better-educated young Germans suffered from deep anxiety about their future career prospects, and therefore embraced a movement that pledged to break the logjam in German society, do away with Marxist fantasies of egalitarianism, and promote opportunities for the strongest and most able.[32]

The masculine mystique of the NSDAP as a party of action-minded political fighters made membership not especially attractive for women before 1933. The male-supremacist ideology of National Socialism, which relegated women to the roles of mother and homemaker, and which was championed by the National Socialist Women's League, was a further discouragement to female membership. Between 1925 and 1932, only 7.8 percent of new party members were women.

While quantitative data regarding the composition of the party's membership and electoral constituency are extremely valuable, we must also look to more impressionist forms of evidence and "ego documents," such as diaries, memoirs, and correspondence, in order to understand the motivations of Hitler's supporters before 1933. A particularly valuable set of sources is a set of 683 brief autobiographies of Nazis collected by means of an essay contest organized by the American sociologist Theodore Abel in 1934. Many of the essays were submitted by Germans who had joined the NSDAP during its "time of struggle" before January 30, 1933. The documents are compelling on account of their contemporaneousness. They show that many Nazis were drawn to the movement by the mystique of action and strong leadership, which they believed would help Germany out of its economic and political morass. Many mentioned a yearning for the restoration of national greatness after the humiliations of Versailles and the Young Plan. A further common theme was a longing for social harmony and an end to bitter class conflict, which they blamed on Marxism. Some of the essays reflected the anticapitalism that had been common in the "left wing" of the party.[33]

Nazism's racial doctrine of Aryan superiority did not figure prominently in the essays, but antisemitism, in numerous forms, did. Many of the essayists stressed the need to break the economic power of the Jews or blamed the Jews for Germany's defeat in the war, its unfair treatment during the 1920s, and the cultural degeneracy of German society. The language used to refer to Jews parroted the words of Hitler's speeches and party propaganda. Although the NSDAP at times intentionally toned down its antisemitism in election campaigns, seeking to broaden its base of voters,[34] there can be little doubt that antipathy toward Jews was an important motivation for a large number of Germans who joined the party before 1933. In addition to being a sincere expression of Nazi ideology, appealing to antisemitism served the instrumental purpose of papering over the contradictions inherent in the party's economic promises. The Nazis offered all things to all men: work for the unemployed, protection against proletarization for the lower middle class, and defense of private property for the capitalists.

The financing of the NSDAP's operations came mostly from its rapidly growing number of dues-paying members. The assertion, often made in Marxist circles both during the Nazi era and since 1945, that the party's rise to power was financed largely by German big business has been disproved by the meticulous archival research of Henry Ashby Turner, Jr. (see Figure 2.2).[35] To be sure, more than a few German capitalists shared the NSDAP's fear of and disdain for Marxism, and they resented the expensive social programs created by the Weimar Republic. But they were also confused and worried by Nazi anti-capitalist rhetoric and the unpredictability of Hitler and his movement. Most capitalists preferred the more traditional conservative right, as embodied by the DVP or DNVP. Thus, they did not lavish funding on the NSDAP before 1933. Once the Nazis were in power, much of the German business world embraced the new regime and channeled generous sums of money to the ruling party.

The End of the Weimar Republic and the Triumph of Nazism

Heinrich Brüning, who had acceded to the chancellorship in March 1930, continued to govern Germany until June 1932. He succeeded in forcing through a moratorium on German reparations payments, which helped bring about a definitive cancellation of the debts shortly after he left office. But despite his executive prerogatives, derived from Article 48, he was unable to halt the deterioration of the German economy. The Nazi movement's visibility on the German political landscape continued to grow. The size of the party's Reichstag delegation, which had grown to 107 as a result of the September 1930 election, was now overshadowed by the prominence the Nazi movement had attained through its rallies and parades in many towns and neighborhoods, and through the frequent street fighting engaged in by members of the SA against Communists. By early 1932, party membership had reached about a quarter-million, augmented by several hundred thousand additional members of the SA.

A potential path to power presented itself in the presidential election of 1932, when Paul von Hindenburg's seven-year term was set to expire.

Figure 2.2 SPD poster depicting the Nazi movement as the enemy of the working class, 1932 (ullstein bild via Getty Images).

Hindenburg, now 84 years old, had not intended to run for re-election, but was persuaded to do so for the sake of the nation. His candidacy was embraced by the Social Democrats and the German Center Party, which recognized him as the bulwark against the far right. Hitler, in his first-ever attempt at elected office, campaigned as the NSDAP candidate. Having not previously been a German citizen, he was rendered eligible for office by an administrative trick in the German state of Braunschweig, where a coalition government with NSDAP participation appointed him a civil servant, granting him citizenship in the process. The Communist Party ran its leader, Ernst Thälmann, while the DNVP, which had lurched to the right since 1928, was represented by Theodor Duesterberg. In the first round of the election, held on March 13, Hindenburg received 49.6 percent of the vote, while Hitler trailed far behind with 30.2 percent. The run-off, held on April 10, featured only three candidates, Duesterberg having withdrawn and the DNVP having thrown its support behind Hindenburg. The incumbent president won re-election with just over 53 percent, while Hitler received 36.7 percent and Thälmann around 10 percent. Although Hitler was not elected, he celebrated the result as a political triumph. His share of the vote was double what the NSDAP had received in the 1930 Reichstag election.[36]

The Reich government now attempted to break the momentum of the Nazi movement by imposing a ban on the SA, a measure that Hitler accepted rather than risk a confrontation with the army. Despite the ban, the Nazi movement emerged with strong results from state elections held on April 24, 1932 in Prussia, Bavaria, Württemberg, Hamburg, and Anhalt. In Anhalt, where the NSDAP emerged from the election as the strongest party, a Nazi was appointed minister president (equivalent to an American governor) for the first time.

Hindenburg, acting on the advice of General Kurt von Schleicher and other confidants from aristocratic-military circles, now decided on a new strategy for containing the Nazi surge. The president dissolved the cabinet of Heinrich Brüning on May 30, betraying the Social Democrats and the centrist political parties that had supported him in the presidential election. Brüning was replaced by Franz von Papen, who was to head a "national government" of non-affiliated ministers acting above party politics.[37] This move marked yet another step away from the parliamentary design of the Weimar constitution in the direction of a more authoritarian presidential regime. Von Papen employed a complex strategy for consolidating power. Whereas Brüning had been loath to deal with Hitler, von Papen hoped to win Nazi acceptance of his new configuration. He made several major concessions to Hitler in June 1932. These included the dissolution of the Reichstag and the scheduling of new elections, which Hitler expected to help his party, and the lifting of the ban on the SA. In July, in a further attempt to consolidate his authority, von Papen used Article 48 to depose the government of Prussia, placing it under the direct control of the national government. In doing this, von Papen intended to balance his concessions to Hitler with a show of force that would pre-empt a Nazi takeover of Germany's largest state in the upcoming Reichstag election.

The fundamental problem with von Papen's strategy was that it had very little popular support. It was essentially a program for aristocratic rule over a society that had become accustomed to mass politics. This problem was underlined by the results of the Reichstag election of July 31, 1932. The NSDAP, with 37.3 percent of the vote, became the largest party in the parliament. As the Communists received 14.3 percent, the totalitarian parties that were dedicated to the downfall of the Weimar Republic together commanded a negative majority in the Reichstag. The two parties would never form a coalition with each other, but, acting together, they could defeat any measure. Von Papen could continue to govern based on Article 48, but with rapidly dwindling popular legitimacy.

Hindenburg and von Papen hoped to address this situation by appointing a government with Nazi participation. Believing they could domesticate the NSDAP by making it share in the responsibility of governance, they offered the position of vice-chancellor to Hitler, who declined. Hitler recognized their tactic and insisted on the chancellorship. In order to prevent Hitler from forging a coalition on his own, and to forestall a vote of no confidence, Hindenburg gave von Papen a blank check to dissolve the new Reichstag at any time. But Hindenburg and Schleicher balked at von Papen's plan for a long-term suspension of the Reichstag, during which the constitution would be altered to institutionalize an authoritarian presidential regime. They feared that, in Germany's tense political atmosphere, such an action could ignite a civil war.

Von Papen promptly dissolved the newly elected Reichstag at its first meeting on September 12 in order to pre-empt an expected vote of no confidence, and yet another election was scheduled for November 6. This time, the NSDAP lost ground, its share of the vote declining from 37.3 percent in July to 33.1. This setback, when considered in the context of earlier developments, suggested that the NSDAP had passed its peak strength and was now in decline. The November election made clear that the party was incapable of attaining an outright majority on the national level, despite pockets of deep support in certain regions. The party coffers had been exhausted by the multiple national election campaigns of 1932, and frustration began to manifest itself in some sectors of the party's rank and file. Intra-party factionalism was inflamed anew by complaints from Nazis aligned with the Strasser wing, who thought that Hitler should have accepted a role in a coalition cabinet after the electoral breakthrough of July. Despite these challenges, the NSDAP remained the largest party in the Reichstag by a large margin, and it was difficult to imagine a viable parliamentary coalition without it.

With no parliamentary solution in sight, von Papen continued his push for an authoritarian reform of the constitution. Schleicher, fearing that such a scheme might provoke a civil war, persuaded Hindenburg to pursue an alternative course. In early December, Schleicher took over the chancellorship himself. His hope was to "tame" the Nazi movement by saddling it with the responsibility of governing. He imagined a broad populist alliance that would include labor unions, Social Democrats, the army, and elements of the NSDAP loyal to Gregor Strasser, whom Schleicher hoped to lure into his cabinet. Such a government would implement aggressive work-creation programs to combat unemployment, and, more generally, set parochial interests aside for the sake of the nation. This plan, which seems highly naïve or even fantastical in retrospect, represented a last-ditch effort to avert a Nazi takeover and preserve a semblance of parliamentary legitimacy for the Republic. The futility of the plan quickly became clear, as the economic and ideological divisions in German society proved too powerful to be overcome. Social Democrats and capitalists could not reconcile their differences, and Hitler refused to permit the NSDAP to participate in a government in which he himself was not the chancellor. As the plan unraveled, Gregor Strasser was compelled to resign from his NSDAP offices.[38]

In order to explain how and why this situation resulted in Adolf Hitler's appointment to the chancellorship of Germany just a few weeks later, on January 30, 1933, we must understand that the Weimar Republic, as envisaged by its founders, had reached a dead end. The German electorate had elected a parliament in which two parties that were fundamentally hostile to the Republic, and to each other, were in control of half the seats. The enduring hostility between the Social Democrats and the Communists prevented the creation of a left-of-center alliance of the sort that emerged several years later with the "Popular Front" in France. Permanent governance based on Article 48 possessed no legitimacy in the party delegations in the Reichstag or among the voters who had sent them there. A fundamental reform of the constitution was regarded as too risky. The Schleicher plan had failed. The prospect of further elections had little appeal after the November election had not substantially altered the balance among the parties.

President Hindenburg, who had by now turned 85, did not see a Hitler chancellorship as the way out of this predicament. He trusted neither

Hitler nor the Nazi movement, which he regarded as plebian and dangerously radical. But von Papen, although no longer chancellor himself, initiated discussions with political allies about bringing Hitler and the NSDAP into a governing coalition with the conservative-nationalist right. Hitler, having previously shunned the possibility of such a coalition, now proved receptive, as the November election had dispelled any hope of the Nazis attaining a majority in the Reichstag. During January 1933, von Papen carried out these negotiations behind the back of Chancellor Kurt von Schleicher, who dreaded the prospect of Hitler in the cabinet. When Schleicher caught wind of the talks, he tried to convince Hindenburg not only to reject Hitler but to ban the Nazi and Communist Parties. Hindenburg, however, who had grown somewhat feeble, was prevailed upon by von Papen as well as by his own son and close advisor, Oskar, to appoint Hitler. After considerable hesitation, he acceded to their wishes.

The essence of von Papen's plan was to simultaneously harness the Nazi movement and to hem it in. A right-wing coalition that included the NSDAP could take on the threat of the Communists, whose support had risen to almost 17 percent in the November election. The Nazis would be useful for this purpose, but would not ultimately be in charge. Von Papen's underestimation of the ruthlessness of Hitler and the radicalism of his movement would have consequences of world-historical significance.

The new government was a coalition drawn from various segments of the German right. It included Hitler as chancellor, with von Papen himself as vice-chancellor. Important ministerial posts with authority over matters of internal security were given to Hermann Göring and Wilhelm Frick, leading figures in the NSDAP. The DNVP provided two ministers, including Alfred Hugenberg, the leader of the party, who had been an ally of Hitler's in the fight against the Young Plan. The cabinet also included several figures who were technically non-partisan but who were drawn from conservative nationalist and aristocratic circles. Nazi propaganda hailed Hitler's appointment as the beginning of a revolution, but, in a practical sense, it did not represent a break with the Republic's system of government, since a reliance on Article 48 had become routine since 1930. The truly revolutionary consequences of the accession to power would become obvious only in the weeks following January 30, 1933, during which Hitler and his movement outmaneuvered their erstwhile conservative allies with astonishing speed.

There should be no illusion that Hitler's path to the chancellorship was the consequence of a democratic process that was in accordance with the Weimar constitution. Beginning in 1930, Germany's slide into authoritarianism was facilitated by a use of presidential emergency powers in a manner that had clearly not been intended by the framers of the constitution. Hitler, an Austrian citizen, had been made eligible for public office in Germany only through a rather dubious naturalization process, which could have been legally challenged, but was not. The NSDAP and its paramilitary wing, the SA, had made extensive use of political violence that was illegal by any definition, something for which Hitler was never called to account. Having attempted a coup against the Republic in 1923, Hitler was given a laughably light sentence, spared from expulsion to his country of citizenship, and permitted to resume his political career. Although he had now pledged to play by the rules, the anti-republican goals of his party were plain to see – at least for some. In 1930, the government of Prussia, led by Social Democrats, prepared a ninety-seven-page memorandum titled "The National Socialist German Workers' Party as a Subversive and Anti-Republican Conspiracy to Commit High Treason." The document laid out an argument for how the NSDAP was preparing a seizure of power by "undermining and disturbing the political and economic life" of the nation, and by creating its own "revolutionary combat troop" in the form of the SA. It concluded with the characterization of the party as a "subversive conspiracy pursuing the aim of undermining the constitutionally established republican form of government."

Prussian officials presented the document to Chancellor Brüning as a brief for declaring the NSDAP an illegal organization, but Brüning balked, claiming a reluctance to use state power to suppress a party that had some basis of popularity in German society. Also in 1930, the highest state prosecutor of the Reich government declined to use the memorandum as a basis for a prosecution of Hitler for high treason. In March 1932, Otto Braun, the Prussian minister president, submitted an updated memorandum on the NSDAP's criminal and anti-constitutional actions to Brüning, but received no response.[39] It is easy to criticize decisions in retrospect, and there is no way to know what might have happened had any of these options been pursued. The point is that there were German officials at a high level who recognized the Nazi movement as a threat to the Republic and who advocated decisive measures of legal and constitutional self-defense, in contrast to the strategy of cooptation that was ultimately pursued, with catastrophic consequences.

Prior to Hitler's appointment to the chancellorship, the Nazi Party's share in a national election never exceeded 37.3 percent of the vote. In Weimar's last election the party received 33.1 percent. Hitler ascended to the chancellorship not as the head of a legitimate parliamentary government, but through "an authoritarian loophole in the Weimar Constitution."[40] By no means can it be said that Hitler was elected. He did not rise to power by democratic means, but rather by virtue of the breakdown of democracy.

3 The Nazi Dictatorship

The government over which Adolf Hitler presided starting on January 30, 1933 embodied a coalition between Nazis and nationalist conservatives. The two groups' visions for the future of Germany overlapped, but also differed in important respects. They shared the desire to restore order to the country based on some form of authoritarian rule, to crush Marxism and radical social-cultural experimentation, and to restore Germany's status as a great power in the international arena. As considerable as these points of agreement were, the differences were also significant. The conservatives, many of whom were rooted in the hereditary aristocracy, championed forms of authoritarian rule based on a hierarchy of traditional elites – in the land-owning agrarian sector, in big business, and in the military. In contrast, Nazism was not a conservative or reactionary movement, but rather a radical one. It was committed to racial and demographic restructuring of German society, subscribed to a virulent variety of biological antisemitism, and employed novel techniques of propaganda and popular mobilization to manipulate a mass following. Nazis regarded their opponents as enemies and traitors, standing ready to resort to physical violence against them. They understood history as an epic conflict for racial survival, and showed little deference to the sense of chivalry and *noblesse oblige* that still served to moderate the political actions of some conservatives. They conceived of themselves not as protectors of narrow class interests, but as animated by a spirit of revolution, fueled by the conviction that they were pursuing a mission to transform Germany on the basis of an ideological truth. Many members of the movement were young, dedicated to the cause, and committed to action. The youthful, populist activism of the Nazis, who were willing to take the political fight to the streets, stood in stark contrast to their conservative allies' preference for back-room machinations and articles in literary magazines.

By the end of July 1933, the Nazi movement had overwhelmed its conservative coalition partners and had abolished political pluralism by establishing a one-party dictatorship and imposing the autocratic Nazi "leader principle" onto the entirety of the country. Non-Nazis in the military, the civil service, the business world, and other elite sectors continued to function as participants in what the historian Ludolf Herbst has termed the "governing compromise" between Nazism and nationalist conservatism. The balance of power within the arrangement would shift continually toward the Nazis during the twelve years of the Third Reich, but this shift was especially dramatic during the first several months of Hitler's chancellorship. The so-called Nazi coordination (*Gleichschaltung*) of the organs of the state and the institutional structure of German society unfolded at a breathtaking pace after January 30, 1933. This "seizure of power" (*Machtergreifung*) was facilitated by physical intimidation and violence targeted against political opponents, many of whom landed in the makeshift concentration camps that were established in the spring of 1933. This political terror unfolded in parallel to the first measures, both official and unofficial, targeted at Jews, and the foundations for a program of institutionalized eugenics were laid shortly thereafter, in July 1933.

Several factors help explain the rapidity with which the Nazi movement was able to marginalize its conservative partners, eliminate left-wing and centrist opposition, establish one-party rule, and unleash racist policies of persecution and exclusion. Despite the fact that the NSDAP had lost some electoral support between the July and November 1932 Reichstag elections, its growth since 1929 had been dramatic, and it had entered the year 1933 as the party with the largest parliamentary delegation. Hitler's appointment to the chancellorship infused new momentum into an action-oriented political movement comprising many true believers who were motivated by a revolutionary fervor. The state terror of early 1933, targeted mainly against Communists and Social Democrats, met with the approval of anti-Marxist conservatives well beyond the Nazi electoral base. But Hitler's conservative coalition partners, thinking they could contain Nazism and harness it to their own agenda, tragically underestimated both the movement's revolutionary energy and the unscrupulousness of its leaders. The illusory self-confidence of the conservatives mirrored a widespread belief in Germany that Hitler, now saddled with the responsibilities of power, would moderate his positions and become a normal politician. Karl Dietrich Bracher, one of the foremost German authorities on the Nazi "seizure of power," famously wrote that "the history of National Socialism from beginning to end is the history of its underestimation."[1] This was true of much of German society in early February 1933, although any illusions that the NSDAP would jettison its ideological priorities for reasons of practical politics were quickly dashed.

A more general factor accounting for the speedy Nazi takeover in 1933 was the acquiescence of much of German society in the face of what seemed increasingly like the fait accompli of Nazi rule. A very large number of Germans who had not previously supported the movement, and even many who continued to harbor severe doubts about it, proved ready to adapt themselves to the radically altered political circumstances. This form of political behavior, rooted in fear, in self-interest, and in the psychological need to not feel out of synch with the times, is referred to as "self-coordination" (*Selbstgleichschaltung*), a bottom-up form of accommodation with the new ruling power.

No factor proved more central to the Nazi "seizure of power" in the early months of 1933 than terror in the form of physical violence and the threat to employ it. This method included state-sanctioned violence on the part of the SA, which was based on an emergency decree of highly dubious constitutionality, and which resulted in the imprisonment of opponents and dissenters, mainly from the political left, in concentration camps. The violence also included acts of intimidation in German everyday life, which were illegal on their face, and which generated the psychological environment of fear to which many German social institutions responded with "self-coordination." The questionable constitutionality and illegality of the changes brought about in large part through the wielding of political violence is worth emphasizing in view of the still widespread notion of the "legal revolution," the idea, promoted by the Nazis themselves, that the profound transformation of German politics and society were grounded in the law and the Weimar constitution. In fact, the events of early 1933 both extended and deepened the collapse of constitutionality and legality that had accompanied the collapse of Weimar and paved the way for the rise of Nazism. The myth of a Nazi "legal revolution" was propagated by the Nazi movement as a means for securing the legitimacy of its rule among civil servants, judges, military officers, and other German elites, many of them of a conservative political bent, who cared about the rule of law, or at least about the appearance of legality. The NSDAP was now applying a lesson that Hitler had learned from the failed putsch of November 1923. It was crucial that Nazi rule be perceived as the consequence of a legal process rather than as some form of coup d'état. But neither Nazi propaganda, nor the self-deception or self-serving dishonesty of those Germans who were prepared to accept it, should be allowed to distract historians from the fundamentally anti-democratic and anti-constitutional process that gave birth to the Third Reich in 1933.

Steps toward Dictatorship

Upon becoming chancellor, Hitler insisted that President Hindenburg dissolve the Reichstag and schedule a new election. Hitler hoped that the voters would give their blessing to his appointment, and more generally to the Nazi agenda, by granting the NSDAP an absolute majority in the parliament. Such a success would mark the culmination of the electoral strategy pursued by Hitler since his release from prison in 1924. Hindenburg once again overcame his aversion to Hitler, granting his chancellor's wish. This would not be the last time that Hindenburg, whose personal and institutional authority might have served as a brake on Hitler's despotic tendencies, exercised his prerogatives to what would turn out to be the benefit of the NSDAP. The Reichstag was dissolved on February 1, 1933, and an election set for March 5.

Hitler lost little time in taking advantage of his control of the levers of power to influence the election in the NSDAP's favor. On February 4, an emergency decree "for the protection of the German people" was issued over his own signature and that of Hindenburg. While the Reichstag Fire Decree of February 28, which will be examined shortly, has correctly been recognized as the foundation for the repressive police state of the Third Reich, the decree of February 4 is often overlooked. Based on Article 48 of the Weimar Constitution, it authorized police to prohibit or break up political meetings, marches, or demonstrations deemed to pose an "immediate danger to public security." The decree further empowered police to ban or confiscate political flyers and newspapers for a multitude of reasons, among them committing "insult" or showing "willful contempt" for the state or its "leading officials." The NSDAP, by virtue of its control of the Reich Ministry of the Interior under Wilhelm Frick, and of the state of Prussia, under Hermann Göring, exercised significant powers over Germany's police forces.

The impact of repressive measures authorized by the February 4 decree has been documented in numerous studies of the Nazi takeover in individual German cities and towns. In and around the small city of Eutin, in the eastern part of Holstein, not far from the Baltic Sea, the police carried out systematic searches of the homes of all Communist Party functionaries. The local party leader was arrested for possessing a revolver and "highly treasonous" literature, while one of his colleagues, though not arrested, saw his Communist songbooks confiscated.[2] In the town of Northeim, in the Lower Saxony region of Prussia, the crackdown against the opposition started in the first week of February. Police raided the homes of local Communists in search of subversive literature and banned the local Communist Party from soliciting contributions or holding meetings of any kind. The disruption of electoral campaigning by the Social Democrats started a bit later but was no less severe. The police confiscated the weekly print-run of the local Social Democratic newspaper on the grounds that it had ridiculed Hitler and referred to the swastika as a "bankrupt symbol." A few days later, a march by 400 members of the Social Democratic *Reichsbanner* organization was broken up by police even as a somewhat smaller march by the local SA troop was allowed to continue without interruption. Further Social Democratic marches and rallies were banned, whereas the local NSDAP was allowed to continue campaigning.[3] Scenes like these played out through much of the country during the month of February.

The intimidating effect of such actions by German police, which carried a patina of legality, was reinforced by violent acts of an outright illegal nature committed by the SA. On February 4, a member of the SA murdered the Social Democratic mayor of the Saxon town of Stassfurt. Eight days later, in the nearby town of Eisleben, 300 SA-men, wielding spades, steel rods, and revolvers, attacked a sports hall where members of the local Communist Party were meeting, killing three of the attendees. To some degree a continuation of the political violence of the last phase of the Weimar Republic, incidents of this kind multiplied throughout Germany after January 30, 1933, resulting more frequently in death or serious injury than they had previously. Hitler's appointment to the chancellorship had emboldened the more violent among his followers, who acted increasingly with a sense of impunity.[4] The political terror was the result of a conscious strategy encouraged from the top, but implemented by Nazi foot soldiers very often on their own initiative.[5]

The process of "grinding the other side into the dirt" – as Hitler characterized the terror to a group of industrialists on February 20[6] – was accelerated by the Reichstag Fire, the dramatic burning of the German parliament building in Berlin on February 27 (see Figure 3.1). The Nazi leadership tried to pin the blame for the fire on an international conspiracy of Communists, while opponents of Nazism and many international observers accused the Nazis themselves of having set the fire to create the pretext for the introduction of severe new emergency powers. Responsibility for the fire remains a disputed matter even today, although the scholarly consensus has tended to reject theories focusing either on Communist or Nazi conspiracies, pointing instead to Marinus van der Lubbe, a Dutch Communist who is believed to have acted alone. What is certain, however, is that Hitler's government would have eventually found (or fabricated) some pretext for implementing the new emergency decree, the draft of which had been in existence for some time.[7] The Decree for the Protection of People and State, to which historians refer as the Reichstag Fire Decree, was issued on February 28.

President Hindenburg signed off on the decree, invoking his authority under Article 48 of the Weimar Constitution, while Franz von Papen,

Figure 3.1 The Reichstag Fire, February 27, 1933 (Historica Graphica Collection/Heritage Images/Getty Images).

the leader of the conservatives in Hitler's cabinet, expressed no discernable objection.[8] The decree went far beyond the February 4 decree in its nullification of civil rights and due process. It empowered police to arrest suspects without evidence or probable cause, to carry out unlimited searches of homes and offices, to intercept and read mail, and to tap into telephone conversations. The decree also provided a basis for the vastly expanded use of "protective custody" (*Schutzhaft*), which allowed police to arrest persons deemed as threats to public security. Although the decree focused on threats posed by Communists, succeeding orders removed all meaningful restrictions on its scope.[9]

The Reichstag Fire Decree remained in force for the entirety of the Third Reich, serving as the main foundation for the Nazi police state in what was essentially a permanent state of emergency.[10] In his book *The Dual State*, published in 1941, the German-Jewish jurist and legal theorist Ernst Fraenkel identified two parallel systems of law in Nazi Germany. On one side stood the "normative state," which encompassed statute law, the police, the established court system, and the established prison system. Starting in 1933, according to Fraenkel, the Nazis set in place a parallel system, the "prerogative state," which, resting on the permanent state of emergency, engaged in unwarranted arrests, imprisonment without trial, and concentration camps. Although these terms were not employed by the Nazi state itself, and even though the distinction between the two legal systems became less clear over time, Fraenkel's model remains useful as a way to understand the system of coercion inside Germany between 1933 and 1945.[11] No law or decree was more important for the functioning of the "prerogative state" than the Reichstag Fire Decree.

The Reichstag election campaigns of 1932 had been accompanied by considerable political violence, but they had been free elections in the conventional sense of that term. The same cannot be said about the March 5, 1933 election, when a single party had come to control both the police and the streets in much of the country. The final days of campaigning unfolded in the shadow of the Reichstag Fire Decree. Communists were arrested by the tens of thousands and thrown into prisons or makeshift concentration camps. Among the arrested Communists was the national leader of the party, Ernst Thälmann, and many other top party officials. Dozens of Communists were killed during roundups and clashes with the SA. Social Democrats were also subjected to arrest and imprisonment, their campaign apparatus either shut down or severely crippled. The major agent of the terror was the SA, which had now been deputized with police powers in much of Germany. As William Sheridan Allen wrote in his classic local study of Northeim, "the Nazis not only controlled the police, they *were* the police." Thirty deputized Stormtroopers patrolled the streets of Northeim in their brown uniforms, marked by white armbands as "auxiliary police" (*Hilfspolizei*).[12] In Eutin, the small city in Holstein mentioned earlier, fourteen members of the local SA who had been deputized in this way reinforced two local police detectives in raiding the houses of Communists on the day before the election. Eight Communists were arrested, beaten, and thrown into the local prison. Three of them were convicted for illegal possession of pistols and sentenced to twelve months in prison.[13] These examples on the local level were microcosms of what took place across the Reich in the days before the election.

The government could have probably gotten away with banning the Communist Party outright, but chose not to do so, probably in order to avoid creating a flow of voters to the Social Democrats.[14]

The results of the March 5 election reflected the deep political divisions in Germany. The NSDAP received 43.9 percent of the vote; in absolute terms, the vote for the Nazi Party amounted to over 17 million votes, 5.5 million votes more than it had received in November 1932. Much of the new support for the NSDAP came from voters who had not gone to the polls in previous elections, but who had now been successfully mobilized behind Hitler during the campaign. The Nazis' conservative coalition partners, consisting of the DNVP and the Stahlhelm paramilitary organization, together garnered 8 percent of the vote, enough to give the coalition a majority in the Reichstag. On the other hand, the Social Democrats managed 18.3 percent and the Communists 12.3 percent, a remarkable showing in view of the systematic repression and terror to which these parties had been subjected during the five-week campaign. The Catholic Center Party won 11.2 percent of the vote, and the ideologically similar Bavarian People's Party 2.7 percent. Thus, in an election with 88 percent voter turnout, the German electorate was split almost evenly between the Nazi Party and its allies, on one side, and parties that were either avowedly anti-Fascist, or which harbored grave doubts about Nazism, on the other.

In the face of this reality, Hitler and his party set about immediately to create the illusion of a German society united behind the government. On March 13, the government created a new Reich Ministry for Popular Enlightenment and Propaganda, placing the NSDAP's chief of propaganda, Joseph Goebbels, at its helm. The personnel of this new ministry came almost without exception from the Nazi Party's propaganda office; hence, from the very beginning, it was a thoroughly Nazified organization, in contrast to the ministries that pre-dated the Nazi government. The competencies of the Propaganda Ministry expanded rapidly in the following months, coming eventually to include extensive controls over the press and most aspects of German cultural and artistic life. These powers would be exercised for the purpose of fostering a popular consensus – and, lacking this, then at least the fiction of a popular consensus – behind the Nazi regime. One of the very first projects of the new Propaganda Ministry was the political choreography of the "Day of Potsdam" on March 21. Potsdam, just outside of Berlin, had been a seat of the Prussian monarchy and nobility. At the elaborate, theatrical ceremony marking the investiture of the newly elected parliament, Hitler presented himself and his movement as the loyal servants of President Paul von Hindenburg, a beloved figure among many Germans

Figure 3.2 Hitler and Hindenburg at the Day of Potsdam, March 21, 1933 (Bettmann/Getty Images).

(see Figure 3.2). The ritual in Potsdam was intended to obscure the radicalism of the Nazi movement behind a façade of Prussian tradition.

An immediate political purpose of the Day of Potsdam was to enhance the aura of legitimate authority around Hitler on the eve of the struggle over the Enabling Act, which was placed on the agenda of the new Reichstag. The democratic legitimation granted to the Nazi–conservative coalition government on March 5 did not satisfy the authoritarian ambitions of Hitler or his partners, who wanted to free themselves from the constraints the parliamentary system. The Enabling Act would accomplish this goal by transferring the power to enact legislation from the Reichstag to the governing cabinet. The drafters of the act titled it the "Law to Remedy the Distress of the People and the Reich."

For such a law to pass, the rules of the Reichstag required a two-thirds majority. On March 23, when the parliament met to consider the Enabling Act, uniformed Nazis patrolled inside and outside of the Kroll Opera, where the parliament met after the burning of the Reichstag building. The votes of the Communist delegates were neutralized by the fact that they were either in prison or had fled abroad. A number of Social Democratic deputies had been arrested prior to the parliamentary session, while others were surrounded by uniformed Stormtroopers on the floor of the parliament during the debate. Despite this kind of intimidation, the Social Democratic delegation held firm in its opposition to the Enabling Act.[15] The deciding role fell, therefore, to the Center Party. The Center deputies were subjected to chanting – "we demand the Enabling Act, otherwise there will be hell to pay" – which came on top of threatening language in Hitler's speech to the parliament. After weeks of political terror targeted mainly at the left, the intimidation produced the intended effect. Fearing that the fate suffered by the Communists might befall them as well, the Center deputies concluded that voting for the Enabling Act would constitute a lesser of two evils.[16] It has often been alleged that the Center's fateful decision had been influenced by the ongoing negotiations between the German Reich and the Vatican over a concordat that would protect the ecclesiastical interests of the Catholic church inside Germany, although the evidence for this assertion is inconclusive.[17] The concordat, which was concluded in July, will be discussed below.

Thus, on March 23, 1933, the Center Party, which had been one of the main pillars of parliamentary democracy in Germany during the 1920s, voted to reduce the Reichstag to window dressing. The Reich cabinet now possessed the authority to promulgate laws. By shifting the power to legislate to the executive, the Enabling Act constituted the second major pillar of the Nazi dictatorship. Much like the Reichstag Fire Decree, it represented a fundamental violation of the democratic spirit of the Weimar Constitution, one made possible through the cynical exploitation of certain provisions of that very document. In an attempt to maintain the patina of constitutionalism, the drafters of the Enabling Act attached to it a four-year expiration period. In 1937, and twice more after that, a Reichstag consisting exclusively of Nazi deputies met to renew the law.

Thus armed with the power to legislate, Hitler took just over a week to issue a pair of laws providing for the "Coordination of the States with the Reich."[18] Striking at the heart of the federalism that had been integral to the German Reich since its founding in 1871, the law formalized the results of a centralization process that had been underway since the formation of the Hitler government. During February and March, the government had posted commissars to the German federal states to ensure their cooperation with the emergency decrees. In Prussia, the largest and most populous German state by far, the Nazis exercised authority by virtue of the system of direct rule that Franz von Papen had imposed on the state in 1932. After January 1933, Prussia was ruled by Hermann Göring, one of Hitler's closest and longest-standing confidantes in the Nazi movement. Outside of Prussia, in places where the NSDAP had built considerable popular support at the regional level, the work of the commissars had also proved relatively simple. But in other locations the commissars needed help from the SA in the streets to overcome local resistance. Nowhere was the resistance greater than in Bavaria. The Bavarian capital of Munich had been the birthplace of the NSDAP and still served as its national headquarters, but the strength of political Catholicism in the region lay in the way of a Nazi takeover. Support for the Bavarian People's Party had remained strong through the March 5 election.[19] Only because of a coup, engineered through a combination of threats from Berlin and the intimation of violence by the SA in the streets of Munich, did the Bavarian government ultimately relent and allow the appointment of a Nazi commissar for the state on March 9. The regional resistance to the centralization of the Reich having been overcome, the two new laws, issued on March 31 and April 7, respectively, replaced the commissars with permanent officials known as "Reich Governors," who were posted to each of the states. The fundamental reform of the structure of the German Reich was eventually concluded in January 1934, with the formal transfer of all sovereignty from the states to the Reich, and with the abolition of the regional parliaments, which had ceased serving any practical purpose.[20]

One of the main targets of the SA's campaign of political terror in February and March had been the socialist-leaning, or "free," labor unions. United under the umbrella of the General German Trade Union Federation (Allgemeiner deutscher Gewerkschaftsbund, or ADGB), this wing of the labor movement had comprised about 3.5 million members at the beginning of 1933. Another 1 million German workers had been organized in an association of liberal-oriented unions, while about half a million belonged to Christian-affiliated (mainly Catholic) unions. In contrast, the Nazi Party's own auxiliary for industrial workers, the NSBO, could claim only about 400,000 members in early 1933, representing less than one-tenth of organized German workers. The NSBO profited from the migration of former Communists into its ranks during March and April 1933, after the Communist Party had been smashed. Some Germans marveled in disbelief and disgust at the defection of Communists to the Nazi movement. In his diary, Karl Dürkefälden of Hanover posed and answered the question: "Who are the biggest fanatics? Those who had previously been red!"[21] While some of the defectors were sincere, others were looking for political cover. Moreover, the majority of German workers recognized the antipathy of the new government to the labor movement.[22]

Both Hitler and his conservative coalition partners did, in fact, envisage a German future without an independent labor movement. They did not move against organized labor immediately upon coming to power, however, perhaps fearing the potential consequences of a general strike. But as the seizure of power progressed, the unions were subjected to increasing violence at the hands of the SA that was tolerated by the authorities.

In March, activists of the NSBO began to occupy local union halls and rough up union officers, illegal acts against which the police were ordered not to intervene. These actions spread and intensified in April.[23] At the same time, the Reich government, equipped with the Enabling Act, unleashed a series of new laws designed to undermine the unions and to empower employers to fire workers for engaging in "subversive activity."[24] The leaders of the labor unions responded with a sense of resignation, hoping to salvage what they could of the labor movement in an extremely inhospitable political environment. On March 17, the Liberal and Christian unions pledged their loyalty to the new order. The leaders of the ADGB, for their part, had attempted to build bridges to the labor-oriented "left wing" of the NSDAP, sensing that the Nazis would be sympathetic to government-financed work-creation programs, but the prospects for cooperation of this sort had been damaged by the purge of the working class–oriented Strasser brothers from the Nazi movement prior to Hitler's appointment. By April 1933 the ADGB leaders had been reduced to pleading with the nascent regime just as the Liberal and Christian unions had done. The ADGB promised to abstain from politics and focus on the social needs of their members if the government would, in return, permit their continued existence as independent actors.

The totalitarian impulses of the Nazi leadership ruled out any such compromises with the unions, and it moved forward with a two-pronged strategy for dissolving them. The plan called for an ostentatious display of Nazi support for German workers, which would be followed immediately by the forced dissolution of the unions. The government appropriated the traditional May 1 observance of working-class solidarity – May Day – transforming it into an official holiday, on which workers would receive a paid day off. The new "Day of Labor" included massive ceremonies and rallies intended to show workers that they would occupy an honored position in the new Germany. On the next day, the offices of the socialist unions were occupied and their officers arrested. These actions were carried out by members of the NSBO, supported by units of the SA and SS. The Christian and Liberal unions were spared this treatment, but then dissolved themselves in short order. The entire operation had been organized by Robert Ley, the Reich Organizational Leader of the Nazi Party, whom Hitler had also placed in charge of labor-related matters.[25]

A few days later, Ley was appointed leader of a new official labor organization that would encompass all German workers, the German Labor Front (Deutsche Arbeitsfront, or DAF). The concentration of the German working class into a mass organization that would operate under state supervision was presented as a measure that would put an end to corrosive, Marxist notions of class conflict but nevertheless promote workers' interests and help provide for their material and social needs. Understood in the context of the history of the Nazi movement, it was a step toward the realization of the neo-corporatist vision that the Nazi Party had spelled out in its original program of 1920: "the formation of corporations based on estate and occupation for the purpose of carrying out the general legislation passed by the Reich." Over the next several years, the DAF grew into a mammoth organization encompassing 25 million members, and administering a sprawling network of banks, insurance companies, publishers, residential and consumer cooperatives, and industrial enterprises.[26]

The demise of political parties other than the NSDAP, Propaganda Minister Joseph Goebbels had predicted, would be merely a matter of time once the unions were out of the way. The Communist Party had already been crushed after the Reichstag Fire. The liberal parties (DDP and DVP) had lost most of their electoral base even before 1933. The nationalist conservative DNVP had been outmaneuvered and been rendered politically impotent by its Nazi coalition partners. Only the Social Democratic Party and the Center Party presented any real competition for the loyalty of the German population. Together they had received about 30 percent of the vote in the March 5, 1933 election. The SPD, which had been the only party to oppose the Enabling Act on March 23, had been significantly weakened by the emigration of many of its leaders and the dissolution of the unions. The desperate predicament led to internal disputes over the best strategy for dealing with the crisis, pitting those advocating accommodation with the Nazi regime against those determined to resist. The latter group consisted of leading Social Democrats who founded a party-in-exile in Prague. The Nazi government cynically exploited the existence of this organization to, first, confiscate the assets of the SPD in Germany on May 10, and then to ban the party altogether on June 22.

After the dutiful self-dissolution of the DNVP on June 27, only the Center remained. By this juncture, the negotiations between the Vatican and the Reich over a concordat had reached an advanced stage, and were most certainly a factor in the Center's decision to dissolve itself. When compared with the situation at the time of the Enabling Act in late March, the Nazi government was more audacious and the Center Party far more isolated. Seeking to avoid a dangerous and probably futile conflict with the regime, and hoping to clear the path for an agreement between the German government and the Vatican that would preserve the ecclesiastical, educational, and spiritual prerogatives of the Catholic church in the country, the Center dissolved itself on July 5. Three days later, the concordat was initialed in Rome by Vatican Secretary of State Cardinal Eugenio Pacelli (the future Pope Pius XII) and German Vice-Chancellor Franz von Papen.[27]

The regime placed the capstone on the destruction of political pluralism in Germany with a new law on July 14, the "Law against the New Formation of Parties." The NSDAP was declared "the only political party" in Germany, and anybody attempting to found another party would be subject to imprisonment. Even by the severely eroded legal standards of the day, this law was illegal, inasmuch as it violated a provision of the Enabling Act protecting the institutional integrity of the Reichstag. The parliament would exist henceforth as a one-party monopoly, enabling the regime to exploit the propagandistic effects of unanimous votes to rubber-stamp its policies (but also reminding the regime's opponents of the farcical nature of the proceedings). The historical irony of the date on which Germany officially became a one-party dictatorship is striking. As the anniversary of the storming of the Bastille in Paris in 1789, July 14 had come to be celebrated in many societies as the victory of the people against political absolutism.[28] In its July 15 edition, the Nazi Party newspaper, *Völkischer Beobachter*, hailed the government's repudiation of this tradition: "The practical significance of our current authoritative government (*Autoritätsregierung*), its fundamental difference from the disastrous parliamentary system of government, has perhaps never been more manifest to the German people."[29]

In less than six months, the German system of government had been transformed from a (to be sure shaky) multi-party parliamentary system into a one-party Nazi dictatorship. Due process had been abolished, and opponents of the regime were subject to arrest on the flimsiest of justifications and incarceration in concentration camps. That this could happen in spite of the Nazi Party having never received more than 44 percent of the vote in a multi-party election testifies to the fervor and ruthlessness of the Nazis, the fragmentation of their opponents, and the overconfidence and ultimate incompetence of their conservative allies.

Measures laying the foundation for racial persecution and eugenics, both of which were highly ranking priorities of the Nazi movement, were woven into the process of creating and consolidating the one-party dictatorship. On April 7, 1933, the same day on which German federalism was dealt its death blow, the government issued the Law for the Restoration of the Professional Civil Service (usually referred to as the Civil Service Law), making possible the dismissal of Jews from government employment. On July 14, the day on which the one-party state was made official, the government approved the eugenics law that provided the legal basis for the mass sterilization program of the Third Reich. (The government approved the concordat on the same day, and thus delayed announcing the eugenics law by a week so as not to offend the Vatican.)[30] As these policies will be examined in detail elsewhere in this book, what merits emphasis here is the swiftness with which they were put in place after the formation of Hitler's cabinet. The readiness to turn against Jewish colleagues also quickly became a litmus test for loyalty to the emerging new regime.

Coordination and Self-Coordination of German Society

The means by which Germany's social and economic institutions were brought into line with Nazism was anything but the bureaucratic or technical process suggested by the term "coordination." It unfolded in stages, beginning in March and April of 1933, when organizations pledged their loyalty to the new regime, removed Jews and anti-Nazis from positions of responsibility, and implemented the Nazi "leadership principle" to replace democratic practices of governance. These organizations included educational and cultural institutions, professional associations, sport and hobby clubs, and private businesses. Subsequent stages of coordination, extending through the 1930s, involved a more comprehensive Nazification of leadership and a more thoroughgoing purge of Jewish members or employees. During the initial stage, in 1933, behaviors were profoundly influenced by a widespread sense of resignation in the face of the country's rapid transformation into a dictatorship, as well as by the fear induced by the political terror of the SA. In this atmosphere, the preservation of institutional self-interest often, but by no means always, seemed to lie along the path of least resistance. Many organizations or companies that were already inclined toward right-wing, nationalistic politics coordinated themselves with relatively little internal upheaval. Others hoped to preserve a degree of autonomy by implementing a limited self-coordination, which often involved the conspicuous removal of Jews from leadership positions. In some cases, resistance to coordination was overcome only through Nazi threats and intimidation. This subject has been of interest to German scholars in particular, as it involves the question of German society's response to the Nazi takeover at the very earliest stage, just as the dictatorship was beginning to consolidate itself. The factors and patterns mentioned above are discernable in a large number of case studies centering on a broad variety of organizations and institutions, several of which will be described here.

The two major football clubs in Munich offer starkly contrasting examples. The "TSV Munich 1860" had already had nationalist leanings and possessed ties to the *völkisch* movement before 1933. On March 22, 1933 – the day after the Day of Potsdam – the club issued a statement welcoming the "patriotic endeavors of the leadership of the German Reich." Long-standing members of the Nazi Party were now added to the management of the organization. In the case of the other club, "Bavaria

Munich," the transition to Nazism was a good deal less smooth. The club's political orientation was more liberal, and its president, Kurt Landauer, was a Jew. Landauer resigned his position on March 22, citing the "political reorganization" taking place in the country. To signal its lack of sympathy for the emerging regime, the club replaced Landauer with an anti-Nazi police official. He did not last long, however, and by 1935 reliable Nazis had taken charge of the organization. Thus, one of the football clubs coordinated itself enthusiastically, the other only reluctantly.[31]

As exemplified by Kurt Landauer, the removal of Jews from leading positions, often in the form of resignation-under-duress, was a salient characteristic of coordination in early 1933. It was a way of paying tribute to the Nazi movement without necessarily making deeper changes to the organization. This practice applied equally in institutions large and small. Shooting clubs (*Schützenvereine*) played an important role in the social life of many small, rural communities. Although relatively few Jews were active in these associations, they were quickly sacrificed in order to demonstrate fealty to the new regime. At the same time, the shooting clubs outwardly instituted the Nazi leadership principle, but changed little else.[32]

The strategy of surrendering to Nazi concerns over the "Jewish Question" while otherwise preserving as much as possible was also adopted by Germany's largest corporation, the chemical conglomerate IG Farben. A significant number of the concern's top managers were Jews. In 1933, several of them were reassigned to positions at Farben affiliates in other countries, a form of "paid exile" intended to appease the regime while continuing to profit from the experience and expertise of the persons in question. Although some of Farben's top managers remained in their positions in 1933, they had all been removed under government pressure by late 1935, despite efforts to protect them. While Farben, judging by its history and personnel, had not been an antisemitic organization before 1933, its success as a business institution depended heavily on maintaining a cooperative relationship with the regime in power, whatever its ideological tendencies. Its profitability would be profoundly affected by policies in the areas of taxation, labor, currency exchange, and the allocation of raw materials. Management had to think not only about the interests of shareholders, but also the welfare of its tens of thousands of employees. The pragmatic approach adopted by the cartel in 1933 included the beginning of large cash contributions to the Nazi Party. This protection money was less an endorsement of the Nazi program than an attempt to preserve autonomy over business decisions.[33]

In many instances, organizations succumbed to the pressure to self-coordinate as the direct result of threats of violence. A well-documented example is that of the physicians' association in Bavaria. On March

21 – the Day of Potsdam – a group of 200–300 Nazi-affiliated physicians assembled in a restaurant in Munich to plan the takeover of the regional physicians' association. They demanded the dismissal of Jews and political opponents from official positions in medical organizations, hospitals, and university medical faculties. They insisted on the introduction of the Nazi leader principle in all medical institutions, and on the reorientation of medical practice in accord with Nazi racial-biological principles. In a formal statement summarizing their intentions, they declared their readiness to employ "ruthless" methods to achieve their aims. After the non-Nazi director of one medical organization refused to resign from his position, a visit to his home from thirty uniformed Stormtroopers persuaded him to change his mind. The Nazi physicians' group then made clear that it would not hesitate to mobilize the SA once again should it prove necessary.[34]

A month later, the blunt instrument of the SA was wielded in a similar fashion to impose Nazi leadership on the Brandenburg regional branch of the League of German Architects. In a meeting held on April 24, the architects elected a new three-member board, two of whom were not Nazis. The Nazi members present at the meeting demanded the resignation of the two non-Nazis, who refused to capitulate. At this point, about twenty uniformed Stormtroopers entered the meeting-room and gathered around the table where the board members were seated. The two non-Nazis now relented and departed from the room. Two Nazis took their place at the board table. The assembled membership took another vote, and the new board, consisting entirely of Nazis, received 80 percent of the votes. The meeting closed with the singing of the Nazi anthem, the Horst Wessel Song. In no way can this process fairly be described as a voluntary self-coordination. The architects were brought into line through an act of raw physical intimidation, one that repeated itself countless times around Germany in March and April of 1933.[35]

This dialectic of coercion and accommodation was not necessary for accomplishing coordination in the public sector. The Nazi government's controls over Reich, state, and municipal institutions were secured through the elimination of federalism, the creation of the Reich Governors, and the emergency decrees. It was a relatively simple matter to place "politically reliable" people in charge of the police, the civil service, the universities, and the education system. This did not, of course, mean that these large organizations did not continue to comprise persons who opposed Nazism, or at least harbored serious doubts about it. Thorough Nazification of government institutions would require a good deal more time. A means for accomplishing this goal was put in place on April 7 in the form of the Civil Service Law, which empowered the government to dismiss civil servants for political reasons, and, just as important, for racial ones. The Law's "Aryan clause" was among the first official acts of the Nazi government targeted at Jews.

Stabilizing the Regime

The initial stage of coordination had left the Nazi movement in charge of the commanding heights of the German state and German society. This had occurred remarkably quickly, but the election of March 5 had demonstrated that the enthusiasm of the German people for Nazism was limited. Moreover, there still remained important centers of power outside the grasp of Nazi control. These included the army, the churches, the civil service below the ministerial level, and most privately owned businesses. Each of these sectors would eventually enter into its own complex *modus vivendi* with the regime. For its part, the Nazi movement itself was hardly a monolithic entity, and its internal divisions soon emerged as a serious problem.

In late 1933, developments on the foreign policy front offered Hitler an opportunity to make a bold gesture calculated to shore up popular support for the regime. The Treaty of Versailles and other components of the post-war peace settlement remained broadly unpopular in Germany, despite Weimar diplomacy's successes at negotiating reparations payments downward and integrating Germany into the community of European neighbors. Hitler's desire was not to commit Germany to a slightly more advantageous set of restrictions than had applied before 1933, but to break free from international agreements restricting Germany's options, and ultimately to transform the country into a dominant, expansionist military power on the European continent. He understood that breaking the shackles of Versailles would be received positively inside Germany. During multi-lateral negotiations over disarmament in the autumn of 1933, Hitler alternated threats to withdraw from the talks with reassurances about Germany's peaceful intentions. He then intentionally torpedoed the discussions and, on October 14, announced Germany's withdrawal not just from the negotiations but also from the League of Nations, citing Germany's unfair treatment at the hands of the international body.[36] In addition to creating space for rearmament and a more unilateral foreign policy, the withdrawal from the League removed Germany from the jurisdiction of agreements protecting ethnic and religious minorities.[37]

Germany's departure from the League was accompanied by the announcement of a public referendum, which was scheduled for November 12. This ploy was designed to underscore popular backing for the regime and its policies well beyond issues of foreign policy. The Nazi regime would employ this technique of plebiscitary legitimation several times. The question on the ballot was formulated as follows:

Do you, German man and German woman, approve of the policies of your Reich government, and are you prepared to declare them as the expression of your own beliefs and your own will and to solemnly identify yourself with them?

Voters faced the simple choice of checking "yes" or "no." The weeks between October 14 and November 12 were dominated by a large-scale propaganda campaign. Appeals to vote "yes" were made by the German Labor Front, industrialists, and professional associations. Campaigning in favor of a "no" vote was not permitted. The official result announced after the referendum was a "yes" vote of 90 percent. There is, however, considerable evidence of manipulation of vote counts by local officials.[38] Moreover, many Germans were afraid to vote according to their conscience, notwithstanding an official guarantee of secrecy of ballots. A pervasive sense of intimidation prevailed, especially in smaller communities; the former Communists and Social Democrats were well known, and would therefore be suspected of having cast the negative ballots. It was also telling that actual voting returns by precinct were not published until after 1945. They showed that in locations dominated by Catholic and working-class voters, almost 30 percent voted "no."[39] Had the critics of the regime been free from duress, the rate of disapproval would undoubtedly have been higher.

In late 1933 and early 1934, the regime laid the foundation for its systemic intervention in the German economy. The approach might best be described by the term *dirigiste*, connoting a significant degree of state control over economic matters while preserving the essential ingredients of a capitalist system. Hitler preferred to harness the capitalist economy to his racist ideological program rather than to overturn it and had already initiated his collaborative relationship with circles of German big business earlier in 1933. Although this relationship drew the ire of anti-capitalist members of his own movement, most of Hitler's supporters (like the majority of German society) wished to preserve the capitalist system in some form. Thus, in contrast to the methods of nationalization or collectivization that had been implemented in the Soviet Union, the Nazi regime would steer the economy by means of controls on international trade and currencies, allocations of raw materials, the regulation of conditions in the labor force and in the professions, and government contracts for infrastructure projects and armaments.

The Nazi government inherited publicly financed work-creation programs that had commenced under Chancellor Kurt von Schleicher in December 1932. These programs, kept and expanded during 1933, involved large-scale construction projects and repair work on existing buildings. By early 1934, unemployment had been reduced by about one-third when compared with a year earlier. The work-creation measures were accompanied by a propaganda campaign intended to convince the German people that the economy had turned a corner. The propaganda included a major emphasis on the Autobahn project, which did not actually employ a large number of workers, but which was photogenic and reflected a society moving into the future.[40]

Two major steps allowing for greater state intervention in the economy were taken in September 1933. Upon the creation of the Reich Agricultural Estate (*Reichsnährstand*) on September 13, about 14 million Germans involved in every branch of agriculture were organized under a single umbrella. In the blood-and-soil ideology of National Socialism, peasants were seen as the wellspring of German racial purity, values of hard work and clean living, and traditional gender roles. The official placed at the head of the Agricultural Estate, Richard Walther Darré, had been among the leading exponents of racial theory in the Nazi movement before 1933. The presence of the Agricultural Estate in the everyday lives of German farmers was, however, felt most strongly in the realm of market regulation. Through price guarantees and guaranteed purchases of produce, the Agricultural Estate sought both to safeguard the livelihoods of farmers and to optimize agricultural production with the goal of making Germany self-sufficient.[41]

With the creation of the Reich Chamber of Culture on September 22, all Germans professionally active in cultural and artistic life were forcibly organized into a so-called "professional estate." Like the German Labor Front, the Chamber of Culture was touted as progress toward Fascist-inspired occupational corporatism. The Chamber of Culture, organized into subchambers for music, theater, film, and other sectors of cultural endeavor, provided a mechanism for delivering work-creation programs and imposing economic regulations aimed at ameliorating suffering in a segment of German society in which unemployment was especially high. Additionally, the Chamber would serve as a mechanism for ideological control over the arts and for the purging of Jews and political opponents from German cultural life.[42] A closely related measure, the Reich Editors Law of October 4, imposed ideological and racial conditions on the profession of newspaper editing.[43]

Perhaps of greatest economic importance was the Law on the Organization of National Labor of January 20, 1934, which has been described as "one of the most all-embracing and rigorous products of National Socialism."[44] The law served as a kind of constitution for the organization of industrial enterprises. It imposed the Nazi leader principle on companies, declaring the owner as the Führer of the organization and the employees as the "following" (*Gefolgschaft*). Although the law stipulated the creation of employee councils to advise the owner, the supremacy of capital over labor was clear. Thus, much in the same way that the conflict inherent to multi-party democracy was eliminated by the creation of the dictatorship, industrial peace would be achieved through authoritarian arrangements in industry.[45]

Although Nazis of all shades were delighted to see the demise of class conflict as understood in the Marxist tradition, more than a few were disappointed by the Hitler government's strong tilt toward the capitalist establishment. More generally, they resented Hitler's readiness to throw in his lot with German elites in the economy, the military, and the civil service. At the center of these grievances was the leader of the SA, Ernst Röhm, and a substantial number of his Stormtroopers. Röhm fancied the SA, and not the Reichswehr, as the future army of the new Germany. As the size of the army had been limited by Versailles, it was a good deal smaller than the SA, which by mid 1934 had grown to about 3 million members. Stormtroopers were well aware of the instrumental role they had played in placing the Nazi movement in power, and for some, now was not the time to give up on the revolutionary zeal that had motivated them. Many of the SA's working-class and lower-middle-class members held negative views of big business, and resented the aristocracy that dominated the Reichswehr officer corps. Moreover, they were dissatisfied with what they regarded as the slow progress with which Jews were being removed from positions of power and privilege.

For his part, Röhm was not shy about his ambitions for the SA or his criticism of the Nazi movement's compromises with established elites. He expressed them openly and in print, creating nervousness in the upper echelons of the Reichswehr, among industrialists, and in the NSDAP itself. Many ordinary Germans, too, were made nervous by the continued militancy of the SA. After months of upheaval, they desired normalcy and sense of predictability about the future. Even the majority of Hitler's supporters did not want a "Second Revolution."

Hitler had intentionally refrained from coordinating the Reichswehr, the one organization in Germany possessing the physical ability to stop the Nazi takeover, and one that was answerable not to the chancellor but to President Hindenburg. Hitler appreciated the professional expertise of the military officer corps (even as he harbored resentment toward its aristocratic snobbery). He did not think Germany could fight a modern war with the SA, which was a populist militia rather than a disciplined military organization. In an attempt to appease Röhm, Hitler offered a division of labor: The Reichswehr would be responsible for national defense externally, while the SA would tend to matters of internal security. This offer failed to satisfy Röhm's ambitions. Röhm persisted in his militant rhetoric, and pressure to act mounted on Hitler from the army and elsewhere. The solution would come at the end of June 1934 in the form of a bloodbath, but efforts to isolate the SA and discredit its leadership started in January 1934. These included having the secret police collect compromising material regarding Ernst Röhm's homosexuality.[46]

A less formidable but nevertheless real threat to Hitler's authority emanated from a circle of conservatives based in the office of Vice-Chancellor Franz von Papen. The leader of this group was Edgar Jung, an influential figure among anti-republican, anti-democratic intellectuals associated with the so-called Conservative Revolution during the Weimar Republic. Jung's book *The Rule of the Inferiors* (*Die Herrschaft der Minderwertigen*), published in 1927, comprised an attack on the individualistic legacy of the Enlightenment and the French Revolution. Its argument was antisemitic, although it downplayed questions of race, emphasizing instead the materialistic individualism of Jews as a cultural problem.[47] As conservatives with an authoritarian bent and some monarchist leanings, combined with a strong dose of social snobbery, Jung and his colleagues loathed the primitive populism and violence of the Nazi movement, but had come reluctantly to recognize its utility for bringing down the Republic and ushering in something new. Like von Papen, they believed that Hitler could be controlled. During the Nazi takeover, they looked on with dismay as von Papen failed to block, or even object to, Hitler's more aggressive acts. Gradually Jung shifted from collaboration to opposition. He and his colleagues worked behind the scenes to mobilize opposition to the Enabling Act, collected disparaging materials on Nazi leaders, and provided the foreign press, especially in Britain, with material that could be used to mobilize public opinion against the Hitler government. By early 1934, the group had cultivated an opposition network consisting of people in the military, the churches, the press, industry, the diplomatic corps, the disbanded political parties, and the Stahlhelm (which was undergoing an involuntary, phased integration into the SA).[48]

In early 1934, Jung and his colleagues developed a plan to strike at the Nazi government in a kind of conservative counter-revolution. Franz von Papen, they hoped, could be persuaded to convince Hindenburg to declare martial law and order the Reichswehr to dissolve the government. Some Nazi leaders would be arrested, but not Hitler and Göring, who would be brought into a governing directorate that would also include von Papen and Heinrich Brüning, and which would be dominated by generals. Ultimately a new constitution would be put in place, based on a limited franchise and rigged to favor the privileged classes. An elected monarch, based on the historical precedent of the Holy Roman Empire, would be entrusted with executive power.[49] When Hindenburg took ill at the beginning of June 1934 and left Berlin for his country estate in East Prussia, the conspirators modified their plan, now intending to trigger the military coup with a provocative speech by Franz von Papen, who had grown critical of the regime's totalitarian ambitions and excesses, including those of the SA. The speech was delivered by von Papen at the University of Marburg on June 17, but, rather than serving as a rallying point for an anti-Nazi coup from the conservative side, it helped set in motion a series of events culminating with a consolidation of Hitler's hold on power.[50]

After von Papen's speech, Hitler felt compelled to seize the initiative.[51] With Hindenburg's blessing, he instructed Göring and SS leader Heinrich Himmler to prepare a strike against his opponents. The dirty work would be performed by the SS, but logistical support in the form of weapons, transport, and billeting would be provided by the Reichswehr, and the minister of defense, General Werner von Blomberg, was involved with the planning. The operation was launched on June 30. About 200 leaders of the SA were arrested across the Reich. A total of about 100 persons were murdered, mostly high-ranking members of the SA. Ernst Röhm was arrested while on holiday in Bavaria and killed on direct orders from Hitler. But the murders extended well beyond the SA. Edgar Jung was killed for his role in the conservative anti-Nazi plot. Hitler also used the operation to settle a number of old scores. Among those murdered were General Kurt von Schleicher, Hitler's predecessor as chancellor, who in late 1932 had worked to avert Hitler's participation in government. Another victim was Gregor Strasser, the former leader of the worker-oriented wing of the Nazi Party, whom Hitler had continued to suspect as a potential threat to his primacy in the movement. Also murdered was Gustav von Kahr, the Bavarian politician whose actions in November 1923 had contributed to the failure of Hitler's attempted putsch in Munich. The prominent Catholic politician Erich Klausener, who had recently criticized government actions toward the church, was counted among the victims, as was Walter Häbich the former leader of the banned Communist Youth League, and Adam Hereth, a former Social Democratic official.[52] One of the SA officers who was killed, Karl Ernst, had been a fierce critic of the Reichswehr, but some have alleged that he was silenced on account of knowledge about the SA's role in the torching of the Reichstag.[53] The German term often used to refer to this operation, the *Röhm-Putsch* (Röhm Coup), obscures the ideological diversity among the victims, and is therefore a less accurate label than the "Night of Murder" (*Mordnacht*), or its commonly used English-language equivalent, the Night of the Long Knives.

The absence of any significant protest over the killings testified to their very effectiveness in bolstering Hitler's authority. The murders were explained to the public as a pre-emptive action against a coup by the SA, and Nazi propagandists did not shrink from disparaging Ernst Röhm and several of his similarly slaughtered comrades for their homosexuality, signaling the beginning of a broader campaign against homosexuality in the party and in German society.[54] The Reichswehr did not publicly object to the murder of one of its generals, who was also a former Reich chancellor. Minister of Defense von Blomberg, a general himself, personally thanked Hitler at a cabinet meeting. The Reich cabinet issued a law declaring the operation a legal and legitimate act of "state self-defense." Consequently, the legal system took no action to investigate the killings or to hold anyone to account for them. The prominent legal theorist Carl Schmitt, a supporter of, and apologist for, the Nazi regime, gave his imprimatur to the summary executions, arguing that "the Führer is not subject to the system of justice, but is himself a higher form of justice." While, to our eyes, such attempts to place a legalistic gloss on the outright political murder of dozens of people might seem absurd, it accorded with the pattern of illegality and rationalization that accompanied the Nazi takeover, providing psychological cover for the self-deception in which many Germans continued to engage regarding the constitutional legitimacy of the regime.[55]

After the purge, the SA was no longer in a position to pursue an ideological agenda of its own, but it continued to perform important functions in German society, some purely ceremonial, but some, such as the intimidation and physical abuse of Jews, of considerable importance to the goals of Nazism.[56] Meanwhile, the SS, having originated as an organization within the SA, emerged from the Night of the Long Knives as a formidable entity in its own right. It took over responsibility for administering the concentration camps from the SA, and during the 1930s gradually established control over a broad constellation of police and intelligence agencies. It also, during the late 1930s and into the war, played a progressively greater role in the formulation and implementation of the regime's Jewish policy, culminating in its central position in the Final Solution.

The passing of President Paul von Hindenburg on August 2, 1934, just a month after the Night of the Long Knives, facilitated the final step of Hitler's monopolization of political power. The death came as no surprise, as the elderly Hindenburg had been ailing. A law, prepared beforehand and implemented on the day of the president's death, abolished the office of the Reich president, transferring its powers to Hitler. Hitler assumed the title Führer and Reich Chancellor. No member of the Reich cabinet questioned whether that body possessed the authority to implement such a profound change to the constitution that was still theoretically in force. Hitler, exercising the prerogatives of the presidency, now counted supreme command over the German armed forces among his powers. Also, on August 2, the Reichswehr ordered its members to take an oath of personal loyalty to Hitler, departing from the established practice of pledging loyalty to the constitution. Hitler had cemented his alliance with the one German institution that could have genuinely threatened his power, and without which he believed he would not be able to conduct his intended wars of expansion.

Hitler now again employed the device of the referendum to win popular legitimacy for his actions. On August 19, the German people received the chance to express their opinion about the melding of the chancellorship with the presidency. The atmosphere of intimidation was no less intense than it had been before the November 1933 referendum. The result – 90 percent in favor – was lopsided enough to provide fodder to the regime's propaganda, but also reflected the persistence of internal dissent from Nazi rule among a substantial minority of Germans. It is impossible to know what percentage of Germans would have voted in the negative had the playing field been level.[57]

4   The Nazi Economy, 1933–1939

Nazi efforts to transform German society beginning in 1933 proceeded on two parallel tracks. On one track, Germans who were deemed to be racially and politically acceptable were embraced by a regime intending to integrate them into an ostensibly emergent *Volksgemeinschaft*, a People's Community, united by bonds of blood, culture, and nationhood. On the second track, members of society who were regarded as alien (e.g., Jews), degenerate (e.g., gay men), or disruptive (e.g., Marxists) were subjected to increasingly severe policies of marginalization and exclusion. They could, by definition, not be members of the People's Community.

People's Community is not an objective category of historical or social scientific analysis, but rather, as used by the Nazis, a concept denoting a society based on Social Darwinism, biological racism, and authoritarian rule.[1] It was not an egalitarian concept, even with regard to Germans who were deemed worthy of inclusion in the community. Much as Nazism posited the existence of fundamental racial differences among nations or peoples, it subscribed to the belief of a natural hierarchy within each race. Members of the German People's Community, therefore, would need to know and accept their place within this hierarchy and to accept the authority of the layers of leadership arrayed above them. This did not rule out the possibility of upward mobility based on natural ability, however. Many leading Nazis, including Hitler himself, possessed non-elite backgrounds, and they often disparaged the old hereditary nobility, which they regarded as biologically degenerate. The People's Community, as they saw it, would be a racially pure society led by an aristocracy of talent.

In addition to its use in Nazi rhetoric and propaganda as a concept of racial or political exclusion, People's Community was often invoked as a shorthand for a certain type of socio-economic system (see Figure 4.1). In speeches, Hitler painted the People's Community as the solution to the social disunity that he saw as endemic in the liberal order, which he associated with Jews. It would do away with the deep social divisions

Figure 4.1 Nazi poster: "The NSDAP Protects the People's Community," 1936 (Universal History Archive/Universal Images Group via Getty Images).

engendered by capitalism and modernity. On March 23, 1933, in his speech to the Reichstag during the debate over the Enabling Act, a pivotal event in the birth of the Nazi regime, Hitler mentioned the term *Volksgemeinschaft* four times. He called for the creation of a "genuine People's Community, which rises above the interests and conflicts of estates and classes."[2] In his speech on May 1, 1933, the first Nazi "Day of Labor," he blamed Marxism for fomenting social strife based on class resentment. In a People's Community, racial unity would replace class conflict.[3] In January 1934, in an interview with the Nazi writer Hanns Johst, the Führer offered a stream-of-consciousness definition that nicely encapsulated the anti-liberal and anti-Marxist essence of the term as the Nazis applied it to social and economic life. The People's Community, he stated, is "the community of all productive labor, that is, the unity of all vital interests, that is, the overcoming of private citizenship and the mechanical organization of the masses into labor unions, that is, the unconditional equating of individual fate and nation, of the individual and the Volk."[4]

While the policies of exclusion, which would ultimately culminate in genocide during World War II, will be examined in detail later in this book, this chapter and the one following it will focus on the Nazi regime's attempts to transform People's Community from an ideological and propagandistic notion into a social and economic reality. They will employ familiar categories of Germans that have long been employed by historians of German society, such as the working class, the middle class, peasants, women, men, youth, and families. It should be obvious that in a modern society of 60 million inhabitants, which until 1933 had suffered from severe political fragmentation, Germans approached Nazism with very diverse perspectives based on background and experience.

Disagreement with the regime's social and economic programs could be rooted in political philosophy, religious faith, personal ethics, adherence to tradition, youthful rebelliousness, or material self-interest. The regime had several tools at its disposal to promote its priorities in the face of the kind of foot-dragging and outright opposition that was bound to occur. It could exploit its control over legislation and regulation (the "normative state") to redefine the legal framework for work, education, family life, or sexual relations. It could use coercive measures (the "prerogative state") to punish, or intimidate, recalcitrant and dissenting members of society. It could use its control over financial and material resources to reward compliance or to penalize non-compliance with its economic reforms. And it could engage in propaganda and other techniques of mobilization to manufacture popular support, or at least to create the illusion of popular support, for its policies.

As Germany did not have public opinion polling in 1939, it is impossible to quantify the extent of support enjoyed by the Nazi regime on the eve of World War II. Class resentment bred by economic inequality remained widespread, despite official efforts to paper over them with propaganda, pageantry, and expanded access to beach vacations. Peasants and merchants bucked at regulations imposed by an increasingly interventionist state. Some women expressed frustration with the limitations imposed on their educational and occupational opportunities. Some youth rebelled against regimentation and imposed conformity.

All of this having been said, however, German society enjoyed significantly greater internal peace in late 1939 than it had just under seven years previously, at the time of the Nazi seizure of power. Although the regime did not attempt to affect a fundamental alteration in the class structure of the country, it made meaningful and psychologically effective gestures of solidarity toward the working class. Unemployment had been erased in no small measure as the result of a massive program of rearmament and militarization of the society, and many workers compared their situation favorably to that of the Depression, which was still a very recent memory. Children and teenagers responded positively to the sport and games offered by the Hitler Youth, and to the attention lavished upon them by important adults in uniforms. Adding to the general base level of contentment with the social and economic situation, Hitler's repudiation of the Treaty of Versailles and his restoration of Germany to great-power status was overwhelmingly popular (even though most Germans had little appetite for another war). The systematic persecution of Jews also met with widespread approval, repelling a significant number of Germans only when it deviated from legal and economic measures to assume violent forms.

The social peace enjoyed by the country by the end of the 1930s was also, to be sure, a consequence of the expansion of the "prerogative state" since 1933. The concentration camps provided for the imprisonment of opponents, dissenters, and even complainers, and the very existence of these camps, which the regime did not try to hide, served as a deterrent to potential objectors.[5] But while the breadth and depth of such dissent should not be underestimated, and while the reality of the Nazi People's Community was nothing resembling the utopia of social harmony depicted in the regime's own propaganda, the peacetime years of Nazi rule did meet with the general approval of the majority of Germans.

The German Working Class

Upon assuming power, Hitler and other Nazi leaders were keenly aware of two realities. First, the crisis of the capitalist economy, and the political polarization that it had brought about, had been key factors in the growth and ultimate political success of their party. Second, their party did not enjoy majority support in Germany, as reflected most dramatically in the March 1933 Reichstag election. The goal of stabilizing the new regime, establishing legitimacy on a broad basis, and building a pro-Nazi consensus necessitated granting high priority to economic measures designed to combat unemployment. The Nazi-led economic recovery of the 1930s, which would become a major pillar of the regime's popularity inside Germany, resulted from a complex combination of factors. These included government-supported programs for work creation, a massive program of military rearmament, and some lucky timing.

The last-mentioned of these factors is easy to overlook. The low point of the Depression already lay in the past by the time that Hitler became chancellor, and a recovery in the business cycle had already started. The turning point had occurred in the summer of 1932, when measured by corporate investment, orders for new industrial machinery, and other important indicators. But the upswing that had already begun only became apparent after January 1933. Once it did, there then ensued a positive change in market psychology resulting from Hitler's chancellorship. The perceived end of labor strife and class warfare fueled optimism among consumers and investment by firms. Although there is no way to test the counterfactual alternative, it is likely that the German economy would have recovered without Nazi policies. But if Nazi policies did not fundamentally cause the recovery, they helped to sustain it, and did much to shape it.[6]

In January 1933, about 6 million Germans were classified as being unemployed. By the autumn of 1933, the number had been reduced to 3.7 million. That number in turn had been more than cut in half by late 1934, when 1.8 million were unemployed. By the autumn of 1937, the number stood at only a half-million.[7] The psychological response of workers to these developments must be understood in the context of the suffering and desperation of the immediately preceding period of the Depression. It was almost inevitable that the Nazis would profit politically from the decline in unemployment. Previously unemployed workers who now re-entered the workforce in 1933 and 1934 were, in many cases, grateful. And those who were not grateful were fearful of the consequences of political opposition. The German labor force was, thus, disciplined and the underground labor movement was undermined. Socialist and Communist resistance did persist but did not significantly affect the lives of most workers.

Government-sponsored programs for work creation were less significant for their macroeconomic impact than for their psychological effects. The Nazi regime inherited the work-creation program that had been

initiated under Chancellor Schleicher in January 1933. Hitler's government supplemented the funding in June. This was accompanied by a
massive and effective propaganda effort, reinforcing the impression that
an action-oriented government was in power, one that was focused on
addressing unemployment. The Autobahn construction project further
reinforced the perception that the new government was committed to
decisive action on the economic front. Based on plans developed during
the 1920s, the project was initiated in the spring of 1933. The number of actual workers on the project was not great – it never exceeded
12,000 – but the audacious modernity and physical dimensions of the
project could be exploited to celebrate the regime's commitment to
creating jobs. By end of 1939, 3,300 kilometers of Autobahn had been
constructed. The regime planned to make a low-cost car available to
German consumers in the form of the so-called "Strength through Joy
Wagon," but resources originally envisaged for this purpose were ultimately diverted into military spending, and by late 1939 only 1.3 million privately owned automobiles were on the road. (In contrast, the
United States did not construct a system of superhighways equivalent
to the Autobahn until after World War II, but by 1939 privately owned
cars were far more common in the US than they were in Germany.)
The German economic recovery did, however, spur a modernization and
expansion of the national rail system, the *Reichsbahn*, which carried more
freight and served ever-greater numbers of passengers.[8]

The impression of action was reinforced by the expansion of the Reich
Labor Service, a publicly financed work-creation program for young
men that had been created at the end of Weimar Republic. By 1934,
the Labor Service was the largest work-creation program in Germany.
Membership rose from 182,000 in 1935 to 300,000 in 1939. Although
the Labor Service was made technically compulsory for young men (and,
at the beginning of the war, for women as well), many exemptions were
granted for economic and military reasons, and the majority of eligible
men did not serve in it. Nevertheless, the Labor Service gave an important assist to large numbers of young men, especially those who would
have otherwise been unemployed between 1933 and 1937. In addition
to providing work, the Labor Service glorified the dignity of labor and
endeavored to instill a sense of pride in young men who were working
to build their country. Contrary to a widely held belief, the Labor Service did not play a major role in Autobahn construction, although it was
involved in the building of other kinds of roads. Its activity lay mainly in
land reclamation (soil improvement, irrigation, drainage), reforestation
projects, firefighting, flood amelioration and clean-up, and the construction of airfields, air-raid shelters, and military installations.[9]

Figure 4.2 Members of the Reich Labor Service (Universal History Archive/Universal Images Group via Getty Images).

The Labor Service was organized on a military model, and its members were subjected to ideological indoctrination and military-style regimentation and drilling (see Figure 4.2). A striking scene in *Triumph of the Will*, the well-known propaganda documentary chronicling the 1934 Nazi Party rally in Nuremberg, depicts columns of Labor Service members marching in military formation, their spades balanced on their shoulders like rifles, chanting nationalistic slogans and pledging their readiness to serve Führer and Fatherland.[10] In addition to preparing men for later enlistment in the armed forces, Labor Service indoctrination underscored a traditional notion of manhood. There was an antisemitic component to this effort, as the masculine, Aryan soldiers of physical labor were contrasted with the Nazi stereotype of effeminate, degenerate Jewish men who shunned physical work while exploiting the honest labor of others. In the Labor Service camps, members also received instruction in the basics of Nazi ideology, including "race science" and antisemitism.

While the focus of work-creation programs was placed on men, the regime provided incentives, such as marriage loans, for working women to resign from their jobs in the economy and retreat into domesticity. In practice, however, millions of women remained in the workforce. Significant numbers of women needed to work, most notably single women aged 18–25. Married women accounted for only about 30 percent of women in employment. In certain industrial sectors, women constituted a significant part of the workforce. These included textiles (50 percent); paper production (35 percent); food production (30 percent); and the electro-chemical sector (20 percent). Women could not be driven out of jobs in these branches without great economic disruption and without fostering widespread resentment toward the regime.[11]

Although the cyclical upswing in the German economy in 1933–34 reduced unemployment significantly, economic historians doubt that the rate of recovery could have been sustained without the implementation of full-scale rearmament and the militarization of the workforce, that is, the conscription of large numbers of young men into the expanding armed forces. The militarization of the German economy was the key difference between the economic performance of Germany and that of the United States, which had also instituted work-creation programs, but where unemployment remained much higher.[12]

The financing of the work-creation programs, and, later, rearmament, was achieved through an unconventional and underhanded accounting method introduced by Hjalmar Schacht, president of the Reichsbank and, as of July 1934, economics minister. While unemployment was still high, the regime was loath to raise taxes or to engage in conventional borrowing, which would have created inflationary pressure. The government, therefore, employed a method of off-budget financing involving government-guaranteed IOUs issued in the name of shell companies, with capital provided by private firms that would ultimately profit from the economic recovery. This technique was first introduced to finance work-creation programs. To finance rearmament, which was far more expensive, the Reichsbank created a shell company called the Metallurgische Forschungsgesellschaft (abbreviated as MEFO), or Metallurgical Research Society, which issued IOUs called MEFO Bills backed by capital provided by armaments manufacturers.[13]

Large-scale rearmament was accompanied by a push for economic self-sufficiency, or autarky, which officially took the form of the Four Year Plan, initiated in 1936. Focusing on petroleum, rubber, and iron ore, the Four Year Plan was intended to replace imported raw materials with domestic production.[14] The underlying logic of the plan was both strategic and ideological. It would prepare the German economy for war in four years, based on the assumption that such a war was inevitable in view of Nazism's expansionistic ambitions and the unlikelihood that Germany's neighbors would accept them. The drive for self-sufficiency was grounded, in part, in Hitler's personal memory of World War I, when a blockade of Germany had led to economic shortages, which, in Hitler's view, had broken the will of the German people and opened the door to the "stab in the back" by its internal enemies.[15]

Figure 4.3 Women in a factory producing Nazi flags and banners, 1933 (Imagno/Getty Images).

In an economy bolstered by rearmament and the Four Year Plan, unemployment virtually disappeared. The regime, which just a few years earlier had tried to encourage women to leave the workforce, now faced the challenge of luring women *into* the workforce. But several obstacles stood in the way of this goal. Wages for women were lower than those for men, women faced poor prospects for promotion in their jobs, and working hours were inflexible. Moreover, many traditionally minded women preferred homemaking to entering the workforce, and such sentiments had been reinforced by Nazism's traditionalist rhetoric about gender roles. More generally, there remained a broadly based cultural aversion to women in industrial jobs. The German Labor Front pushed for higher wages for women as one approach to the problem, but employers resisted. Despite such obstacles, the number of female workers in German industry rose over 50 percent between 1933 and 1938, from 1.2 million to 1.85 million, while there was a parallel increase of women in clerical and white-collar jobs from 1.6 to 1.9 million between 1933 and 1939 (see Figure 4.3).[16] Nevertheless, only 52.8 percent of all women eligible for the workforce were actually in it in 1939, and for work-eligible married women the figure was only 36 percent.[17] Thus, the regime's efforts to mobilize female labor enjoyed limited success. The mobilization of the German economy in preparation for war necessitated a level of female participation in the economy that was inconsistent with the regime's ideological vision for women. The problem would become even more acute during the war years, contributing to the regime's increasing dependence on forced foreign labor.

While the economic upswing put Germans back to work, the German working class possessed relatively little purchasing power when compared, for example, with American workers. Food and dwellings were expensive, and consumer goods were in short supply in an economy driven by the priorities of rearmament and infrastructure development. In the classic choice between guns and butter, the former was clearly the higher priority. The Nazi regime addressed this problem by enabling the mass production of certain products.[18] Among the best known of these was the inexpensive "People's Radio" (*Volksempfänger*). This item brought entertainment into the homes of millions of Germans while also vastly extending the reach of Hitler's speeches and other regime-produced propaganda.[19]

The desire to provide entertainment and recreation to the masses of the German population otherwise deprived of access to consumer products led to the creation of "Strength through Joy" as a part of the German Labor Front. The organization was designed to satisfy desire for mass consumption without raising wages to a level that might threaten rearmament. It addressed working-class concerns by sponsoring a variety of programs aimed at making industrial work more satisfying. These included, for example, attempts at the beautification of factories. Strength through Joy expanded opportunities for attending concerts and other cultural activities, and offered workers affordable vacations (see Figure 4.4). In the grander scheme of things, the goal of such initiatives was industrial peace, a balancing of class interests in the capitalist economy, and the creation of a happy workforce for the sake of the optimization of productivity and efficiency. As the historian David Schoenbaum argued in his still-relevant book published in 1966, *Hitler's Social Revolution*, the Nazi regime did little to alter the class structure of German society but did take very seriously the task of raising the social status of workers, reassuring them of their value to the People's Community.[20] Strength through Joy was central to this effort, and arguably proved to be the most popular institution introduced by the Nazi regime. Strength through Joy vacations and cultural programs were open only to racially acceptable Germans; thus, they must also be seen as an element of the regime's institutionalized racism.[21]

Figure 4.4 Vacationers on a "Strength through Joy" cruise, 1935 (ullstein bild/ullstein bild via Getty Images).

The British historian Tim Mason has identified four general strategies pursued by the Nazi regime for taming and controlling the German working class: the use of terror to repress opposition and resistance; a readiness to make concessions to working-class interests in order to quell dissent; the exploitation of divisions by rank and ideology within the working class; and the integration of elements of the working class into the system of domination.[22] The Nazi government destroyed the institutional infrastructure of organized labor as one of its very first measures in early 1933. Circles of working-class Germans who had been connected with the Social Democratic and Communist Parties became important loci of dissent and resistance to the regime, which reciprocated by targeting such individuals and groups as dangerous enemies of the people. State terror loomed as a continual factor.

This did not mean, however, that the regime ignored working-class interests. After January 1933, it implemented a form of managed capitalism aimed at balancing the interests of labor and capital for the sake of preserving industrial peace and avoiding class warfare. An important role was played by the so-called Trustees of Labor, a group of officials based in the Reich Labor Ministry. The Trustees were charged with promoting the interests of the nation as a whole by enabling management to operate efficiently, productively, and profitably, while simultaneously protecting labor from a level of exploitation that could lead to unrest. During the Weimar Republic, wages and working conditions had been enshrined in "wage contracts" (*Tarifverträge*) that had been hammered out through a process of collective bargaining. The Trustees transformed these wage contracts into "wage orders" (*Tarifordnungen*) and, over time, revised and re-adjusted them. Although labor had lost its ability to bargain collectively, and employers had been empowered as autocratic Führer by the Law for the Organization of National Labor early in 1934, the Trustees did, in fact, constitute a check on the power of employers to exploit their workers.[23]

The German Labor Front, into which the labor unions had been forcibly "coordinated" in 1933, was an additional element in the regime's system for the regulation of working-class interests. The Labor Front continued to provide benefits and services that had previously been the domain of the unions, such as social insurance, labor exchanges, and arbitration in cases of conflicts between labor and management. A good example of how the Labor Front advocated for working-class interests can be found in its effort, ultimately unsuccessful, to fundamentally alter the German system of old-age pensions to the advantage of blue-collar workers.[24] Considered together with the popular programs of Strength through Joy, these activities of the Labor Front exemplify Mason's observation regarding the success with which the Nazi regime integrated elements of the working class into its system of domination.[25]

The Nazi regime also attempted to use antisemitism as a means for depicting itself as the champion of the working class. Relatively few German Jews belonged to the industrial working class, while, for historical reasons discussed in Chapter 1, they were represented in commerce and the professions in percentages beyond their share of the general population. Playing off long-standing stereotypes, Nazi propaganda targeted at workers depicted Jews as greedy, elitist, and exploitative. Propaganda extolling the dignity of physical labor singled out the Jews for their supposed aversion to such forms of honest work.[26] While such antisemitic tropes may have been effective among workers who had already supported the Nazi movement before 1933, there is no evidence that the German workers who had previously been aligned with the Social Democrats or Communists became antisemites in large numbers during the Nazi years. When, for example, Nazi activists unleashed a wave of vandalism against Jewish-owned shops in Berlin in the summer of 1935, they were met with minimal support in the working-class district of Wedding.[27] The Social Democratic Party in Exile believed that experience in the labor movement and in Marxist parties had preconditioned workers to regard antisemitism as a "diversionary tactic" used by the capitalist class to distract attention away from concerns over wages and working conditions.[28] This ideological position, a common feature of contemporary Marxist critiques of Nazism and Fascism, seriously underestimated the importance of antisemitism as a genuine motivating factor, and not merely a tactic, of Nazism. But it also rang true to workers facing longer working hours, increased production quotas, rising food prices, and the loss of union representation.

Peasants, Agriculture, and Rural Life

In 1930s Germany, about one-third of Germans lived in rural areas and were dependent on agriculture for their livelihoods. During the rise to power, Hitler and the NSDAP had enjoyed their greatest electoral support in such regions, specifically in rural, Protestant ones. Nazism glorified the peasantry as the salt of the earth and bastion of Germanic racial purity. The scholarship on this subject nevertheless remains relatively limited, not nearly commensurate to its historical importance.[29]

According to Nazi ideology, "the racial health of the German people depended on strengthening the peasantry."[30] Nazi leaders championed the cause of preserving the traditional peasantry as a wellspring of Aryan virtue. But the lip-service paid to this ideological tenet in official propaganda did not necessarily make it a high policy priority of the regime. In the end, the preservation of traditional peasant culture took a back seat to the requirements of a highly industrialized nation that was in the process of mobilizing for war.

Agricultural prices had dropped precipitously between 1929 and 1933, while farmers maintained a fairly level rate of production. By 1933, farmers were massively in debt, leading to bankruptcies and foreclosures. The crisis was seen by farmers as not merely economic, but as a threat to a way of life. This helps to explain the turn to support the NSDAP in rural regions before January 1933. Hitler appealed to farmers with promises to address their economic plight, but also by praising the peasantry as a bulwark against racial degeneracy. Richard Walther Darré, who was appointed leader of the Reich Agricultural Estate and Minister of Agriculture in 1933, had trained in agronomy at the university level as a specialist in livestock selection, insights from which he extrapolated onto humans. He embraced the concept of Blood and Soil (*Blut und Boden*) as the encapsulation of the connection between racial purity and rootedness in the soil. German's decline, he claimed, had been caused by forces connected to the city. A regeneration of Germany would come from the peasantry.[31]

Darré had orchestrated the creation of the Reich Agricultural Estate in 1933 in order to promote the interests of agricultural producers. He portrayed it as the fulfillment of a long-standing yearning among agricultural producers for a united front against low prices and debt. Closely linked to the Agriculture Ministry, the Agricultural Estate was organized according to the top-down Nazi leader principle, with a large administrative cadre extending into the villages in the German countryside.[32]

In concert with the Agriculture Ministry, the Agricultural Estate sought to implement a system that Darré called the "Ordered Market" (*Marktordnung*). This system would be a form of managed capitalism applied to the German agricultural economy. "The Ordered Market," Darré stated in 1935, "does not interfere with private initiative, but orders it internally for the common good." Similar to the logic behind the creation of the Trustees of Labor, the Ordered Market would balance the interests of agricultural producers with those of German society more generally. It would protect farmers from the vicissitudes of the market while securing a steady and sufficient food supply for a modern, urbanized society. The Ordered Market aimed to rationalize agricultural production, contain seasonal fluctuations in agricultural prices, and reduce damage to the economic interests of producers caused by the importation of agricultural goods. It controlled the flow of imported foodstuffs not by imposing tariffs, but rather by having the German state purchase foreign products and then release them only gradually into the market at prices that would not undermine domestic producers. Imported products falling under this system included cereals and feed, milk, oils, fats, eggs, cattle, fruit, and wine. In addition to the import controls, the Ordered Market placed production limits on German producers, which were enforced by compulsory, state-controlled producer cartels.[33]

The Ordered Market led to positive results for most farmers. Agricultural prices in Germany returned to pre-Depression levels in the mid 1930s, even while they remained depressed globally. The system also succeeded in averting serious price fluctuations. German consumers did pay more for grain, vegetables, fruit, beef, and pork than they had in 1933, but prices remained fairly stable between 1935 and 1939.[34] Although farmers objected to the intrusion of government bureaucracy into the management of their businesses, they mostly profited from the regulated market.[35]

A different pillar of Nazi agricultural policy proved more disruptive and controversial among farmers. The Law of Hereditary Entailment, issued in September 1933, stipulated that family-owned farms of modest size, between 7.5 and 125 hectares, be bequeathed to only a single heir. Farm holdings were to be passed along to the oldest or most deserving son. The land could neither be sold nor mortgaged. The brainchild of Darré, the law aimed to create a hereditary rural farming aristocracy consisting of racially pure peasants. The owner of the entailed farm carried the title of "hereditary farmer" (*Erbbauer*), a classification for which farmers would have to apply, and which was restricted to racially pure Germans who could demonstrate their upstanding character.[36] The law rested on the historical foundation of entailment and primogeniture, which had been common in Europe, including in Germany. In earlier times, these practices had been designed to ensure the financial viability of farms that might otherwise have been divided into ever-smaller, economically untenable parcels. Applied in the 1930s, however, a policy of enforced entailment produced unintended negative economic consequences for the affected farmers.[37]

The implementation of the Entailment Law drew criticism in rural communities and in government circles. Younger siblings and others who did not stand to inherit land felt aggrieved. Existing owners feared that if their landholdings were classified as inalienable, they would never be able to use the land as collateral for bank loans. Without such credit, they would not be able to modernize their farms for the sake of profitability.[38] Meanwhile, some Nazi economic experts objected to an arrangement that extended too much protection to a significant segment of the agricultural economy. The hereditary farmers could not borrow against their land, but neither could they lose their farms to bankruptcy, resulting in a toleration of inefficient farming methods. Such a situation, it was feared, would undermine the entrepreneurial spirit of the farmers and perpetuate inefficient farming methods. But Darré, with Hitler's support, pushed the Entailment Law through on account of its racial and demographic significance. Darré bragged that removing peasant farms from market forces represented a victory over the "Jewish spirit" of commercialism.[39] Ultimately, 689,635 entailed farms were officially recognized, encompassing a total of 16 million hectares. An additional 300,000 farms were eligible for entailed status but never received it. Either the farmers were rejected for being insufficiently "upstanding," or they did not apply, fearing a coercive bureaucracy and the limitations on commercial freedom to sell or mortgage land.[40]

Economic developments in Germany in the late 1930s placed a squeeze on farmers. Rearmament and the Four Year Plan accelerated industrial expansion, which drew workers from the countryside into cities, creating a serious labor shortage in agriculture. At same time, the goal of self-sufficiency, when applied to food, increased pressure on farmers to produce. Increasing agricultural productivity in a tightening labor market could be achieved partially through advancements in mechanization and the expanded application of chemical fertilizer. In addition, Reich Labor Service workers were assigned to help with harvests, supplemented by paid foreign labor, mainly from Italy and Poland.[41]

Food prices rose in the second half of the 1930s, which was good for farmers, but not necessarily for consumers, who, having grown used to the low food prices of the Depression era, complained incessantly about the cost of butter, fat, eggs, and meat. Some regions experienced frequent shortages of meat and butter, which produced a lot of grumbling, but did not seriously undermine confidence in the Nazi regime.[42]

Nazi agricultural policies failed to enable the country to meet the nutritional requirements of a modern industrial economy preparing for war. Increases in agricultural output never rose to a point that was even close to where Germany could feed itself without imports. The country continued to import 16–20 percent of its foodstuffs, especially in the form of grains, fats, and oils.[43] Hitler and others in the leadership objected to this situation, which, as they saw it, placed Germany at the mercy of other countries. Determined to avoid a repetition of World War I, Hitler resolved that Germany would conquer agricultural land in Eastern Europe in the next war.

The Middle Classes

The German middle class during the 1930s can, for analytical purposes, be divided into two main groupings. The "old middle class" consisted largely of artisans and shopkeepers, while the "new middle class" encompassed white-collar workers and civil servants. The latter had expanded considerably since the beginning of the twentieth century as the result of the growth of corporations and the state bureaucracy.[44]

Germans anchored in the old middle class had formed the backbone of the Nazi Party before 1933. The Nazi movement had proved effective in exploiting their grievances against both large-scale capitalism and Marxism. Members of the commercial middle class had focused much of their resentment against large-scale retail in the form of department stores, which were widely associated with Jews, and against consumer cooperatives, which were championed by the Social Democrats. Germans who gave the Nazi movement their support for one or both of these reasons expected that, once in power, a Nazi government would act decisively to protect their interests.

But they were soon disappointed. As early as July 1933, Rudolf Hess, Hitler's Deputy Führer, ordered Nazi Party members to refrain from demonstrations, vandalism, and other actions targeted against department stores.[45] Between January 1933 and the Night of the Long Knives of June 1934, the militancy of the anti-capitalist faction within the Nazi movement was at a high point. Expectations about the forced closing of department stores ran high. But not only did the owners and managements of these large businesses resist, their workforces also expressed strong opposition to closing the stores.[46] There were too many jobs at stake, an estimated 90,000, and the shutdown of department stores would have also had a damaging effect on the banking system. Similarly, the elimination of the consumer cooperatives would have had severe repercussions on their 3.7 million members. The disappointment of the commercial middle class was pronounced, and complaints flowed into party and government offices.

The regime did nevertheless try to satisfy the commercial middle class with specific concessions intended to safeguard the interests of small-scale retailers. As a form of protectionism on behalf of existing shops, regulations issued in 1933 made it more difficult to open new small businesses. Although existing department stores were not closed down, a prohibition was imposed on the opening of new ones in an effort to slow the concentration of retail commerce that had begun decades earlier. The regime also gradually constricted the operations of consumer cooperatives, ultimately dissolving them in 1941.

While rearmament and the Four Year Plan placed increased emphasis on economic productivity, some German economic officials came to regard protectionist policies as outmoded and, in a literal sense of the term, counterproductive. Several of the protections were scaled back, but small retailers and artisans generally profited from the recovery of the economy.[47] For the old middle class, this recovery must also be understood in the context of Nazi anti-Jewish policies. Between 1933 and 1939, the number of retail businesses in Germany fell from 850,000 to 689,000. The dissolution of thousands of Jewish-owned businesses accounted for a substantial share of this decline. The process of Aryanization, in which Jewish-owned property and businesses were transferred to Aryan hands, was carried out in tandem with the implementation of protectionist policies in the retail sector. The authorities, for example, made sure that certain Jewish businesses were closed rather than transferred to Aryan ownership. Many of the closings occurred in 1938, and then radicalized further after the Kristallnacht pogrom of November 1938.[48]

The economic situation of German artisans also improved considerably during the 1930s. The Nazi regime allowed them to impose a form of neocorporatism, a kind of modern-day guild system, which diminished competition by restricting the number of workshops. Artisans gained more power over their own workshops, owing largely to the destruction of the labor unions. They appreciated the recognition granted to them in their roles as carriers of long-standing traditions. And, generally speaking, they approved of the regime's assault on Jewish retail establishments, which had been targets of demonization in artisanal circles since the nineteenth century.[49]

Among white-collar workers – the new middle class – incomes and job security both increased in the mid to late 1930s, especially in the industrial sector. They received better wages than industrial workers, and could also take advantage of cheap vacations and other programs offered by the Strength through Joy organization. Civil servants at all levels were vulnerable to dismissal because of the Civil Service Law of April 1933. Many joined the Nazi Party to demonstrate loyalty, an act of mass collective opportunism, but one that was perhaps understandable in the situation. Civil servants served the Nazi regime effectively out of ideological conviction, fear, opportunism, or a sense of professional obligation. Civil servants were instrumental to the functioning of the Nazi state, including those agencies that bureaucratically implemented the regime's policies of persecution.[50]

The Professions

Professionals – those who practiced in fields such as medicine, the law, engineering, and education – constituted a relatively small segment of the German population. Historically they had been paid well, possessed a relatively high level of job security, and occupied a prestigious position in German society. But their financial standing and self-confidence had been destabilized since the time of the German Empire by war, revolution, inflation, and depression. These developments had been especially tough on male professionals belonging to the "war youth generation," who proved particularly susceptible to the lure of Nazism. These men, who were born between 1900 and 1910, experienced World War I as children, then lived through the tumult of defeat, revolution, inflation, and depression. Successful in school and at university, their hopes for financial success and social recognition were dashed by hard economic times and political tumult. Recent university graduates were especially hard hit by the Depression, unable to find employment after having invested years of study. Older colleagues, although already in secure practices or positions in the civil service, faced pay cuts and diminished possibilities for promotion. Many at the time perceived a "crisis of professional consciousness."

In many cases, social attitudes reinforced such feelings of precariousness. Professionals were drawn disproportionally from the middle and upper classes, and so in many cases they reproduced the nationalist or conservative attitudes with which they had grown up. Already before 1933, some professionals were attracted to National Socialism by the promise of a restoration of order and hierarchy. For those whose political leanings were conservative, the political empowerment of the working class during the Weimar Republic deepened anxiety over their own declining status. Their self-perception as individuals of high ability and social standing did not comport with their predicament. Additionally, in fields such as law and medicine, some harbored resentment toward what they regarded as a disproportionately high, and therefore illegitimate, Jewish presence in their profession, especially in certain major cities.

Many professionals, to be sure, were repelled by the crudeness, anti-intellectualism, and bigotry of the Nazi movement. Most did not become Nazis before 1933, but a significant number were drawn to the movement. This was especially the case among physicians.[51] Many others, who had kept their distance to Nazism, succumbed after the NSDAP's success in the September 1930 election. After the seizure of power, many flocked into the party, some out of purely opportunistic reasons, others having arrived at the conclusion that National Socialism would be the antidote to the nation's ills.

As with the artisans examined above, the readiness of German professionals to support Nazism derived from a desire to pursue a neocorporatist restructuring of their fields. They hoped, with the backing of the state, to establish greater collective control over key aspects of their professions, such as education, standards for practitioners, compensation, and economic regulations. The neocorporatist rhetoric of National Socialism lured professionals who were prepared to give allegiance to a regime that protected their interests. This arrangement seemed to work on the surface. The regime orchestrated the creation of national organizations, known as chambers, in which membership would be compulsory for persons wishing to practice particular professions. The centralization of professional life in this manner was a complex undertaking that did not proceed at the same pace everywhere. The Reich Attorneys' Chamber was founded as early as March 1933, for example, whereas the Reich Chamber of Culture followed six months later, while the Reich Physicians' Chamber came into existence only in April 1936. Theoretically these organizations would advocate for the professional interests of their members, and in some important respects they did indeed do so. But they also became mechanisms for the downward transmissions of orders from the regime, and the hoped-for professional autonomy never materialized.

The disappointments, however, did not outweigh a degree of prosperity and stability that had been established by the late 1930s. A large number of professionals experienced these years in contrast not only to the Depression but, in the case of the more senior ones, to the entire period since 1914. By 1937, for example, the average gross income of German physicians was almost 50 percent higher than it had been in 1933.[52] Lawyers were also doing quite well in general, although those at the bottom suffered under a serious imbalance in the distribution of income. Teachers were dissatisfied by salaries that remained quite modest when compared with those earned by other professionals, but they benefitted from good job security.[53] The 1930s was no Golden Age for German professionals, but it was good enough for them to accommodate themselves, in the phrasing of historian Konrad H. Jarausch, to an "abnormal Nazi normality."[54]

Most German professionals did not eventually become Nazi war criminals, but a good number were drawn into some of the more ethically problematic activities of the Nazi regime. Lawyers, for example, drafted and enforced exclusionary racial legislation, physicians administered the regime's eugenics program, and teachers preached Nazi propaganda to their pupils. When it came to the purge of Jewish professional colleagues, a few spoke out while the majority looked the other way or applauded the elimination of Jewish competition. In some major cities, Jews were highly represented in the legal and medical professions especially, so their purge from these professions served the interests of Aryan professionals. In Berlin alone, 1,880 Jewish lawyers, constituting just under one-half of all lawyers in the city, were purged from the legal profession in 1933 and 1934.[55] The purge of Jews from the ranks of physicians in Berlin required a lengthier process that did not conclude until 1938, but the numbers were even more dramatic. In 1933, 2,000 of the capital city's 3,600 insurance-approved doctors (*Kassenärzte*) were Jews. Their removal from the practice of medicine created significant opportunities for non-Jewish physicians, including young doctors who had struggled to establish a practice during the Depression.[56]

By 1939, Germany had attained full employment while joblessness continued to plague the United States, Britain, and other countries with highly developed economies. Nazi leaders could boast credibly of this achievement. But the conquest of unemployment had created a different set of problems that generated discontent: shortages of consumer goods, longer hours for workers, bureaucratic intrusions into economic decisions, and fear of a coercive regime. The class structure of German society in 1939, and the resentments that this generated, was not fundamentally different from what it had been in 1933. The Nazi regime, which had come into existence in large part as a reaction against Communism, had not attempted to change the nation's class structure, but it made conspicuous gestures of solidarity to the working class. It would be an exaggeration to say that the regime had succeeded in subsuming class differences under the integrative idea of a People's Community, but it would also be an exaggeration in the other direction to deny that it had established broad legitimacy across classes. Germans could believe that a rising tide had lifted all boats. Germans interviewed after World War II often had positive memories of the peacetime years of Nazi rule, which they recalled as a time of peace, prosperity, and national unity.[57]

The economic recovery had been enabled by rearmament and the militarization of German society. As the country became militarily stronger during the 1930s, it also achieved significant and popular victories in foreign policy, which liberated the country from the shackles of the post-war settlement and restored it to the status of Great Power. The restoration of national greatness, as it was understood, further enhanced the regime in the eyes of many Germans (and sympathetic foreigners as well).

Antisemitism was embedded in many elements of Nazi economic policy, even those that were not primarily targeted at Jews. Germans were largely sympathetic to non-violent Nazi anti-Jewish measures. These included the purge of Jews from the German professions and the Aryanization of Jewish-owned property. German Jews had been widely perceived as having wielded too much economic influence in the country before 1933. There were, of course, dissenters from this view, but the Nazi regime's accomplishments in economic and foreign policy, and its creation of stable, seemingly effective government, caused many to accept antisemitism as an unfortunate but also unavoidable byproduct of an otherwise successful system.

5   Nazi Society, 1933–1939

In the previous chapter we observed how the Nazi regime applied *dirigiste* methods to the German economy, the fundamental capitalist structure of which it did not alter. Complaints and pushback, while common, did not translate into widespread rejection of the system. This chapter will describe a similar pattern while focusing on cultural and demographic categories such as women, men, youth, and university students. With regard to sex roles, gender identities, and family issues, much of Nazi policy embodied continuity with the past, but this continuity was overlaid with Nazism's cult of masculinity, glorification of motherhood, and cultivation of racially healthy young people. Incessant propaganda and frequent, heavy-handed attempts to mobilize the population behind this shift in consciousness generated their own pushback, based sometimes on ideological opposition, sometimes on irritation with inconvenience, and sometimes on discomfort with the official imposition of a suffocating conformity. But never did the objections amount to a widespread fundamental rejection of the system.

Nazi Conceptions of Masculinity and Femininity

Inasmuch as Nazi Germany was a society in which personal aspirations and expectations for personal conduct followed gendered norms that were deeply entrenched, it did not differ essentially from other societies in Europe (or beyond). Starting in the 1970s, historians have been exploring the regime's policies toward women as well as the daily experiences of German women under those policies.[1] More recently, the study of women has evolved into a more capacious consideration of gender and sexuality, which has included the study of how the behavior and experiences of men were shaped by specific notions of masculinity and by non-heteronormative sexualities. While the Nazi regime's persecution of homosexual men and women will be considered in the following section, we will focus here on how Nazi ideology and policies shaped the gendered order of the majority, those deemed in good standing in the People's Community.

National Socialism posited the existence of a "natural" gender order, one of gendered spheres for men and women, of male breadwinners and female homemakers.[2] Traditional gender roles were overlaid with a reinforcing logic of racist determinism and demographic necessity. Nazi ideas about gender were a reaction against challenges to traditional gender expectations that had emerged in the Weimar period. The progressive ideals of Weimar regarding abortion, homosexuality, women's work, and sexology had had a high profile but only a limited degree of acceptance in German society. In *Mein Kampf*, Hitler had rarely mentioned the family or reflected upon women's roles. But he was obsessed with the "crisis" of German manhood posed by "feminized men" and the need for masculine regeneration. He and other Nazis regarded the restoration and strengthening of traditional gender roles as a prerequisite for national defense and national rejuvenation. This idea was based on the Social Darwinistic view of the world as an arena of struggle. The performative elements of the Nazi movement, including its violent rhetoric, were primarily masculine. Once the Nazis were in power, the antifeminist element of ideology and propaganda had to be balanced against the need to mobilize a large, complex society for war – a society in which more than half the population was female. While feminism was regarded as alien and associated with liberalism, socialism, and Communism, the Nazis envisaged a place for women and girls in the People's Community. Within the Nazi movement and government, there were disagreements and arguments over precisely what this place should be, and ideological positions pertaining to gender could sometimes take a back seat to other priorities, such as economic productivity.

Like Fascist movements elsewhere, Nazism in Germany may be understood, in part, as "a solution to a felt crisis in gender relations in Weimar."[3] In the aftermath of the Weimar Republic, which right-wing Germans associated with feminism and tolerance of homosexuality, Nazism intended to restore masculine authority and to celebrate heroic masculinity, promoting it in education, culture, and propaganda.[4] The Third Reich elevated male camaraderie to a "state virtue" by promoting a romanticized nostalgia for the soldierly comradeship of the trenches of World War I.[5] The all-male units of the Hitler Youth and the Reich Labor Service were dubbed "*Kameradschaften*" to underscore the intention that they would help overcome class divisions and differences in social status. This masculine community would be forged further by means of negative integration, with the Jews identified as a common enemy to German men of varying backgrounds. Within the Nazi movement, such notions of male comradeship had been deeply embedded in the culture of the SA since the beginning.[6] By 1939, the Nazi regime had set up a pathway for boys and men to prepare them for entering the so-called "circle of men" (*Männerbund*), starting with the Hitler Youth for boys, then the Labor Service, and finally the Wehrmacht, with membership in the SA along the way for many.[7] Life in these organizations promoted conformity and helped young males find their place in the social hierarchy through sports, physical competitions, and brawling. The development of "manliness" was accompanied by ideological indoctrination intended to reinforce the male-dominated gender order and an authoritarian mindset. The masculinity promoted in these organizations was oriented toward struggle, violence, and war. While not all German men were immersed in this comradely culture, the segments of male German society that were influenced by it were large and significant. Arguably it helped enable the genocide perpetrated by Germans during World War II.[8]

Just as it had bemoaned the feminization of men during Weimar, the Nazi movement had also condemned the masculinization of women. This critique was not limited to issues of women in the workplace or reproductive freedom. The Nazis also attacked gender-neutral fashion trends that had caught on during the 1920s, placing a good deal of the blame on Jews who had been active in the German fashion industry. During the Third Reich, however, the aesthetic construction of femininity was not limited to dirndls and other traditional styles, contrary to the impression often conveyed by Nazi propaganda films. While steering clear of the gender-neutral or masculine-inspired designs that had been in style during the 1920s, female fashion during the 1930s could be elegant, sophisticated, and conscious of international trends. Even the uniforms for female members of Nazi mass organizations were seen by many as stylish.[9] This approach to female fashion exemplifies a broader reality about Nazi policy toward women who were deemed acceptable for the People's Community. The Nazi regime, while irredeemably hostile to reproductive freedom, coopted the rhetoric and some of the goals of early twentieth-century German "bourgeois" feminism. Before 1933, most German women had remained traditional in their attitudes toward gender and sex, and they did not experience the Nazi years as a dystopian patriarchal nightmare.

The Attack on Homosexuality

German law had prohibited homosexual sex among men since the inception of the German Empire in 1871. Article 175 of the Reich Criminal Code proscribed the act of "sodomy." Homosexual acts between women had not been formally criminalized, in part because they did not threaten the masculinity of the country's patriarchal political class, and in part because of the fear that normal affectionate physical contact between women could be misconstrued as lesbianism. Article 175 remained on the books during the Weimar Republic, but authorities in some places took a very permissive approach to enforcement, allowing gay subcultures to arise in cities like Berlin and Hamburg. After the Nazis came into power, Article 175 was already available to them as a key weapon in their campaign against homosexuality.

Because discrimination against homosexual persons both preceded the Nazi takeover and continued after the collapse of the Third Reich, Nazi measures targeting them were part of a longer historical pattern, but they also represented a new level of persecution. Nazism's hostility to homosexuality embraced and went beyond traditional forms of homophobia based on religion and conservative morality. Homosexuality was believed to undermine the Nazi ideal of martial masculinity, a sentiment based on the stereotype of gay men as being effeminate. Homosexuality was also believed to conflict with Nazi pro-natalism. Many Nazis feared that homosexuality might be an inherited trait that could be passed down by bisexual men or by closeted gay men who married and had children. Finally, many Nazis associated the liberal acceptance of homosexuality during the Weimar Republic with the prominent Jewish sex researcher Magnus Hirschfeld. During the Nazi era, medical researchers and psychiatrists unanimously regarded homosexuality as an abnormality, but they debated whether its causes were hormonal, psychological, genetic, or some combination of all these factors.[10]

The onslaught against homosexuality began in the spring of 1933, when authorities ordered police and SA units to raid and close down bars and clubs connected to the gay and lesbian subculture.[11] Gradually, legal authorities increased the frequency of prosecutions under Article 175. Whereas there had been 464 prosecutions under that statute in all of Germany in 1932, in 1933 the number rose to 575, and in 1934 it rose still further to 635.[12]

An important turning point was the murder of the leader of the SA, Ernst Röhm, in June 1934. Röhm, who was homosexual, had embodied a contradiction between the homophobic rhetoric that was dominant in the Nazi Party, on the one hand, and the reality of gay life within an important sector of the Nazi movement, on the other. Röhm and the men in his immediate circle rejected the notion that the ideal of militarized masculinity had to be coupled with heterosexuality. Their conception of comradeship embraced a homoerotic element. This view was not uncommon among German veterans of World War I and was openly promoted in veterans' circles during the Weimar Republic.[13] While the murder of Röhm on Hitler's orders was motivated primarily by Hitler's desire to appease the military leadership, it also conveniently solved the dilemma posed by Röhm's homosexuality.

In 1935, the Nazi government revised Article 175. Consummation of homosexual sex was now no longer required for prosecution and conviction; the mere intention of initiating sex between men now sufficed. Moreover, the definition of homosexual sex was broadened beyond "sodomy" to include intimate touching of various kinds.[14] The new version of Article 175 came into force on September 1, 1935, inaugurating a dramatic rise in prosecutions. The crackdown on homosexuality extended into many sectors of German society, including the officially homophobic Christian clergy, and even the SS, an organization comprising the ostensible Aryan elite.[15] The German press churned out stories emphasizing the dangers of homosexuality and the importance of combatting it, creating an environment in which Germans were encouraged to denounce suspected homosexual activity to the police.[16] During the years 1936 to 1939, approximately 30,000 German men were convicted under the statute.[17] Prosecutions under Article 175 dropped during the war years, when millions of men served in the armed forces, which clamped down on homosexuality through its own disciplinary and court system.[18]

Whereas during the Weimar Republic men convicted under Article 175 had often received fines, after 1933 the penalties usually included incarceration of at least one year.[19] Longer sentences were meted out in cases involving minors. Having been prosecuted under statute law and been convicted by a court, the gay men served their sentences mostly in prisons rather than in concentration camps. Many, however, ultimately landed in the camps anyway. Heinrich Himmler, the head of the SS and all German police, was a fanatical homophobe[20] under whose authority many gay men were taken into "preventative custody" and sent to camps, sometimes to await trial while Article 175 charges were in preparation.[21] Starting in 1940, on Himmler's orders, gay men deemed to be continuing threats were taken into "protective custody" upon the completion of their prison sentences and transferred to concentration camps without additional legal process. Some gay men who had been convicted of having sex with young boys were able to avoid the camps by agreeing to have themselves castrated. In 1941, the national sentencing law was revised so that courts could pass down death sentences in Article 175 cases involving minors. The number of gay men executed under this legal provision is not known.

Both in the prisons and in the camps, gay men were singled out for abusive treatment by guards and by other inmates. Conditions for them were especially bad in the concentration camps, where the SS guards held them in contempt.[22] The gay inmates were assigned to especially difficult and humiliating forms of labor, such as cleaning the latrines. But far worse were the beatings, hazardous work assignments, and outright murders by guards. Of the approximately 6,000 gay men who were sent to camps, between 3,000 and 3,600 perished there, mostly during the war years.[23]

Although early in the Nazi regime the German authorities contemplated a revision of Article 175 that would have criminalized homosexual acts between women, the change was never adopted. The Ministry of Justice feared that it would, among other problems, lead to the unjust harassment of women who engaged in innocent embraces and hand-holding. In the absence of a statute aimed directly against lesbianism, the Nazi campaign against homosexuality did not extend to women in any systematic way. There were, however, cases in which lesbians were arrested and imprisoned for violating anti-lewdness laws or for subverting military readiness. More broadly, lesbians were sometimes subjected to shaming, harassment, and intimidation by the police and local Nazi Party offices.[24] An important regional exception to the pattern described here was Austria. Prior to its annexation by Germany in 1938, Austria had combatted homosexuality with a statute – Article 129 of the criminal code – that was framed a good deal more broadly than Germany's. This law remained in force even after the annexation, providing a legal basis for the prosecution of women for acts of homosexual sex. Between 1938 and 1945, women comprised about 5 percent of the defendants convicted under Article 129 in Austria.[25]

Women in Nazi Society

In 1931, in an effort to attract female voters, the Nazi Party created the National Socialist Women's League (NS-Frauenschaft). While attempting to mobilize female support, the Women's League did not question the subordinate position of women. The leader of the Women's League, Gertrud Scholtz-Klink, was an effective organizer who, while committed to a hierarchical gendered order and traditional conception of the family, saw herself as legitimately serving the collective interests of German women (see Figure 5.1). Once the Nazis were in power, she advocated her understanding of women's interests to a male leadership that was indifferent, if not hostile, to the perspective of women. Women, she argued, should be regarded as a resource to be harnessed. By late 1939, the Women's League counted 1.4 million members.[26]

The Women's League (along with a larger organization that it controlled, the Deutsches Frauenwerk) was active in areas that had been

Figure 5.1 Gertrud Scholtz-Klink, mid 1930s (ullstein bild/ullstein bild via Getty Images).

emphasized by the middle-class women's organizations of the pre-1933 period. These included the education of girls and young women in household management activities such as cooking and cleaning, and education about childcare, which encompassed the proper ideological indoctrination of children. The training in household management targeted women in their roles as consumers with an eye to the broader economic policy goal of reducing demand for consumer goods and especially imported products. The regime recognized that women were usually in charge of household consumption in their families. A Reich Mothers' Service (Reichsmütterdienst), established in May 1934, celebrated motherhood as a form of national service, sponsoring educational activities on housework, child-rearing, and "racial hygiene." The Women's League promoted women's involvement in social assistance as auxiliary nurses, as social workers, and in air-raid protection. These programs met with limited success. Not a few women expressed frustration with policies relegating them to domesticity, thwarting the intellectual, academic, and occupational ambitions of themselves and their daughters. Such criticisms were even expressed from within the ranks of the Women's League. At the same time, there were also many German women who embraced, sometimes enthusiastically, the roles assigned to them by the Nazi regime.[27]

Although there were elements inside the NSDAP that were captive to inhibited, prudish attitudes toward sex, the regime was not, on an ideological level, anti-sex. Sex was necessary for reproduction, so the regime emphasized and promoted heterosexual sex among Aryans. Fashionably dressed women, as described above, were consistent with this goal.[28] The regime was pro-natalist, and it policed sex and reproduction with the aim of increasing the fecundity of "hereditarily fit Aryans." Reproduction was promoted in propaganda and the education system, and was incentivized in the tax code. The Nazi regime modified divorce laws to facilitate the breakup of childless couples when the prospect existed that one or both partners would reproduce with different partners.[29] These pro-natalist measures, it should be emphasized, were closely intertwined with the national program for eugenic sterilization, introduced in 1933, which aimed to impede reproduction among people considered to be racially unhealthy. Moreover, the connection between sex and reproduction was one reason, among several, that the regime took such great pains to suppress homosexuality.

The birth rate in Germany did increase significantly during the peacetime years of Nazi rule. Starting with 14.7 births per thousand people in 1933, the rate rose to 19 per thousand in 1936, and reached 20.3 per thousand in 1939. It is impossible, however, to determine the degree to which the upward trend was a result of pro-natalist policies or the consequence of the general economic upswing of the 1930s; it was probably a bit of both. The climbing birth rate does not necessarily reflect ideological support for Nazism, but it can fairly be interpreted as a sign of rising confidence in the future.[30]

During the Weimar era, German women enjoyed expanded access to birth control advice and to contraceptives. The Reich Criminal Code inherited from the Empire by the Weimar Republic criminalized abortion and provided for stiff penalties for the woman and the abortion provider. The relevant legislation was liberalized in 1926. While abortion remained illegal in Weimar, the prescribed punishments were dramatically relaxed.[31] After the Nazi seizure of power, the manufacture and sale of contraception remained legal, but prohibitions on display and advertising were hardened. The regime shut down birth control centers, many of which had been run by the Communist Party. Access to birth control became more difficult, and much of it moved underground. The crackdown on abortion was much harsher. The intensified enforcement of abortion laws must be seen not only in connection with eugenics measures, but also with the destruction of the Weimar-era sex reform movement and the persecution of leftist and Jewish doctors who were seen as the promoters of reproductive freedom. In May 1933, stiff penalties on abortion were reintroduced. From 1932 to 1933, Germany saw a dramatic decline in referrals for legal therapeutic abortions from 44,000 to 4,000. In 1936, the government created a Reich Central Office for the Combatting of Homosexuality and Abortion, underscoring how those two concepts were connected in Nazi thinking. The intensified enforcement of the prohibition on abortion led to a nine-fold increase in prosecutions in 1937. The pattern of increasingly severe enforcement continued during World War II, when the death penalty was added as an allowable punishment.

Nevertheless, illegal abortions continued to be performed in significant numbers; according to (probably exaggerated) Gestapo estimates, between a half-million and a million such procedures occurred annually.[32] Even as voluntary abortions, desired by women, were ruthlessly suppressed, eugenically motivated abortions for the "racially undesirable and unfit" remained not only legal but could be ordered by the state. Such compulsory abortions were authorized by the very same committees of physicians who decided on eugenic sterilization cases.[33]

Indoctrinating German Youth

During its rise to power, the Nazi movement had cultivated an image of youthful vigor and a promise of renewal. The elite of the NSDAP, like that of the Communist Party, was younger than that of the established political parties, and the national association of university students had been the first major national organization to fall under Nazi control. After 1933, the Nazi regime established the mobilization of young people as a national priority. Here again, the regime's approach was to embrace inherited traditions and mentalities, overlay them with a stratum of Nazi racism, antisemitism, and militarism, impose an unprecedented degree of centralized control, and apply the power of the state to enforce conformity. The system promoted the gendered socialization of boys and girls in separate youth organizations, preparing the former for life as fathers and warriors and the latter for life as mothers and homemakers. In the schools, Nazi ideology was infused into the curriculum, and teachers were subjected to political criteria for appointment and promotion. As in other sectors of German life that were subjected to Nazification during the 1930s, there was plentiful evidence of reluctance, non-compliance, and resistance among German youth. But there was also widespread acceptance and conformity, especially when it came to programs for youth that were considered to be fun, such as sports, games, and outdoor activities. The degree to which such conformity resulted in the conscious adoption of Nazi ideology is difficult to measure, but the internalization of the main principles of National Socialism inevitably took place on a broad scale.

The main vessel for the mobilization of German children and teenagers was the Hitler Youth.[34] At the time of its creation by the Nazi Party in 1925, this organization was one youth group among many along a broad ideological spectrum. Originally targeted at boys, the Hitler Youth was expanded to include girls in 1931 with the creation of the League of German Girls (Bund deutscher Mädel, BdM). This occurred against the wishes of the Women's League, which had laid its own claim to the mobilization of girls and young women.[35] In 1931, Baldur von Schirach, a 24-year-old leader of the National Socialist Student League, was placed at the helm of the youth organizations, receiving the lofty title of "Reich Youth Leader."[36] In 1931, the Hitler Youth, including all of its suborganizations for boys and girls, had an enrollment of 35,000 members aged 10 through 18. During the final phase of the Weimar Republic, these groups, like the NSDAP more generally, profited from the polarization of German society. The youthfulness of the NSDAP and its leadership signaled a future-oriented movement not bound by the failed formulas of the past.[37] By January 1933, membership stood at around 100,000.

During the process of "coordination" after January 1933, the Hitler Youth gobbled up many of the non-Nazi youth organizations. By the end of 1933, it counted 2 million members, and by December 1936 this figure had climbed to 5.4 million.[38] By the end of 1937, 64 percent of eligible youngsters belonged to the Hitler Youth.[39] Membership rates remained especially low in Catholic Bavaria, where Catholic youth organizations persisted, and where many anti-Nazi Catholic parents and clergy discouraged young people from joining. Technically, membership in the organization was still voluntary. Although a law issued in 1936 declared that "the entire German youth within the territory of the Reich is coordinated within the Hitler Youth," it was not until 1939 that membership was made truly compulsory.[40]

Before 1939, decisions about whether to join were subject to a complex set of incentives and disincentives. Young people were drawn to the organization by the prospect of adventure, excitement, and sport. Peer pressure in schools and communities could be considerable. Moreover, certain occupational and educational opportunities, such as apprenticeships and the *Abitur*, the secondary school degree required for admission to a university, were made dependent on membership in the Hitler Youth. These attractions and pressures did succeed in drawing a majority of German youth into the organization before it was made compulsory,

Figure 5.2 Hitler Youth members learning to fire a rifle, mid 1930s (Keystone/Getty Images).

although membership rates were lower for girls than for boys, as the girls were, as a general rule, under less pressure for educational and occupational advancement.[41] A byproduct of the incentive structure was the problem posed by nominal members who avoided attendance at meetings and participation in activities. Many young people with an individualistic bent resented conformity and indoctrination, and many came from families that were critical of Nazism. They joined because they had to, but avoided genuine involvement.[42]

Nevertheless, a great many young Germans valued their time in the Hitler Youth. They were flattered by the attention heaped on them by adults and enjoyed the ritualized aspects of many of the activities. The Hitler Youth offered an escape from constraints imposed by parents at home. The experience was exciting and new. Many of the teenage boys enjoyed the military-style training offered by some of the sports and games, and derived pride and a sense of belonging from their uniforms (see Figure 5.2).[43]

Ideological indoctrination was integrated in one way or another into most Hitler Youth programs. While active roles in promoting ideology were limited to a relatively small number of members in leadership positions, most members were exposed to propaganda on a regular basis. Antisemitism and doctrines of race were systematically infused into all sorts of activities. Ideological content, for example in the form of antise-mitic songs, was introduced into chapter meetings and overnight camp-ing. Male Hitler Youth members accompanied adults during antisemitic actions such as boycotts and vandalism against Jewish-owned businesses. Notably, male members of the Hitler Youth were involved to a signifi-cant degree in the anti-Jewish violence of the so-called Kristallnacht, the November 9–10, 1938 pogrom.[44] This pattern continued into the war as teenage boys from the Hitler Youth were recruited into assisting with the deportations of Jews from Germany.[45] Aside from antisemitism, the ideological training focused on chauvinistic lessons about German his-tory and on the Fuhrer cult.[46]

The nationalist and traditional masculine values of the Hitler Youth were reinforced in publications like *Die Kameradschaft* (*Comradeship*), which was intended for reading by boys at home after school. The maga-zine urged its young readers, in the description of a scholar who has studied it, to "be a man, be a soldier, be hard, be ready to sacrifice for the *Volk*, be loyal to one's *Volk* and one's friends, work hard, produce, achieve, focus on deeds rather than words." The magazine drew con-trasts between heroes and merchants, with the Jewish merchant depicted as cowardly, greedy, dishonest, and not rooted in the soil or the Volk.[47]

Because members of the Hitler Youth ranged in age from 10 to 18, those who were in the organization during the Nazi period had been born as early as 1916 and as late as 1934. One can therefore not really speak of a uniform "Hitler Youth Generation." Germans born within that wide chronological window underwent very diverse personal experiences. It was nevertheless the case that a large number of boys spent formative years of their youth in the organization before joining the Wehrmacht (and in many cases the Reich Labor Service) and were thus subjected to years of unremitting indoctrination before going to war.

Young people, whose identities and beliefs were still in the process of being shaped, were susceptible to these attractions. While some youths could appreciate the adventurous elements of the Hitler Youth without simultaneously buying into the ideology, others embraced the sense of certainty about the world that was offered them. Members who ascended into leadership positions cherished the opportunities for personal growth and the exercise of authority.[48] Alfons Heck, who distinguished him-self as a particularly fanatical member and then official of the Hitler Youth, later recalled that he and his comrades had "received an almost daily dose of nationalistic instruction, which we swallowed as naturally as our morning milk."[49] Melita Maschmann, a similarly ambitious and successful member of the League of German Girls, who eventually participated in the Nazi colonization project in Eastern Europe, was grateful for how the youth organization had imparted meaning to her life. "Everything that was *I* had been absorbed by the Whole," she explained after the war.[50]

For the members of the League of German Girls, the emphasis was less on physical exertion and drills, and more on "friendship," fun, and communal play. Activities emphasized hiking, singing, puppet shows, folk dancing, handicrafts, and needlework. Political indoctrination took forms that were less heavy-handed than among the boys, although it remained omnipresent in ways that were more implicit. The girls did engage in sports, but this was organized in a less competitive way than it was for the boys. The focus was on gymnastics and swimming, with a greater emphasis on gracefulness than on power. Female sport was regarded as a showcase for femininity, and specifically for a traditional ideal of feminine beauty. Many girls enjoyed wearing the BdM uniform, the design of which had been given great attention. Girls regarded it as fashionable and attractive. In addition to standard uniforms, there were special uniforms for dances, ceremonies, and other occasions. The beauty ideal promoted by the BdM included lipstick, make-up, styled hair, good grooming, neat dressing, and an overall healthy look (see Figure 5.3). Girls, it was believed, needed to learn how to be attractive to men as potential wives and bearers of children.[51]

The memoirs of Germans who spent time in the Hitler Youth reveal a complex set of reactions to that phase of their lives. Many young people had been swept away by the adventure, ceremony, and flattery that they experienced. They had been gratified to be part of something larger than themselves, and to participate in a process of national renewal. They had positive memories of the pre-war years, fondly recalling games like "cops and robbers" and "capture the flag," sports, and hikes. In their memoirs, they repressed, or ignored, the ideological indoctrination and antisemitism, although some did claim that they had found the incessant drilling and indoctrination offensive or boring. Many recalled having been subjected to peer pressure to join the Hitler Youth by their friends, a dynamic that frequently generated intergenerational tension within anti-Nazi families. The death and destruction that Nazism brought down on the country enabled many to ultimately recognize that they had worshipped a false idol. Later in life, they resented having been seduced by a movement that had exploited their idealism.[52]

While cases of open opposition among youth were the exception rather than the rule, they did demonstrate the potential for nonconformity. The most common way to buck the system was for individual dissenters to

Figure 5.3 Members of the League of German Girls at the Nazi Party rally in Nuremberg, 1937 (Photo by Max Ehlert/ullstein bild via Getty Images).

withdraw from the Hitler Youth.[53] Organized acts of nonconformity, while less common, could be more effective in rankling the authorities. Organized dissident youth fell into two general categories. First, there were the Christian, liberal, or Communist-inspired youth groups, which had continued to function illegally after their formal dissolution in 1933. They engaged in their various activities – such as hiking, sports, and music-making – while wearing the uniforms of their now-banned organizations. These groups were monitored by the Hitler Youth and the Gestapo, and were often shut down. Their opposition to National Socialism was idealistic or ideological, and not merely a pushback against a suffocating conformity. The siblings Hans and Sophie Scholl and other students who organized the famous White Rose resistance movement (discussed in more detail in Chapter 10) at the University of Munich during World War II had belonged to this kind of dissident Christian youth movement during the 1930s. The second category of dissident youth tended to be less ideological and not affiliated with any pre-1933 political party or tradition. They were characterized more by rebellion against conformity and social control imposed by the Hitler Youth. They arose mostly in the late 1930s and continued into the war years. Some possessed the character of gangs, which roamed specific localities or regions. They consisted of both young men and young women, but were dominated by male leadership, and some came to be known for sexual promiscuity. The groups cultivated a romantic image, as reflected in the name of the best-known of the groups, the loosely organized Edelweiss Pirates, a network of gangs of mainly working-class boys in the northern Rhineland and Ruhr basin regions.[54]

The Edelweiss Pirates (and similar groups elsewhere in Germany) cultivated an alternative youth culture to the official one, framed intentionally to provoke and outrage the Hitler Youth and mainstream adults. They despised the pressure for conformity, but were also motivated by a working-class resentment toward the middle-class and elite backgrounds of much of the Hitler Youth's leadership cadres.[55] The Pirates, who consisted mainly of boys in the 14–18 age group, mocked, ridiculed, and often disrupted official Hitler Youth functions. They gathered in parks, bars, and town squares in groups of about a dozen, singing protest songs, some of them profane. When on hiking or cycling trips, they would confront and taunt members of the Hitler Youth. They celebrated drinking, smoking, sex, and other behaviors that the Hitler Youth discouraged (although often without success). While the Pirates were primarily non-ideological, an outwardly similar network of gangs in Leipzig, "The Packs" (die Meuten), was anchored in the local tradition of Communist, working-class youth.[56]

An additional form of dissent from official youth culture that emerged during the 1930s was the Swing Youth. These young people rejected the sentimental and nationalistic folk music promoted by the Nazi regime, preferring instead to listen and dance to jazz records or bands. Official

Nazi culture regarded jazz and swing as racially inferior and morally depraved on account of their connections to the African American community. The adherents to this movement consisted mainly of young people drawn from the upper middle class. Many were students at the *Gymnasien*, the elite secondary schools. Thus, the Swing Youth had a different social basis from the Edelweiss Pirates. They preferred fine liquors over beer, and their form of rebellion required financial means to purchase clothing, phonographs, records, and liquor. Their modes of dress, hairstyles, and female make-up were inspired by American and British fashion, and their self-conscious foreignness was an additional feature making them objectionable to the regime. The Swing Youth was not an explicitly political or ideological rebellion, but rather a revolt against an officially prescribed national culture characterized by the demonization of Blackness and a provincial nationalism.[57]

Education under Nazism

While Hitler and other leading Nazis sang the praises of Germany's impressive cultural accomplishments over the centuries, they tended to reject intellectuals as decadent, internationalist, and Jewish-influenced. In the education system, they preferred practical training and political indoctrination over a critical intellectualism. The learning outcomes emphasized by official education policy included character building, personal discipline, nationalist sentiment, racial consciousness, and physical fitness. To achieve these aims, the country needed to develop an effective corps of "teachers for the Volk" (*Volkserzieher*). Teacher training academies were placed on an ideological basis with respect to admissions and curricula.[58]

The National Socialist Teachers League (Nationalsozialistischer Lehrerbund), founded by the party in 1929, embodied such a politicized approach to education. The League expanded rapidly after the onset of Germany's deep political polarization in 1929, attracting a disproportionately high number of younger, nationalist-oriented teachers. Growth accelerated after the Nazi takeover of the country, and by 1937, 97 percent of Germany's 320,000 primary and secondary school teachers were members.[59] An important function of the National Socialist Teachers League during the Nazi era was to police the political loyalty of teachers, who, under the provisions of the Civil Service Law of April 7, 1933, could be fired for reasons of political unreliability.

Social Democratic, Communist, and Jewish school teachers were subjected to harassment from the very start of the Nazi regime. Jewish teachers were fired *en masse* in 1933, while teachers who were politically (as opposed to racially) objectionable were subject to case-by-case review. The number of teachers who were dismissed on political grounds varied greatly according to location and level. In Germany's largest state, Prussia, for example, 3,343 teachers, roughly 3 percent of the total, were either fired, forced into premature retirement, or demoted for ideological reasons between 1933 and 1937. But at the *Gymnasium* level in Prussia, a full 46 percent of teachers were adversely affected by the purge of politically or "racially" objectionable people.[60]

Teachers who were kept on had to undergo ideological instruction. The National Socialist Teachers League sponsored courses and retreats where teachers could receive training in Nazi race theory, antisemitism, and international politics. In courses targeted at teachers of biology, race science and eugenics received special emphasis. By 1939, two-thirds of all teachers had attended at least one such League-sponsored program. Not surprisingly, the reactions of teachers to these compulsory indoctrination programs were mixed. Some appreciated the sense of camaraderie experienced during the retreats, which included sports, hiking, and other outdoor activities. They valued the esprit de corps engendered at the retreats. Others, however, were repelled by the racism and ideological stridency. This was especially the case with some teachers who were practicing Christians.[61]

The pervasiveness of Nazi ideology in the instruction received by young Germans was reflected in the pages of *Hilf mit!* (Help Out!), a magazine distributed to millions of students between the ages of 8 and 18. The magazine, which reinforced the content of classroom activities, drove home the basic tenets of Nazism. It described male and female sex-role expectations, demonized Jews and Communists, glorified the national leadership, and documented the achievements of Nazi-created organizations like the Reich Labor Service. The magazine presented the propaganda in an attractive form, with many photographs and illustrations, and mixed in riddles, word games, and other features targeted at young people.[62]

As a matter of social science methodology, measuring the influence of official propaganda on the worldview and attitude of young people is an exceedingly complicated and uncertain undertaking. Such a task is made even more challenging by the fact that the systematic public opinion surveys that we take for granted as a facet of modern societies did not exist in Germany in the 1930s. Such surveys were, however, conducted in post-war West Germany, and their results underscore important generational differences. According to a 1949 survey, Germans who had been socialized during the Nazi period showed higher levels of antisemitism than Germans who had been born before 1885. In 1949, over 40 percent of Germans younger than 65 were openly antisemitic, emotionally rejected Jews, or were reserved toward Jews. But the figure for those who had been in the Hitler Youth was roughly the same as for other Germans younger than age 65, suggesting that the influence of the Hitler Youth and the schools was, in and of itself, less important than the more general experience of having lived in Nazi Germany. Later surveys show that many of the younger Germans who had been in the Hitler Youth had subscribed to antisemitic ideas but became open to changing their minds after 1945. This finding is consistent with the personal accounts of Germans who admitted to having absorbed antisemitic notions during the Nazi period, but who later expressed resentment at their brainwashing by the Hitler Youth.[63]

University Students

The Nazi approach to higher education, too, was characterized by anti-intellectualism, ideological indoctrination and mobilization, and an emphasis on practical training. The regime never formulated a centralized or unified policy toward science and scholarship (which are embodied together in the German concept of *Wissenschaft*). Nevertheless, starting in 1933, a series of improvised measures consistent with Nazi values aimed to bring about a shift in teaching and scholarship at the university level. University faculties gradually surrendered their autonomy to political authorities, who wielded the levers of control over funding and personnel to affect a gradual Nazification of institutions. This occurred over the objections of many established professors who, while not necessarily hostile to the agenda of National Socialism, objected to the overt politicization of scholarship and to the erosion of intellectual standards.

Nazism regarded scholarship as an instrument of politics, rejecting the liberal notion of scholarship as the pursuit of pure knowledge. As the influential Nazi pedagogue Ernst Krieck wrote in 1933, in an essay titled "The Renewal of the University," "We acknowledge for the future no intellectual spirit, no culture, and no education that does not derive its meaning from service to the self-actualization of the German Volk."[64] In the biological sciences, scholars who had already promoted racist theories and eugenics before 1933 received promotions, increased funding, and praise in the Nazi-controlled press.[65] In the field of physics, a group of scientists promoted a so-called Aryan physics, which rejected the theories of Albert Einstein, who was Jewish.[66] The majority of scientists did not succumb to such a blatant ideological perversion of scholarship, but many nonetheless made themselves useful to the Nazi regime by contributing to weapons research and other endeavors that were considered to be in the national interest. In the humanities, the established professoriate was politically conservative to begin with, and while most did not shift their scholarship and teaching to be explicitly in support of Nazism, their work was, in many cases, already compatible with right-wing nationalist concepts of history, literature, and philosophy.[67]

The politicized Nazi conception of higher education was embodied in the activism of the National Socialist Student League. Created in 1926, the Student League at first aligned itself with the "left wing" of the NSDAP, led by Gregor and Otto Strasser. It was anti-liberal and antisemitic, but also critical of capitalism and the traditional German establishment. This radicalism limited its appeal to students from middle-class backgrounds, who constituted the majority of students at German universities. When Baldur von Schirach took over the leadership of the organization, he brought its program more into line with the *völkisch* right and with the mindset of the traditionally nationalistic fraternities, to which over 50 percent of male university students belonged. Women belonged to the Student League, albeit in small numbers and not in leadership roles, and participated in the agitation at German universities. While they supported an ideology and movement that championed the very opposite of promoting women into elite circles, they were nationalistic or were attracted to other elements of the Nazi program.[68] Under von Schirach, the League enjoyed a series of successes in student elections at universities, and ultimately it prevailed in the elections of the national student organization, the German Student Union, in 1931. This victory marked the first time that National Socialists seized control of a national organization of any kind.

German university students, who constituted but a small segment of society, regarded themselves as a social elite. They expected to take over leadership positions in state, society, and the economy. They saw themselves as "creators of a nationalistic, patriotic, self-confident upper class."[69] Many were anti-democratic, showing special hostility to the egalitarian programs of the left-wing parties of the Weimar Republic. The Depression deepened their pessimism about their prospects for attaining positions commensurate with their abilities and expectations. As the job market dried up, enrollments increased, leading to overfilled classes and eroding conditions for study.

Right-wing students saw universities and their faculties as representatives of outmoded mentalities and ideologies, as flabby, tired old institutions that were not engaged with the national crisis. They saw themselves as a generation that had been betrayed by their elders and deprived of their patrimony by a failed, weak system. They were highly critical of what they saw as foreign influences in German culture. Antisemitism had been a feature of the German student fraternity scene since the nineteenth century, and this attitude dovetailed nicely with Nazi depictions of Jews as spiritually alien and parasitical. The students denounced the crisis-prone Weimar Republic as a degenerate system that was subject to influence by Jews, Freemasons, Marxists, and other alleged enemies of the German nation. They demanded that universities be closed to Jews, Communists, and others who did not belong to the People's Community. Local chapters of the Student League agitated on campuses against Jewish and left-wing professors. Finally, the students demanded a transformation of scholarship, which, once liberated from a political disinterested intellectualism, would serve the interests of the German Volk.[70]

Once in power, the Nazi government banned all student organizations other than its own. Nazi students disbursed leaflets and organized boycotts of Jewish and left-wing professors, leading in many cases to the "voluntary" departure of faculty members even before the Civil Service Law of April 7, 1933 institutionalized the purge of objectionable professors. In addition, during the years 1933 and 1934, a total of 548 students were expelled from universities on account of their political connections to Communist organizations.[71]

The Nazi-dominated German Student Union played a critical role in the planning and carrying out of the notorious book-burnings of May 1933. Dubbed the "Campaign against the Un-German Spirit," the students framed the burnings as a response to the "shameless atrocity propaganda of foreign Jewry." Around the country, students fed books written by Jews, Marxists, and liberals into pyres, ritualistically accompanied by chanting and slogans. Thus, the university students were responsible for one of the most notorious acts of anti-intellectualism in the modern history of Europe.[72] Nazi students lobbied for a formal role in the appointment of professors but were rebuffed because such a practice would have conflicted with the Nazi leader principle in the administration of the university.[73]

The Nazi students were more successful in maintaining power over student life. The fraternities were folded into the Student League in the mid 1930s. But sources of friction remained between the Nazi student leaders and the fraternities. One of these involved the implementation of the so-called Aryan Paragraph. The fraternities had banned Jews in the nineteenth century, but their rules were less strict than Nazi racial laws when it came to defining people as Jews on the basis of their ancestry. The fraternities tried to protect members who did not regard themselves as Jewish, but who were considered to be such under Nazi race laws. An additional source of disagreement was the fraternities' code of honor. The Weimar Republic had banned dueling in 1925, but that practice was reinstated after January 1933. The Nazi Student League preferred a code of honor for fraternities requiring the duel as a means for settling disputes, but some fraternities actually discouraged dueling, preferring non-violent rituals instead.[74]

The amount of time that students had to commit to ideological indoctrination and other activities outside their studies was considerable. Starting in the summer of 1933, all students in their first four semesters were required to attend a ten-week labor camp. In 1934, in an attempt to bring the future elite closer to "the people," the regime ruled that, before their matriculation, all university students were to spend six months in the Reich Labor Service.[75] Later during the 1930s, students were encouraged to move into residential "comrade houses," which would serve as sites for political training. By the end of the decade, however, only 20 percent of male students lived in them.[76] Students were also urged to focus more on sports and physical fitness. The typical male student had to devote more and more time to camps, retreats, and training sessions, which distracted from their academic studies.

Some students resented these demands on their study time and complained. Even students who gave their political loyalty to the regime felt put upon by these new demands on their time.[77] Policies that were designed to mobilize students behind the cause resulted instead in widespread apathy and resentment.[78] The politicization of student life caused concern among professors, who noticed a decline in student performance. Government economic officials also expressed concern that the quality of technical education could be undermined by too many distractions to study.[79] One high-profile initiative, the Reich Vocational Contest, which was designed to show off the contributions of students to the German economy, attracted very disappointing levels of participation, underscoring the reluctance of many students to participate in political gimmicks.[80]

Between 1933 and 1939, the total number of university students in Germany declined from 115,000 to just over 50,000. Students were drawn into the workforce as employment levels increased, and male students were drafted into the armed forces as Germany remilitarized. Many professors welcomed the declining numbers, believing that the universities had been overcrowded during the Depression. In 1933, the vast majority of students had come from middle-class and upper-middle-class backgrounds, while only 3 percent came from the much larger German working class, and almost seven years of Nazi rule during peacetime did little to change this class structure at the universities, Nazi rhetoric about solidarity with the working class notwithstanding. What did change substantially was the representation of women among the students. During the first semester of Nazi rule, in 1933, women accounted for 11.1 percent of the student body. One year later, the figure stood at 9.1 percent, and by 1934 at only 7 percent. As a consequence of the military draft, however, the percentage of women had once again reached 11 in 1939.[81]

Female students, like their male colleagues, were subjected to constant demands to participate in non-academic activities. Although a general law mandating time in the Labor Service for women was not promulgated until 1939, starting in 1934 there was a clear expectation of time spent in the Reich Labor Service for women who desired to enroll at universities (with the exception of Jewish students). Some joined voluntarily in order to demonstrate their commitment to the Volk and to the overcoming of class divisions. Female students, like the men, were pressured to attend political indoctrination retreats and camps, participate in the Reich Vocational Contest, and live in politicized dormitories. Their responses to these pressures were also similar to those among the men. They resented the extracurricular mobilization as a time-consuming distraction from their studies. Their frustrations were typified by a letter sent to the rector of the University of Munich by the mother of a female medical student. Her daughter worked a fifty-eight-hour week, including fifteen for sports, air-raid training, and volunteering for the Winter Relief charity (see Chapter 6). With all of these demands on a student, not enough time was left over for laboratory work or learning physics.[82]

Jewish university students were excluded from such political activities. After January 1933, they were made to feel increasingly unwelcome at universities before they were definitively banned in late 1938. At the time of the Nazi takeover, there were 3,336 Jewish students at German universities, making up 3.8 percent of the national total. Although this number was small, Jews (still defined by religion) constituted only 0.9 percent of the German population, and the disproportionately high percentage of Jews studying at universities had featured prominently in the antisemitic propaganda of the Nazi Student League. Representation of Jews differed significantly from one university to the next. Jews made up 10.7 percent of the student body at the University of Berlin, 9.6 percent at the University of Frankfurt, and 8.7 percent at the University of Heidelberg. They were also represented in significant numbers at the Universities of Freiburg and Breslau. At the same time, at other German universities, the Jewish presence was minimal. Jewish students also tended to concentrate in certain fields, most notably law and medicine. (In the German system, these were, and are, undergraduate courses of study.) The percentage of women among Jewish students was an exceptionally high 32.8 percent, roughly three times the percentage of all female students.[83]

The Nazi assault on Jewish students after January 1933 began with the occupation of Jewish fraternity houses by activists from the Nazi Student League. In February and March, university administrations and regional governments followed this with a ban on the admission of new Jewish students, but these measures were not uniform or nationally coordinated. Finally, in April 1933, the Reich government acted by promulgating the Law against the Overcrowding of German Universities, which stipulated that the number of Jewish students should be systematically reduced so as to equal the percentage of Jews in the overall population. Although the law allowed for exceptions and had loopholes, its implementation was taken seriously. From the beginning of 1933 to the beginning of 1934, the number of Jewish students at German universities declined from 3,336 to 812. One year later, the number had declined further to 538. These numbers reflected not only the changes to admissions policies, but also the flight of Jewish students, who were no longer eligible for financial assistance and had been banned from student cafeterias. Subjected to constant harassment from Nazi students, they felt threatened at their own universities. Many Jewish students left Germany to study in other countries. Over time, as Jewish students either completed their degrees or departed, their numbers dwindled. In late 1938, after the Kristallnacht pogrom, German universities banned Jewish students entirely. Some foreign Jews were exempted from the prohibition for diplomatic reasons, but by this point few remained, as university administrations had also quietly and unofficially refused entrance to foreign Jews in the mid and late 1930s.[84]

Germans who were interviewed after 1945 frequently shared positive memories of the pre-war years of Nazi rule, which they remembered as a time of peace, prosperity, and national unity.[85] In the current chapter (as in the previous one) we have noted numerous instances of griping and complaining, but in the vast majority of cases these attitudes did not amount to a systemic rejection of the Nazi regime. Despite the often-overbearing demands for ideological mobilization, life for Germans offered a level of stability that would have seemed unimaginable in 1932. While German society under Nazi rule was hardly the harmonious People's Community depicted in official propaganda, many Germans approved of the political, social, and cultural direction of their country, while many more managed to accommodate themselves to the "new normal" that had been erected in Germany since 1933.

6   Policing the Boundaries of the People's Community

The creation of a People's Community necessarily involved creating and enforcing a distinction between "People's comrades" (*Volksgenossen*) and "community aliens" (*Gemeinschaftsfremde*).[1] While the German state – through laws, ordinances the police, courts, prisons, and concentration camps – presided over policies of exclusion, the process by which outsiders were defined and marginalized also involved German society much more broadly. By denouncing neighbors to the authorities, purchasing the property of Jews at bargain-basement prices, shaming acquaintances for failing to give the Hitler salute, or expressing enthusiasm for a regime that had thrown thousands of fellow citizens into concentration camps, millions of ordinary Germans enabled the degradation and persecution of their fellow citizens. This chapter will examine both the mechanisms and policies employed by the Nazi state, as well as the social history of exclusion, in order to present an integrated picture of how persecution functioned in the Third Reich. This chapter makes no attempt to offer comprehensive coverage of the exclusionary policies of the regime, which constitute an exceptionally well-researched area of modern European history. Rather, it will seek to explain how the various strands of persecution fit together in the context of Nazi ideology and how they unfolded in their social contexts.

National Socialism defined "aliens" broadly to include persons deemed objectionable by their behavior, by their "race," or by their sexuality. The groups targeted for exclusion on the basis of their behavior included persons who subscribed to ideologies that were deemed dangerous, such as Communism and (Marxist) socialism, adherents to nonconformist religions, such as the Jehovah's Witnesses, and persons of any ideological stripe who were engaged in resistance against the regime. The two main groups targeted as racial aliens were Jews and Sinti/Roma (i.e., "Gypsies"). "Aryans" who had (or were believed to have) hereditary disabilities were targeted by a eugenics program intended to purge the German race of dangerous impurities. The victims of Nazi exclusionary policies were, therefore, a very diverse group of individuals, most of whom had little in common with each other. They were united only by the hostility directed at them by the Nazi regime.

The Apparatus of Coercion

For decades after 1945, scholarly and popular understandings of Nazi Germany emphasized the regime's apparatus of suppression, or what we have been calling the "prerogative state." This focus was consistent with the widely accepted paradigm of totalitarianism, which posited essential commonalities between Nazi Germany and the Soviet Union (especially during the era of Stalin). The ability of the Nazi regime to mobilize German society behind it, according to this view, lay mainly in its capacity for instilling fear in the population through such means as the Gestapo and concentration camps. A ruthless, fanatical movement relied on terror to control the majority of the population. The exculpatory logic of this interpretation led many Germans to embrace it after 1945. As the Nazi era receded further and further into the past, and as historians subjected one sector of German society after another to detailed, critical analysis, the coercion-focused model for explaining Nazi society gave way to a consensus-based understanding. The emphasis now lay on ideological support for many of Nazism's goals within the population and on a convergence between the regime's policies and the material self-interests of many Germans. One historian has labeled this new approach, which became dominant after 1990, the "voluntarist turn."[2] The scholarship produced in this vein has produced a fuller, more nuanced, and more accurate picture of German society under Nazism. But the coercive aspects of Nazi rule inside Germany may have been obscured in the process. While being careful to avoid resurrecting the old apologist narrative, we must try to understand the role that coercion played in the creation of the pro-Nazi consensus inside Germany between 1933 and 1939. We should not underestimate the means of coercion at the disposal of the regime, and the regime's readiness to make use of them. The regime could, and often did, treat its real and imagined enemies severely. While, seen statistically, only a small fraction of the German population spent time as inmates in concentration camps, the prospect of doing so was a horrifying one that served as a very real deterrent against dissent, opposition, and resistance.

The origins of the Nazi "prerogative state," which rested on the foundation of a permanent state of emergency, and which provided for arrests on the basis of "protective custody," imprisonment without trial, and the creation of concentration camps, have been discussed in Chapter 3. The new Nazi government used these methods to smash its opposition during the nascent phase of the dictatorship in March and April 1933. We can now look at the development of the concentration camp system from its origins to the end of the 1930s in a more systematic way.

The first concentration camps were makeshift, improvised installations set up to house Communists and other anti-Nazis. A leading historian of the Nazi concentration camps has estimated that as many as 200,000 political prisoners were arrested during the year 1933. As the arrests were improvised actions, they were carried out with little thought as to where all the prisoners would be housed. The first camps arose as the temporary solution to this problem. They were set up inside existing prisons, in pubs, and even in apartments. Some of these early camps were operated by police or prison officials, while others were administered by the SA. Conditions for prisoners were significantly worse in the facilities run by the SA, where the Nazi guards felt free to act on their long-standing resentment of leftists. The purpose of the early camps was not genocidal, although beatings were commonplace and hundreds of prisoners were murdered.[3]

The mass arrests of spring 1933 overwhelmingly targeted Communists, of whom as many as 50,000 were arrested in March and April. By late June the arrests had broadened to include around 3,000 Social Democrats and conservative leaders who were regarded as anti-Nazi. The vast majority of those arrested were men, but some women were also caught in the dragnet. Most of the prisoners were released after a short time but were replaced by new ones. In late July 1933, the camps housed a total of around 37,000 inmates, but by October the number of prisoners had fallen to around 22,000.[4]

Jews as a group were not systematically targeted for arrest during this early phase. Nevertheless, in 1933, about 10,000 of them landed in concentration camps on account of their political affiliation, because they had voiced criticism of the new government, or because they had offended Nazi activists at one point or another. Some of the Jewish prisoners were prominent lawyers or businessmen. Even the questionable standards of "preventive detention" were violated by Nazi guards eager to lash out at Jews, whom they subjected to ritual humiliation and beatings. In 1933, most of the Jewish prisoners stayed in the camps only a short time, and it would not be until 1938 that Jews again became a significant part of the inmate population.

The improvised concentration camps were mostly closed by the end of 1933, giving way to a system of more elaborate, permanent camps located in different regions of the country. Whereas many of the original, improvised camps had been SA operations, these permanent ones fell under the authority of the SS. The most notable of these camps were Dachau, outside of Munich, which had been established in March 1933; Sachsenhausen, outside of Berlin, which was founded in 1936; and Buchenwald, near Weimar, which went into operation in 1937. After the German annexation of Austria in 1938, a new camp was created at Mauthausen, in Upper Austria near the city of Linz. In 1939, a camp for female prisoners, Ravensbrück, was established north of Berlin. Dachau served as the model for the network of camps, perfecting a system based on psychological terror and severe discipline designed to instill fear into the prisoners.[5]

Once the Nazi movement had consolidated its control over the country, the number of camp prisoners dropped considerably from the levels of 1933. In 1935, the average daily prisoner count for all camps stood at 3,800. This number rose to 4,761 in 1936, and then to 7,746 in 1937. These figures will strike many readers as surprisingly low, but the intended deterrent effect did not necessarily depend on large inmate populations in the camps. The regime systematically publicized the existence of the camps, and while it did not boast about specific acts of cruelty, it sent clear signals that prisoners faced tough conditions (see Figure 6.1).[6] Moreover, the number of inmates climbed significantly in 1938 as a result of two developments that will be discussed later in this chapter: the roundup of "asocial" and "work-shy" persons in June, which drove the prisoner totals up to 24,000, and then the mass arrest of Jews in November, after the Kristallnacht pogrom, which increased the total number of camp inmates to 50,000. The release of most of the Jewish prisoners after a few days or weeks left the camp system with 31,000 inmates at the end of 1938. When World War II started in Europe on September 1, 1939, 21,400 Germans were imprisoned in the camp system, a number that would increase by many orders of magnitude during the war years.

The camp inmate population comprised several major categories of prisoners during the 1930s. Political prisoners constituted the largest category. Additional categories included opposition figures from the churches, including a significant number of Jehovah's Witnesses; men accused of violating the statute against male homosexuality; Germans classified as "asocial"; the so-called work-shy, who were rounded up in June 1938; and Jews.[7] In most cases, time in a camp was associated with forced labor. Inmates worked in construction, camp maintenance, agriculture, and in quarries. While it was (and remains) an established practice in many countries to subject prisoners to labor, some of the work assignments in the camps, especially the quarries, were unusually arduous and lethal.[8]

The consolidation of the German police under the SS and Himmler unfolded in parallel to the development of the camp system. Both sets of developments marked a growth in the size and power of the "prerogative state" and a further blurring of the lines between the NSDAP and

Figure 6.1 Prisoners at the Dachau concentration camp depicted on the cover of a magazine, 1936 (Galerie Bilderwelt/Getty Images).

the German state. The SS, which had originated as a unit of the Nazi Party responsible for protecting Hitler, eventually came to control police forces at all levels in Germany. These included the SD (Sicherheitsdienst, or Security Service), which had begun its existence as an NSDAP intelligence-gathering unit that carried out surveillance targeting Jews, Freemasons, and other supposed internal enemies of the German Volk. During the 1930s, the SD kept tabs on Jewish organizations and on the remnants of the Marxist parties and the labor movement.[9] Meanwhile, the Secret State Police (Geheime Staatspolizei), better known by its acronym of Gestapo, investigated political dissent and opposition, and carried out arrests. Contrary to a widespread belief that its agents were omnipresent in German society, the Gestapo was relatively small. Its effectiveness as a political police force lay in the readiness of Germans to denounce one another. Such denunciations were motivated by ideology, personal agendas, and fear – including the fear that one would be denounced for not denouncing someone else. The Gestapo's ability to intimidate and induce Germans into denouncing one another is a prime example of how the policing of German society could be as much a social process as an exercise of state power.[10]

Rituals of Conformity

Further insight into how practices of coercion and exclusion functioned as components of normal life can be gained from an analysis of everyday rituals that became ubiquitous in Germany after 1933. Through their participation, or refusal to participate, in these rituals, Germans signaled their feelings toward National Socialism and the national leadership. The complex ways in which Germans engaged in these rituals on a daily basis served as gestures of approval, deference, acquiescence, fear, or disapproval toward the regime. We will briefly look at three such rituals: use of the Hitler salute, the display of flags, and charitable contributions to the Winter Relief.

The "Hitler Greeting," consisting of a salute with an outstretched right arm accompanied by the acclamation *Heil Hitler*, had been required practice inside the Nazi movement before 1933. After the seizure of power, it was adopted as the standard greeting throughout all of German society, replacing more traditional greetings such as *guten Tag* (good day) or, in southern Germany, *grüß Gott* (may God greet you). Millions of Germans recited the phrase multiple times daily in their routine interpersonal interactions in public, for example entering a shop or meeting an acquaintance on the street. Among Nazi Party members of long standing, doing so simply continued an established practice of expressing loyalty to their Führer. To explain why millions of other Germans began to employ the Hitler salute after January 1933 it is not sufficient to point to political and social pressure from above, which was certainly considerable. Many adopted the practice as an autonomous personal decision to conform to the new order, whether they believed in it or not. By virtue of its ubiquity in everyday life, the greeting colonized and politicized the sphere of routine interpersonal communication with a Nazi principle, underscoring the Nazi claim to power over ordinary people in their private lives.[11]

Precisely because the use of the Hitler salute became normative, Germans could voice criticism of the regime by using a more traditional greeting, exclaiming "Heil Hitler" with demonstratively little enthusiasm, or crossing the street to avoid acquaintances expecting to hear it. Friedrich Kellner, an anti-Nazi civil servant in the small town of Laubach in north-central Germany, wrote in his diary about being scolded by the town's former mayor for greeting him with "good day." "You say 'Heil Hitler,' young man!" Kellner vented in his diary: "When this tyranny by Nazi big shots has broken down, and I am asked which Nazi requirement gave me the biggest headache, I will say without hesitation it was the greeting 'Heil Hitler.' This criminal of all criminals forces even those he has suppressed to worship him daily in greeting."[12]

The practice of displaying flags (*Beflaggung*) also, for a time, offered opportunities to express a range of opinions toward the regime. On Nazi holidays, such as Hitler's birthday, and on other politically significant days, the regime rallied the population to fly flags from their balconies, in front gardens, and on building entrances. The flags would create a colorful visual accompaniment to parades and other forms of public celebration. They would give an impression of national unity, or, in the words of Propaganda Minister Joseph Goebbels, that the German people formed "a single giant living organism."[13] The preferred flag, of course, was the red, white, and black Nazi banner with a swastika at its center, while the red, black, and gold flag of the Weimar Republic (which had been based on the flag of the liberal revolution of 1848) was no longer tolerated.

During the early phase of the regime, many Germans who desired to distance themselves from Nazism did not display flags. Some, as a means for avoiding the swastika, hoisted the red, white, and black flag of the old German Empire. Some raised the flags of their states or municipalities. This method of signaling dissent continued even after 1935, when the government issued the Reich Flag Law, which declared the Nazi flag as the sole valid flag for the Reich. To bring people into line, local Nazi officials, who kept close tabs on who flew which flag, would issue threats, sometimes veiled, sometimes explicit. Over time, as it became clear that failure to display the Nazi flag could result in negative consequences, people began to display the Nazi flag defensively, to pre-empt stigmatization by the authorities. Citizens found imaginative ways to satisfy the party while continuing to distance themselves from Nazism. One could, for example, display a large flag of the German Empire while appending a much smaller swastika flag to its side. Such practices ended in 1937, when a new decree expressly banned the flying of flags other than the Nazi one. Meanwhile, Jews were prohibited from hoisting the Nazi flag under any circumstances.[14]

Our third example of ritualized obeisance to Nazism in everyday life is found in the charity drives of the Winter Relief Organization (*Winterhilfswerk*). This project was launched in 1933 by the Nazi Party's official social relief organ, the National Socialist People's Welfare Organization (NS-Volkswohlfahrt), which would, by the beginning of World War II, develop into a mass organization with 14 million members. The Winter Relief drive ran annually from October 1 through March 31, soliciting donations of both money and goods to support needy cases. The collection drives were elaborately orchestrated campaigns, organized in cooperation with the Propaganda Ministry, which dubbed the Winter Relief "the greatest charity of all time." During the first couple of years of Nazi rule, when unemployment in Germany remained high, and the number of needy cases was, in fact, high, even anti-Nazis could give to the Winter Relief with a clear conscience. But for the regime, encouraging personal charity was not enough. It framed the Winter Relief politically, as an opportunity to demonstrate one's readiness to sacrifice for the Volk.

Collectors stationed themselves with their donation boxes on streets and in front of shops (see Figure 6.2). Such practices were, and are, common in many countries, but the Nazi Winter Relief employed additional methods that were quite coercive. Collectors armed with lists of donors appeared at people's homes soliciting contributions. They often wore uniforms of the party or the SA, presenting themselves not as representatives of a private charity but as agents of the regime. Donors were rewarded with a certificate posted on their door, in the process stigmatizing neighbors whose doors remained unmarked. The Nazi Party maintained records of who contributed and how much, and this information was included in evaluations of political reliability provided by the party to Germans applying for jobs or educational opportunities. Not uncommonly newspapers published lists of citizens who had not contributed, which sometimes resulted in angry demonstrations of Nazi activists in front of homes. Even as it brought such pressures to bear on its citizens, the regime maintained the fiction that giving to the Winter Relief was a voluntary act. From the very

Figure 6.2 Collecting for the Winter Relief (ullstein bild/ullstein bild via Getty Images).

beginning, the Winter Relief served as a demonstration of the power of the Nazi order to infringe on the private lives of its citizens.[15]

Resistance during the 1930s

The term "resistance" can be defined in many different ways. Having earlier in this chapter, and in the preceding ones, described multiple forms of dissent and non-compliance, we will employ a relatively narrow definition of the term, limiting it to instances of Germans who acted with the intention of openly defying the government, undermining the legitimacy of the regime, disrupting the implementation of policies, and, in the most dramatic cases, replacing the national leadership. Resistance in Nazi Germany is the subject of a very large literature. But while it is important to recognize and explain the conduct of those who resisted, we must also not exaggerate their numbers. This section will focus on the period up to September 1939. Some of the more dramatic instances of resistance occurred during the war years, and they will be addressed in Chapter 10.

Historians classify resistance by the social sector in which it took place. The largest category is that of "the left," which included the remnants of the two Marxist parties – the Communist (KPD) and Social Democratic (SPD) Parties – and the pre-1933 labor movement. Then there was the resistance within the German aristocracy, prominent families descended from the former German nobility that were well connected in the civil service, the diplomatic corps, and the officer corps of the military. The two final categories comprise the military and the churches, which were conservative, elite institutions with long institutional histories.

On the political left, Communists, who had a history of operating illegally in small cells, were in a better position to operate clandestinely than were Social Democrats. The Communists also tended to be more ideologically committed to their cause. Many adherents of the larger, more moderate SPD had resigned themselves to Nazi rule in 1933 and withdrew from the struggle, although a core of leaders left the country to carry on from Prague, Paris, Switzerland, and Scandinavia. Among them was Willy Brandt, who would later serve as the chancellor of the Federal Republic of Germany from 1969 to 1974. Important KPD leaders also fled the country, in their case taking up residence mainly in Moscow. While few Social Democrats deluded themselves into believing that they could bring down the Nazi regime, the Communists regarded Fascism as a transitional phase to the proletarian revolution. The Communist resistance focused on disseminating anti-Nazi materials in factories and other industrial facilities, hoping to counteract official propaganda, especially as it pertained to the welfare of the German working class. Many Communists engaged in this activity were caught and spent considerable time in prisons and concentration camps, where some of them, like KPD Chairman Ernst Thälmann, were ultimately executed. In addition to Communist resistance among the working class, well-educated Germans with Communist ideological sympathies exploited their skills and connections to undermine Nazism. The wartime resistance and espionage activities of the married couple Arvid and Mildred Harnack, both intellectuals with close ties to Communism, will be discussed in Chapter 10.

The SPD leadership in exile maintained a network of informants inside Germany who reported on the popular reception of a host of Nazi policies. The SPD did not have a resistance network inside the country analogous to that of the KPD, although there were individual figures, such as Wilhelm Leuschner in Hesse, who maintained contact with multiple circles of the regime's opponents, and who paid with his life for his connection to the July 20, 1944 plot to assassinate Hitler. The left-wing opposition also included distinctive subgroupings. One example was the Herbert Baum group, which consisted mainly of Jews.[16] A second example was the "League," also known as the "Community for Socialist Life," which operated in the Ruhr industrial region. During the 1930s, it functioned mainly as a refuge from Nazi-dominated daily life, although during the war it provided assistance to German Jews facing deportation.[17]

Opposition activities among liberals and anti-Nazi conservatives took the form of social networks and discussion groups. There were several such oppositional "circles," the best known of which met on the estate of the von Moltke family in Kreisau in Lower Silesia. In addition to Helmuth Count von Moltke, a German lawyer with liberal leanings, the Kreisau Circle included other highly educated Germans from aristocratic and cosmopolitan backgrounds who were active in the legal field, the civil service, education, and the churches. Their contacts also extended into the labor movement. Believing that only the German military would be capable of removing Hitler from power, starting in the late 1930s the discussants concentrated on formulating a vision for a post-Nazi era. During World War II, they forged connections with members of the military resistance and participated in the July 20, 1944 conspiracy.[18]

The military and the Christian churches were two powerful sectors of German society where it was potentially possible to mount effective resistance to Nazism. Before World War II, the German military offered little in the way of significant resistance. During the war, military officers were at the center of a plot to kill Hitler and seize power, culminating with the failed coup of July 20, 1944. While many members of the tradition-bound and aristocratic officer corps harbored disdain for what they viewed as the plebian character of the Nazi movement, there were important areas of overlap between their vision for a German military resurgence and Hitler's own plans. Both wanted to overturn the Treaty of Versailles and to rearm the country. They had a shared dislike for the political left, and many officers were antisemitic, albeit often in a more genteel way than the Nazis. In the late 1930s, as Germany became more aggressive on the international front, some anti-Hitler officers feared the prospect of a ruinous war, but they balked when it came to action against their own government. They were held back by their oath of loyalty to Hitler, their sense of duty and honor, and by a lack of support for action among their colleagues. Ultimately, they felt compelled to act when Germany faced defeat and destruction during the war.[19] These events will be described in Chapter 10.

There was also overlap between the program of the Nazi regime and the outlook of many members of the Christian clergy. They shared, for example, a strong anti-Communism, a desire to preserve traditional families and gender roles, and an opposition to what they perceived as obscenity in modern art. Antisemitism was also deeply rooted in the Christian clergy. Even while many priests and pastors rejected Nazism's racial definition of Jewishness and its propensity for violence, they subscribed to theological anti-Judaism and to negative stereotypes of Jews as materialistic, exploitative, or radical. There also were, to be sure, Christian clergymen, both Catholic and Protestant, who held serious disagreements with the Nazi regime about a whole host of issues, but rarely did their objections translate into open hostility to the regime, much less actual resistance, during the 1930s.[20]

In a series of developments known collectively as the "Church Struggle," German Protestantism became deeply divided during the Nazi period. Two factions emerged to challenge the Protestant establishment. The Confessing Church, which accounted for about 20 percent of the Protestant clergy, provided a home to influential critics of the regime, most famously Dietrich Bonhoeffer, who was ultimately executed in a concentration camp in 1945. Meanwhile, the so-called German Christians (Deutsche Christen) formed a strident pro-Nazi wing of Protestantism, going so far as to assert the Aryan lineage of Jesus and to advocate for the de-Judaization of the Bible.[21] Although the Confessing Church is often upheld as a model of courageous resistance to Nazism, its record of opposition to the regime was actually very mixed. Its approach was the product of tactical thinking, fear, internal divisions, compromise, and caution. Much of its focus was on ecclesiastical issues rather than on the substance of Nazi persecution measures, and its criticisms of the regime, including its foundational Barmen Declaration of 1934, were couched in doctrinal and theological language that was not intended to mobilize popular opposition to the regime. Even Dietrich Bonhoeffer was relatively muted in his critique of the regime before the war.[22]

The Catholic clergy, too, exercised a great deal of caution. In 1933, as a provision of the concordat between the church and the German government (see Chapter 3), the church had agreed to withdraw from politics in order to tend to its own flock. Outnumbered by Protestants by a factor of two-to-one in Germany and having suffered from official persecution during the *Kulturkampf* of the 1870s, Catholics had good reason to think defensively. The clergy concentrated on the pastoral care of its parishioners and on preventing government encroachment into Catholic education. When clergy challenged the regime's racial policies, they focused mainly on the persecution of so-called "non-Aryan Christians," Germans who were Christian by faith but Jewish according to official Nazi racial definitions. Although Pope Pius XI published an encyclical, titled "With Burning Concern" (*Mit brennender Sorge*), severely critiquing Nazi racial policies in 1937, few Catholic clergymen inside Germany openly condemned policies aimed against the Jews.

A notable exception was the Berlin-based Catholic Monsignor Bernhard Lichtenberg. In November 1938, after the widespread destruction of synagogues during the Kristallnacht pogrom, Lichtenberg denounced the violence from his pulpit and began to pray daily for the welfare of Jews.[23] As a result of this and other outspoken attacks on the regime, Lichtenberg was arrested in 1941 and ultimately died as the result of damage to his health incurred in a concentration camp. A small number of Protestant pastors also publicly condemned the pogrom. Julius von Jan, a pastor in the small Swabian town of Oberlenningen, unleashed a scandal when, on the annual Day of Repentance and Prayer, he denounced the pogrom in harsh and clear language. Jan served five months in prison for this transgression.[24] While Lichtenberg and Jan were not the only clergymen in their churches who displayed such courage, they were rather the exception than the rule.

Resistance was the norm in only one branch of Christianity, the Jehovah's Witnesses, of whom about 25,000–30,000 lived in Germany in 1933. Because of their radical nonconformism, their American roots, and their steadfast refusal to pledge their loyalty to any human leader, the Jehovah's Witnesses were the targets of oppressive measures from the start of the Nazi regime. Their claim to conscientious-objector status when Germany reinstated conscription in 1935 deepened the official distrust. Their fervent commitment to their principles and their organizational discipline marked them as a threat, leading the authorities to prohibit the distribution of their literature. The Jehovah's Witnesses fought back, launching a massive pamphleteering campaign in 1936. The pamphlets focused narrowly on the regime's treatment of the Witnesses, but the attempted illegal placement of tens of thousands of pamphlets in the mailboxes of ordinary Germans represented a massive act of defiance. Many Jehovah's Witnesses were arrested and sent to concentration camps. By early 1938, over 10 percent of the inmates at the Buchenwald and Sachsenhausen concentration camps were classified as Jehovah's Witnesses. Over a thousand eventually died in the camps, and hundreds more were executed for refusing to serve in the military.[25]

Eugenics to 1939

As an understanding of race lay at the core of the Nazi conception of peoplehood, policies of exclusion targeted members of "alien" races as well as "Aryans" who were deemed biologically defective and sexually deviant. Seen from the ideological perspective of Nazism, the persecution of Jews went hand-in-hand with eugenically motivated sterilization and a campaign against homosexuality. The regime proceeded on all of these fronts very soon after its creation. Between March and July 1933, for example, the government ordered the police to raid and close down gay and lesbian bars, purged Jews from the civil service, and promulgated a law mandating compulsory eugenic sterilization. Such measures, which intended to draw biological boundaries around the People's Community, moved forward on parallel tracks and with increasing severity through the end of the 1930s. As we examine these strands of exclusionary policy individually in the following sections, we must keep in mind that they unfolded concurrently and were rooted in a common set of ideological principles.

Germany was a relative latecomer to institutionalized eugenics, but under Nazi rule it initiated a program of sterilization that quickly placed the country at the forefront of the international eugenics movement.[26] The pioneer in eugenic sterilization had been the United States, sixteen of whose states had put sterilization laws in place before World War I. Additional US states followed during the 1920s, as did a Swiss canton, the Canadian province of Alberta, and the country of Denmark. The Mexican state of Vera Cruz implemented sterilization in 1932. The eugenics movement had also had its setbacks, as in Great Britain, where a eugenics law was rejected by the House of Commons in 1932.

The Nazi movement embraced eugenic sterilization early on. Hitler advocated it in *Mein Kampf* in 1925. "The demand that defective people be prevented from producing equally defective offspring," he wrote, "is a demand of the clearest rationality" and is a task that requires "systematic implementation."[27] But there were also many German supporters of a program of "race hygiene" outside the Nazi movement. They drafted sterilization laws and lobbied for their passage, but failed. The advent of the Nazi government in 1933 opened new possibilities. Not only did the Nazi movement favor sterilization, it was also willing and able to implement it quickly over the moral and theological objections of the critics of eugenics.

The foundation for the sterilization program was laid on July 14, 1933, when the Reich cabinet issued the Law for the Prevention of Hereditarily Diseased Offspring. The law, which followed directly on the heels of the official elimination of all political opposition, belonged to a package of legislation that created many of the underpinnings for the Nazi dictatorship.[28] Unlike the draft for the Prussian law in 1932, which had allowed only for voluntary sterilization, the statute set in place on July 14 provided for compulsory sterilizations to be ordered by state authorities. The new law incorporated key concepts and practices from a model sterilization law that had been promoted in eugenicist circles in the United States.[29] The German law identified seven medical conditions for which individuals could be sterilized: "congenital feeble-mindedness," schizophrenia, manic depression, Huntington's chorea, hereditary blindness, hereditary deafness, and serious physical deformities. It also identified chronic alcoholism as grounds for sterilization. Additionally, the law created a network of so-called Hereditary Health Courts, which would decide who would be sterilized. These courts were grafted onto the existing judicial system. Typically, a local Hereditary Health Court consisted of a judge from a lower court (*Amtsgericht*), a physician from the local public health office, and a second physician possessing expertise in the science of human heredity.[30] The courts assessed referrals (one could also use the term "denunciations") from physicians, public health officials, and the Nazi Party. When the courts decided in favor of sterilization, the ensuing operations took the form of tubal ligation for women and vasectomy for men. In 1935, the sterilization law was modified to allow for castration of male sex offenders, including homosexuals, child molesters, rapists, and exhibitionists.

Three categories of elite professionals were instrumental in the sterilization program. Biological scientists, employed by universities or attached to government research institutions, advised on the formulation of laws and the implementation of policy. They also helped to legitimize eugenic sterilization among the general public through speeches and newspaper articles.[31] Physicians drove the sterilizations both by referring cases to the Hereditary Health Courts and by serving on those bodies.

Moreover, physicians with faculty appointments at universities trained medical students in the methods and technologies of sterilization.[32] At least 183 doctoral dissertations submitted by medical students during the Nazi years studied some aspect of sterilization.[33] Finally, legal professionals, both in the government and the court system, integrated the practice of routine sterilization into German legal practice. The implementation of the sterilization program took place within the "normative state," that is, the normal German legal system.

The phraseology of the sterilization law gave the officials tasked with implementing it a great deal of leeway. This was especially the case for the condition of "feeble-mindedness," which eventually accounted for three-quarters of all sterilizations performed in Nazi Germany. The concept of feeble-mindedness was extremely vague and, we now realize, scientifically unsound. When the members of Hereditary Health Courts decided on such cases, their diagnosis was often based more on social prejudices than on medical thinking. They employed verbal intelligence tests containing questions that pertained more to knowledge than to intellectual ability.[34] Physicians and judges who possessed little understanding of the lives of farmers and workers imposed onto them their own biased notions of intelligence. There was also a gender bias to their decisions. Promiscuity weighed heavily as a factor in cases involving women, and unmarried mothers were sterilized in disproportionate numbers, reflecting a bias against out-of-wedlock parenting that had nothing to do with medical science.

It has been difficult for historians to determine the precise number of Germans who were sterilized under the authority of the sterilization law. Estimates are rendered difficult by the decentralized nature of the Hereditary Health Courts and by the fact that not all sterilizations that were ordered were actually carried out. Despite these uncertainties, a recent careful calculation yielded an estimate of about 300,000 sterilizations carried out in Germany between 1933 and 1945. About two-thirds of these procedures were performed between 1934 and 1937.[35] The 300,000 figure, it should be emphasized, does not include sterilizations performed in areas annexed by Germany in the late 1930s and during the war, so the actual number was somewhat higher. Because the surgical procedures used for sterilization involved a mortality rate of about one-half of 1 percentage point, we can estimate that between 1,000 and 2,000 persons died from complications from their operations.[36] The vast majority of those who were sterilized were "Aryan" Germans, but some Jews and Sinti/Roma ("Gypsies") were also targeted.

Nor does the estimate include several hundred "mixed-race" persons sterilized under a special program in 1937. The disparagingly labeled

"Rhineland Bastards" were the children of German mothers and "colored" fathers who had been stationed with French and Belgian colonial troops in the occupied Rhineland region of Germany during the 1920s. The Kaiser Wilhelm Institute for Anthropology, Human Heredity, and Eugenics, in Berlin, one of Nazi Germany's foremost organizations in the field of "race science," played an instrumental role in the identification and sterilization of these young persons.[37]

Thus, Nazi Germany sterilized about five times the number that the United States did, and during a much shorter period.[38] While in many respects the eugenics movement in Germany was fundamentally similar to that in other countries, the politically repressive atmosphere made it impossible for critics or dissenters to question the policy. There were no moral brakes on the system. This factor helps explain not only the dimensions attained by the German sterilization program but also the escalation, during the war, of eugenics from sterilization to the systematic murder of disabled persons, which occurred in Germany but nowhere else.[39]

The Campaign against Sinti and Roma

In 1933, Germany was home to about 26,000 persons commonly, and often pejoratively, referred to as "Gypsies" (German: *Zigeuner*). The accurate designations for the majority of these persons is Sinti and Roma. Sinti were the Central European branch of the larger population of Roma, the majority of whom lived in Eastern, and especially Southeastern, Europe. A traditionally itinerant people, the Roma had been stereotyped as lascivious, anti-social, and criminal for generations. The Nazi government inherited a patchwork of laws targeting so-called "Gypsies," which had been placed on the books on the regional and local levels. The new regime intensified the enforcement of the existing laws and added new ones. Persecution escalated during the 1930s and, during World War II, Sinti and Roma became one of three categories of people against whom the Nazi regime committed mass murder, the other two being Jews and the disabled.

The persecution and genocide of the Sinti and Roma are less thoroughly documented than that of the other two groups. Their predominantly oral tradition produced relatively few memoirs and diaries. The Nazi bureaucracy generated less paperwork through its measures aimed at Sinti and Roma than it did through its anti-Jewish measures. Post-war trials for Nazi crimes, which created important evidence for historians, paid relatively little attention to the Sinti and Roma. Nazi propaganda treated them as objects of vilification and dehumanization, but not, as in the case of the Jews, as a people aspiring to exercise power over governments, economies, and cultural life. Hitler had made no mention of them in *Mein Kampf*, a work in which, in contrast, his antipathy for the Jews is pervasive. While Nazis expressed anxiety over the possibility of miscegenation, they saw "Gypsies" more as a pest than as a danger.[40]

The Sinti and Roma in Germany, in addition to the laws specifically targeting them, fell victim to laws and edicts aimed at criminals and "asocial" persons. They were also caught up in the eugenic sterilization program; historians estimate that about 500 of them were sterilized between 1933 and 1939. As compulsory alternatives to traditional "Gypsy camps" and caravans, some German municipalities set up new camps, where residents were subjected to strict surveillance and supervision. In 1936, the Reich Ministry of the Interior, which had jurisdiction over policing matters, issued a decree preventing "Gypsies" from entering Germany from the outside, imposing a sedentary lifestyle on Roma and Sinti communities inside the country, and paving the way for more frequent raids on camps and caravans.

Over time, the regime shifted from treating "Gypsies" as an asocial group to defining them as an alien race. The Nuremberg Laws of 1935, which will be discussed in the next section, did not themselves refer to "Gypsies" per se, but an influential commentary on the laws described them as a people with non-Aryan blood. In addition, implementation orders and decrees issued shortly after the Nuremberg Laws extended their most important provisions regarding sex and marriage to "Gypsies."

Anthropological research on Jewish racial characteristics proceeded in parallel to racial research about "Gypsies." In 1936, the Ministry of the Interior set up a special institute within the Reich Health Office for this purpose. Its head, Dr. Robert Ritter, was a physician and child psychiatrist who had become interested in "Gypsies" as a result of his work on the biological bases of criminal behavior. Ritter and his team of anthropologists collected material on "Gypsies" from police records, "Gypsy" camps, and prisons. They interrogated members of Sinti and Roma communities, taking blood samples and anthropometric measurements. By 1939, Ritter's team had collected information on 20,000 persons whom they classified as either "pure Gypsies" or "mixed-race Gypsies." Not surprisingly, Ritter concluded that the "Gypsies" constituted an alien race, an argument that he asserted in lectures and publications.

The campaign against Sinti and Roma intensified considerably in 1938, a year during which the Nazi regime also ratcheted up the pressure on Jews. In June, the German police launched a major roundup of Germans deemed to be "asocial," including habitual criminals and persons thought to be averse to work. Those persons arrested and transferred to concentration camps without any legal process included about 2,000

Jews and several hundred Sinti and Roma.[41] By August 1, 1938, "Gypsies" accounted for 5 percent of the inmates at the Sachsenhausen camp outside of Berlin.[42] In December, Heinrich Himmler issued a "Decree for Combatting the Gypsy Plague," according to which "Gypsies" had to be treated not on the basis of behavior but rather on the basis of racial characteristics. The transformation of Sinti and Roma from an allegedly asocial or criminal population to an alien race was thus complete, laying the groundwork for deportations and mass murder during World War II.[43]

The Persecution of German Jews through 1939

We have attempted thus far in this volume to emphasize the centrality of antisemitism to the theory and practice of Nazism by integrating an analysis of anti-Jewish measures into sections of the narrative analyzing more general political, economic, and social developments. A section dedicated specifically to Jewish policy and its consequences during the 1930s is nevertheless needed as part of the current chapter's examination of how the regime defined, marginalized, and mistreated "community aliens." The following discussion will concentrate on the main ideological assumptions and factors that shaped Nazi Jewish policy, on the main strategies used to implement it, on the responses of "ordinary" Germans, and on the responses of German Jews.[44]

National Socialism was obsessed with the Jews from the moment of its creation to the moment of its demise. The program of the NSDAP issued in 1920 pledged a struggle against the "Jewish materialistic spirit," maintaining that no Jew could be a German citizen. When Adolf Hitler dictated his final testament in the bunker under the ruins of his chancellery in April 1945, he did not neglect to lay the blame for World War II at the feet of "international Jewry." During the intervening two decades, the Nazi movement continually reiterated its antisemitic convictions, in both its rhetoric and actions. That these convictions led a civilized nation to undertake the mass murder of millions of people underscores the importance of recognizing antisemitism not as a byproduct or side-effect of Nazism, but rather as a core element of its worldview.

The ideological, cultural, and psychological roots of Nazi antisemitism were deep and complex, deriving from a combination of traditional European Judeophobia, on the one hand, and a modern, biological-racial worldview, on the other. National Socialism inherited and deployed a panoply of anti-Jewish accusations and stereotypes. In the late nineteenth century, these traditional anti-Jewish biases had merged with the newly emerging "science" of race and Social Darwinism. Rather than understanding the Jews in religious, cultural, or ethnic terms, the new racial antisemitism attributed Jewish behaviors and characteristics to heredity. This fact is of central importance for analyzing the development of Nazi antisemitism and Jewish policy. Although Nazi antisemitic propaganda exploited old-fashioned religious and economic prejudices in order to legitimize anti-Jewish policy among the German public, the policy itself rested on a logic of race. This is what endowed Nazi antisemitism with its radical and lethal potential. Racial antisemitism, by virtue of its emphasis on biological determinism, ruled out the possibility that the Jews could be changed. From the Nazi perspective, then, the "Jewish Question" could be solved only through the removal of the Jews by one means or another.

Although committed to an antisemitic program, the NSDAP had not formulated a detailed plan or blueprint for its Jewish policy before coming into power. That policy, therefore, unfolded after 1933 as a series of improvised measures, initially inside Germany, and eventually on a Europe-wide scale. During the peacetime period of Nazi rule, Jews were subjected to racial stigmatization, occupational exclusion, economic expropriation, and social segregation. At the time of the Nazi "seizure of power" in 1933, there were about 550,000 Jews (defined by religion) in Germany, constituting 0.9 percent of the total population. Jews had enjoyed full civic equality in Germany since the founding of the German Reich in 1871. Although antisemitic attitudes had persisted in many circles of German society after that date, official, institutionalized antisemitism had largely become a thing of the past. During World War I, about 12,000 Jewish men had died fighting for what they had regarded as their German Fatherland. In 1933, the vast majority of Jews were thoroughly integrated into the German language, society, and culture. They were highly represented in the commercial sectors of the German economy, in academic professions such as medicine and law, and in cultural occupations, such as music and journalism. Nazis and other antisemites regarded this level of Jewish success not as something to be admired in a historically persecuted minority, but rather as evidence of the Jewish drive to establish control over Germany.

The purpose of Nazi Jewish policy after January 1933 was the "dejewification" (*Entjudung*) of German society. This would be accomplished in all areas of national life: economic, social, cultural, and intellectual. The overall goal was to promote the emigration of Jews from Germany; concrete plans for mass murder emerged only during World War II. The regime preferred to implement Jewish policy by instituting legal and bureaucratic measures, which would be seen as legitimate by the majority of Germans. Violence and physical intimidation against Jews were officially frowned upon, as such methods would alienate many ordinary

Germans who would otherwise support a peaceful and orderly marginal-ization of Jews. In practice, however, the regime did not always discour-age such illegal actions by its more fervently antisemitic supporters, as occurred, for example, during a major wave of antisemitic vandalism on the Kurfürstendamm boulevard in Berlin in July 1935. At times – most notably during the Kristallnacht pogrom of November 1938 – the regime actively encouraged anti-Jewish violence. Legal anti-Jewish actions undertaken by the state, on the one hand, and illegal (albeit officially tolerated) anti-Jewish actions undertaken by Nazi activists, on the other, thus reinforced one another, producing a spiral of escalating severity.

Dejewification could not occur without defining who was a Jew and who was not. In accordance with its racist ideology, the Nazi regime defined Jews by ancestry rather than by religion. Between January 1933 and late 1935, the racial definitions applied to Jews were improvised and not nationally uniform. The Nuremberg Laws, promulgated in September 1935, put in place the standardized racial categories that would remain in effect through the end of the Third Reich. The system stipulated four racial classifications, all of which were based ultimately on the religious affiliation of one's grandparents in the year 1871. Persons with three or four Jewish grandparents were classified as "full Jews." Persons with two Jewish grandparents were classified as "mixed-race persons of the first degree" (or, colloquially, as "half-Jews"), although they were considered Jews if they had Jewish spouses or were affiliated with the Jewish commu-nity. Persons with one Jewish grandparent were classified as "mixed-race persons of the second degree" (or "quarter-Jews"). Persons with no Jew-ish ancestry were classified as "persons of German blood," who were usually referred to as Aryans. The system produced a not inconsider-able number of "Christian Jews," that is, persons of Christian faith who were categorized racially as Jews, a fact that underscores the racist, as opposed to religious, nature of Nazi antisemitism. The multi-tiered racial hierarchy created by the Nuremberg Laws determined who could prac-tice a profession and who could not, who could own property, and who would be allowed to marry whom. During World War II, when German Jews were rounded up for deportation to camps and ghettoes in Eastern Europe, one's racial classification became a matter of life and death.

"Scientific" studies intended to foster intellectual respectability for the racialization of the Jews accompanied legal steps to reclassify Jews from a religious group to a racial one. A new interdisciplinary field of "Jew-ish research" received official support and funding, gradually insinuating itself into German academic life through the establishment of institutes, professorships, and journals. The scholarship produced in these circles functioned as a highbrow genre of antisemitic discourse, reinforcing the anti-Jewish propaganda pitched through the popular media, the educational system, and mass organizations. It addressed the purportedly undesirable features of the Jewish religion, the occupational structure of Jewish communities, and the supposed Jewish penchant for criminal behavior. All of it, however, posited a racial-biological, rather than a cultural or an historical, basis for Jewish behavior.[45]

Among the most notable anti-Jewish measures of the pre-war period were those designed to purge Jews from professions and occupations. This campaign began with the Civil Service Law of April 7, 1933, which excluded Jews from government employment at all levels. This action encompassed not only the official bureaucracy but also educational and cultural institutions. At the insistence of Reich President Paul von Hindenburg, special exceptions were granted to Jewish civil servants who had been in office since 1914, those who had fought for Germany in World War I, and those who had lost a father or son in the war. In view of the large percentage of Jewish men who had fought for Germany in the war, about half of Germany's 5,000 Jewish civil servants were able to invoke the Hindenburg exception to their dismissal in 1933.[46] But their protection was revoked upon Hindenburg's death in August 1934.

The Nazi regime required more time to organize the dejewification of the professions and the private economy. In the case of the professions, the purge of Jews was carried out not by the government per se, but rather by the neocorporatist professional chambers that had been either "coordinated" in 1933 or set up by the regime as entirely new mechanisms of control (see Chapter 4). Thus, for example, the purge of Jews from the artistic and cultural professions was carried out primarily through the Reich Chamber of Culture, which had been created in late 1933 to regulate activity in the fields of music, theater, the visual arts, literature, the press, film, and radio. The professional ban on Jews functioned similarly in other professions. The membership policies of the Reich Physicians' Chamber, for example, provided the framework for excluding Jewish physicians. Implemented as it was in this decentralized fashion, the professional purge of Jews took several years to complete.[47]

Concurrent with the exclusion of Jews from the professions there took place the coerced transfer of Jewish property to non-Jewish ownership, a process referred to at the time as Aryanization. This practice began early during the Nazi regime. Jews were theoretically not prohibited from owning businesses and real estate, but through official and unofficial forms of economic and personal harassment, many were compelled to sell their property, usually at prices well below what normal market conditions would have determined. Moreover, much of what Jewish emigrants had received from such transactions had to be surrendered to the state in the form of a "flight tax." In November 1938, in the wake of the Kristall-nacht pogrom, the transfer of Jewish-owned property to Aryan purchas-ers was made compulsory. Although most Jewish-owned property had already been Aryanized by that date, a substantial number of Jews had held out. Thus, during the last two months of 1938 and through much of 1939, German Aryanizers enjoyed a feeding frenzy as a great amount of property was made available for sale by Jews, who were now under legal pressure to sell and desperate to emigrate from Germany.[48]

Whereas the purge of the professions and Aryanization aimed to dis-enfranchise the Jews economically, parallel measures were designed to isolate the Jews socially and culturally. One of the Nuremberg Laws, the Law for the Protection of German Blood and Honor, prohibited mar-riage between Jews and Aryans, and criminalized extramarital sex across the racial divide. Other laws promulgated in the 1930s restricted Jewish access to public transportation, parks, and other common spaces. Gov-ernments at all levels took anti-Jewish actions that both intruded into private life and intended to humiliate Jews. In Bavaria, for example, Jews were forbidden from wearing Lederhosen and other traditional costumes of the region. The spitefulness of this gesture was difficult to overlook.

The escalatory dynamic in which illegal violence accelerated legal exclu-sion continued through the decade. Often the culprits of violence were members of the SA, who were nostalgic for the no-nonsense tactics of the pre-1933 period. The year 1938 saw a significant increase in the number of violent anti-Jewish incidents. Two war scares, one in May and one in September, provoked the wrath of antisemitic hardliners, who regarded the Jews as a potential domestic threat in the event of war. Although neither of these waves of violence took on the character of a systematic campaign, they did reinforce a climate of antisemitic mob activism, and by doing so they helped set the stage for Kristallnacht, the night of November 9–10, 1938.[49]

This event was the single instance of large-scale, open, organized vio-lence against Jews in Germany before the outbreak of World War II. It was precipitated by the assassination of a minor German diplomat in Paris, Ernst vom Rath, by Herschel Grynszpan, a Jewish teenager. In October 1938, Grynszpan's family, along with thousands of other Jews with Pol-ish citizenship, had been rounded up from their homes in Germany and dumped into the border zone between Germany and Poland. Grynszpan, who had been living with relatives in Paris, acted to avenge the suffer-ing of his family, but German radio and newspaper reports depicted the assassination as the product of a Jewish plot to intimidate Germany and to undermine French–German relations. The reporting provoked anti-Jewish riots in several German cities on November 7, 8, and 9.

On the evening of 9 November, Hitler and Goebbels decided that the violence percolating up from below should not be halted, but rather embraced and expanded. They had multiple reasons for this decision, relating both to domestic and foreign policy. They wished to facilitate the complete transfer of Jewish-owned property into Aryan ownership; to accelerate the departure of Jews from Germany in anticipation of a coming war; to throw some red meat to antisemitic radicals among the Nazi movement's rank and file; to demonstrate to the German people that certain important national goals would be attainable only through violence; and to discredit anti-Nazi political circles in France, which they disingenuously claimed had orchestrated the assassination of vom Rath.

The violence that unfolded on the night of November 9–10, 1938, and through much of the day of 10 November, was not limited to the major Jewish population centers. It reached into hundreds of communities, even those with only a handful of Jewish families. The main perpetrators consisted of members of the SA, although in many localities the circle of participants was a good deal broader, and included members of the SS, the Hitler Youth, and ordinary citizens who spontaneously joined in. The result of the violence was a catastrophe for German Jewry. Most of the country's synagogues were destroyed or severely damaged, and thousands of Jewish-owned businesses were vandalized and looted (see Figure 6.3). Many Jews were attacked inside their homes or hunted on the streets. Some 30,000 Jewish men were rounded up and sent to the concentration camps Dachau, Buchenwald, and Sachsenhausen (see Figure 6.4). About 100 Jews were killed on November 9–10, but hundreds more died in the camps in the subsequent days and weeks as the result of physical abuse, exposure, and deprivation. Most of the men were released from the camps in late 1938 and early 1939, but only after agreeing to a rapid Aryanization of their property and promising to leave Germany as quickly as possible. In order to finance repairs to the damage to property inflicted on November 9–10, the Reich government imposed a collective fine of 1 billion Reichmarks on the Jewish community.[50]

The reaction of most ordinary Germans to Kristallnacht was negative. They were critical of the destruction of property, the vandalism of houses of worship, and, more generally, the violence and disorder of the anti-Jewish uprising. This does not mean, however, that they had been opposed in principle to the dejewification of German society. To the contrary, a fairly broad consensus of Germans had believed that the Jews had exercised too much collective influence over German economic and cultural life, and since 1933 they had supported anti-Jewish measures that had been implemented legally and bureaucratically. Objections focused mostly on the method, rather than the purpose, of the Kristallnacht.[51]

Throughout the 1930s, the Jewish community in Germany did not respond passively to its treatment at the hands of the National Socialist regime. A response embraced by roughly half of German Jews was

Figure 6.3 The synagogue in Eberswalde burning during Kristallnacht (Universal History Archive/Universal Images Group via Getty Images).

Figure 6.4 Arrested Jewish men being marched through Baden-Baden after Kristallnacht (Mondadori via Getty Images).

that of emigration. Just over 50,000 Jews departed Germany during the first year of Nazi rule. Between 1934 and 1937, the number of Jews emigrating annually averaged about 30,000. In 1938, a year of escalating violence inside Germany and rising tension in international affairs, the number rose to over 47,000. In 1939, in the wake of Kristallnacht and the final stages of Aryanization, 68,000 departed, the most in any single year. Their primary destinations were the United States and Britain, while significant numbers also went to Palestine. As entry into these preferred places of refuge became more and more difficult in the late 1930s, German Jews looked increasingly to less likely destinations, such as Latin America, South Africa, and even China.

Jews who remained in Germany despite the intensifying persecution did so for a variety of reasons. Most came from families that had been present in Germany for generations, and they felt themselves to be deeply German. Until the Kristallnacht, many remained hopeful that the situation in Germany would improve, or at least stabilize. Reluctance to emigrate also stemmed from the practical difficulties involved in moving one's life to another country, such as learning a new language, finding work, and adjusting to a new culture. In addition, Jews who remained in Germany received significant support from Jewish communal institutions, such as schools, hospitals, and cultural associations. Jewish life in Germany had grown increasingly uncomfortable during the 1930s, but for many Jews it reached the point of being intolerable only in November 1938, by which time it had become very difficult to attain visas for the countries to which they desired to flee.[52]

On January 30, 1939, on the sixth anniversary of the Nazi takeover, and less than three months after the Kristallnacht, Hitler delivered a wide-ranging and belligerent speech before the German parliament. It was in this address that he made his infamous "prophesy" about the Jews. "If international finance Jewry inside and outside Europe should succeed in plunging the nations once more into a world war," he warned, "the result will not be the Bolshevization of the earth and thereby the victory of Jewry, but the annihilation of the Jewish race in Europe."[53] This single sentence encapsulated multiple antisemitic beliefs: that the Jews conspired globally; that they controlled international finance; that they controlled Bolshevism; and that they had been responsible for the outbreak of World War I. The prophesy, however, does not mean that the Final Solution became inevitable in January 1939. Historians have attributed multiple tactical motivations to Hitler's statement, seeing it as a form of blackmail against countries that, in his view, complained too much about Germany's treatment of Jews without admitting more of them as refugees.[54] Nevertheless, such a naked threat, issued so closely on the heels of Kristallnacht, starkly reaffirmed the depth of Hitler's hatred of Jews. During the war, as the Jews of Europe were being slaughtered under his command, Hitler and other leading Nazis referred back to his prophesy on multiple occasions.[55] The prophesy, then, is evidence that he entertained the idea of perpetrating mass violence against the Jews of Germany and Europe many months before the onset of World War II. The dejewification of Germany and Europe counted among Hitler's main goals in that conflict.

7   A New Order in Europe

The terms of the peace after World War I generated tremendous resentment in German society across the political spectrum, but it did not lead inevitably to the next war.[1] During the Weimar Republic, German diplomats and statesmen, most notably Gustav Stresemann, worked hard for a sustained peace with a Germany that was fully reintegrated into the European order. Upon achieving power, Hitler was not interested in revising the post-war order but rather in destroying it, so as to allow Germany to pursue a set of expansionist aims that were anchored in the racist and Social Darwinist aspects of Nazism. In its fundamental assumptions and goals, therefore, the Nazi regime's foreign policy was closely intertwined with its domestic priorities. While Hitler's aims in foreign policy were a product of his worldview, they had to be justified on grounds that would resonate both with his own people and with foreigners interested in a fair deal for Germany. The revision of Versailles, fairness for Germany, and equity with other powers were pretexts used to justify steps toward a far more ambitious agenda, one that was based on an ideology of race and space rather than in the traditional considerations of great power politics. World War II, which began in Europe in September 1939, and which would lead to the deaths of tens of millions of people, was not the result of the flaws of the Treaty of Versailles, but rather of Nazi Germany's aspirations for expansion and conquest.

Hitler and German Foreign Policy

Adolf Hitler was undeniably the chief architect of German foreign policy during the 1930s. He devoted much time and effort to international affairs even while he delegated significant authority to subordinates when it came to other areas of policy.[2] Although he was driven primarily by ideological goals, he was opportunistic in his pursuit of achieving them. He did not follow a plan in the sense of a detailed, step-by-step blueprint for action worked out in advance and adhered to scrupulously, but instead improvised his way toward a clear set of goals.

At the core of his thinking were the concepts of race and space, the notion that in a world of racial struggle among peoples, the German Volk required additional "living space" (*Lebensraum*) in order to proliferate, nourish itself, and thrive. The underlying Social Darwinistic premise of this view held that the natural state of humanity is one of conflict. This led Hitler to reject notions of cooperative interdependence among nations in a liberal international order. He saw treaties and international organizations as straitjackets around German power. Germany should instead embrace the inevitability of struggle, conquest, and hegemony as the natural order among races. To prevail in this struggle, Germany required additional territory to allow its population to grow. Such territory lay in the agriculturally valuable regions to Germany's east. Knowing full well that Germany could not acquire these lands peacefully, Hitler regarded a war of conquest as an inescapable necessity. The conquest of living space would be accompanied by a fundamental transformation of the racial composition of the population. Because Nazi racial doctrine ruled out the possibility of assimilating the conquered peoples, Germanization would necessarily involve their eventual expulsion or their eradication by other means, even if during a transitional period their labor would be exploited for the benefit of Germans.

Hitler's vision for German racial expansion overlapped with two important ideas that gained influence in conservative circles during the Weimar Republic. One of these was a field of scholarly research known as geopolitics, which aspired to understand politics and international relations at the intersection of space, culture, economics, and military strategy. In view of the territorial losses imposed on Germany after World War I, the practitioners of geopolitics called attention to Germany's "lack of space," that is, to the discrepancy between the country's needs and the territory it inhabited. National Socialism eventually appropriated concepts and terminology from geopolitics, and after 1933 the key geopolitical journal, the *Zeitschrift für Geopolitik*, published articles about *Lebensraum* that lent scientific credibility to Nazi notions of expansionism. The most prominent scholar in the field was Karl Haushofer, a retired military officer. Hitler's deputy, Rudolf Hess, studied under Haushofer at the University of Munich in the 1920s, thereby providing a key personal bridge between the field of geopolitics and the Nazi movement (although Haushofer himself eventually became an opponent of the Nazis).[3]

The second idea influential among conservatives that dovetailed with Nazi thinking was that of the "large area economy" (*Grossraumwirtschaft*). It, too, was based on an understanding of the world as an arena of struggle rather than cooperation among nations. The proponents of this idea believed that the nations of the world were destined to break up into autarkic economic blocs or zones, including Europe, North America, and the Soviet Union. The European economic area, they argued, should be German-dominated and serve German needs. They rejected the post-war push for free trade and the liberalization of the world's economy, believing instead that the (German-dominated) European economic area should achieve self-sufficiency, or autarky, with regard to raw materials, foodstuffs, industrial production, and markets. The experience of Germany's blockade by Britain during World War I, they argued, justified a shift toward autarky, and they saw the onset of the Depression as a validation of this view. The notion of a German-dominated large area economy in Europe also rested and built upon older visions of "Mitteleuropa" that had been in circulation in the German Empire before World War I and had then shaped the country's expansionist goals during that conflict. Despite the autarkic aspirations of the Nazi regime, Germany remained dependent on imports of food, steel, and many raw materials during the 1930s, a situation made more acute by the production demands of the Four Year Plan. The continued dependency on trade reinforced Hitler's resolve to achieve autarky through the acquisition of additional living space for the German Volk in the war that would eventually come.[4]

Hitler's conscious and very deliberate embrace of war as a tool necessary for the realization of his aims was based on his own understanding of Germany's recent history, and especially of its defeat in 1918. First and foremost, Germany needed to avoid a repetition of a two-front war. This could be achieved by isolating Germany's enemies and fighting them one at a time. The short wars would also avoid placing too much of an economic and psychological burden on the German people. The treacherous "stab in the back," which Hitler understood as the cause of the German collapse in November 1918, had been possible because the German people's will to fight had been undermined by their sacrifices during a prolonged two-front conflict. Hitler drew three additional lessons from the history of the German collapse in 1918. First, all manifestations of pacifism, exemplified by the anti-war novel and film *All Quiet on the Western Front*, had to be expunged from German society. Second, the population required careful psychological preparation for war. And third, the internal enemies who had been responsible for the "stab in the back" at the conclusion of the previous war needed to be removed from German society before the start of the next war. These were, most notably, Jews, Communists, and socialists.

The rebuilding of German military might, and its application toward the desired goals, would require not merely rearmament, but also the militarization of German society. Mass organizations like the Reich Labor Service and the Hitler Youth were used to inculcate martial values into teenage boys and young men. It would, in addition, be necessary to win, or force, the collaboration of traditional elites in the diplomatic corps and the officer corps of the military. Many of these figures embraced priorities and even had ideological proclivities that overlapped with those of Hitler. They believed, for example, that German security was dependent on hegemony on the European continent and on the reacquisition of territories lost in 1918. But many, while sharing the desire to overturn Versailles and re-establish Germany as a great power, distrusted Hitler and feared that he would plunge Germany into a disastrous war. Hitler, for his part, accepted their help when their goals overlapped with his, and dispensed with them when they were no longer useful. Tensions between the Nazi leader and these reluctant collaborators planted the seeds for an unsuccessful attempt to assassinate Hitler and remove the Nazis from power in July 1944.

Hitler employed several basic tactics in his interactions with the leaders of other countries. He proved adept, for example, at exploiting the ongoing ethnic rivalries and territorial disputes in Eastern Europe. These included issues around German ethnic minorities in Czechoslovakia and Poland, which Hitler would use as a pretext for interfering in the affairs of those countries. Hitler also understood the widespread fear of the Soviet Union and Communism among Europeans, portraying Nazi Germany as a key bulwark against those threats. He knew how to manipulate the genuine widespread anxiety about war by engaging in reassuring rhetoric about Germany's intentions even as he violated agreements and annexed Austria and part of Czechoslovakia. He possessed no scruples when it came to signing new agreements that he knew he would eventually violate. He directed this same fundamental and totally shameless dishonesty against his own people, assuring them repeatedly of his peaceful intensions even as he prepared them for a war that he was planning.

Hitler based his views of other countries on their geostrategic characteristics as filtered through his racialized view of the world. Closest to Germany, he saw his native Austria through a Pan-German lens, regarding the separation of the two countries as an historical accident compounded by the opposition of other European countries to a united German Volk. He considered the existence of the binational state of Czechoslovakia as another violation of nature, and also as an arrow pointed into the heart of German-speaking Europe. He was, therefore, determined to annex Austria to Germany and to dismantle Czechoslovakia. With regard to Poland, Hitler's contempt for those he believed

EUROPE IN 1933

Map 7.1 Europe in 1933.

were racially inferior Slavs built upon traditional German stereotypes of the supposedly backward and incompetent Poles. Reacquiring the territories that Germany had been forced to cede to Poland after World War I would not suffice, but the Polish state itself had to be destroyed. The continued existence of the Soviet Union was also unacceptable, as it was, in Hitler's view, a mostly Slavic but also racially mongrelized society governed by Judeo-Bolsheviks. Moreover, the arable land coveted for German living space lay mainly in the western regions of the Soviet Union, Ukraine and White Russia. The smaller states to Germany's east, such as Hungary and Romania, which had long been part of Germany's sphere of economic influence, would be reduced to the status of German satellites.

Looking to the West, Hitler saw in France not only Germany's foe in the last war, but also the birthplace of the Enlightenment and liberalism, the first country to emancipate its Jews, and the country that introduced Black Africans into Europe during World War I. He believed that France needed to be militarily neutralized, but did not see it as a target of German racial colonization, except for the provinces of Alsace-Lorraine, which had been ceded from Germany to France at the end of the war. Whereas Hitler understood from the beginning that his ambitions for Germany would inevitably result in war with France, which would not willingly accept German hegemony on the continent, he hoped to avoid a war with Great Britain. Hitler envisaged a long-term arrangement in which Britain would accede to German hegemony in Europe in exchange for a free hand in its empire. But he always knew there was a good chance that Britain would refuse such a deal, and he, like other Nazis, obsessed over the supposed infiltration of the British governing elite by Jews and people of Jewish ancestry.

In the south, Italy had been the birthplace and homeland of Fascism starting in 1922, giving it prestige in Nazi circles. During the 1920s, Nazi leaders made pilgrimages to Rome, seeking audiences with Mussolini and other Fascist personalities. Despite ideological affinities between Italian Fascism and German Nazism, there were also important points of disagreement. For example, the Pan-German aspiration of Nazism to unite all Germans in one Reich clashed with Mussolini's commitment to maintaining Italian control over South Tyrol, a German-speaking region in the far north of Italy that had been part of Austria until 1918. Moreover, Italian Fascism did not at first pursue an antisemitic program and had even counted some Italian Jews among its most ardent supporters. By the late 1930s, however, Germany and Italy would be drawn together by their common desire to overturn the international status quo in Europe and the Mediterranean. As the two countries drew closer together, Italy instituted anti-Jewish legislation that was motivated at least in part by a desire to ingratiate itself with its larger, more powerful partner.

The United States had figured into Hitler's thinking from early on, but his views of the country were subject to change over time and according to circumstances. In *Mein Kampf*, he attributed the "immense inner strength" of the United States to its control over an entire continent.[5] He saw the history of European emigration to North America and the resulting supremacy of white settlers over indigenous peoples and imported slaves as a key to the country's power. In his second, unpublished book, written in 1928, Hitler credited the power of the United States to its vastness, its fertile soil, and its domination by people of the "highest racial quality."[6] By the late 1930s, however, he had come to believe that the United States, like Britain, had become subject to overweening Jewish power and racial degeneration. By the outbreak of war in late 1939, Hitler had come to hold a diminished assessment of American power, but he continued to regard the United States as a global competitor and believed that a military reckoning between Germany and the United States was probable in the long term.

The Road to War, 1933–39

Once in power, Hitler moved first to extricate Germany from its commitments under Versailles, and then to prepare the country for war. His success in both these respects can be attributed at least partly to the inability or reluctance of other European powers to thwart him. The ineffectual responses of France and Britain to Hitler's transformation of the power alignments in Europe are traceable to several factors. Vivid memories of the horrors of World War I led many in those countries to do everything possible to avoid another war, even if that included appeasing the German dictator by acceding to treaty violations and land grabs. During much of the 1930s, Depression-era domestic issues made it hard for leaders to mobilize decisive responses to German moves. Many Europeans felt more threatened by Communism than by Nazism, and a not insignificant number of people outside of Germany developed a degree of admiration for the Nazi regime's success at taming unemployment while neutralizing the political left. At the most basic level, European leaders, like Hitler's opponents inside Germany before them, failed to comprehend the radicalness of what they were facing.

During the early phase of Nazi rule, Hitler had to maneuver slowly and carefully while consolidating his regime. While clearly signaling that he rejected the status quo, he had to avoid provoking war and create space

for rearming. He took provocative actions followed by rhetoric and diplomatic gestures aimed at reassuring people about German intentions. In
October 1933, for example, he withdrew Germany from the League of
Nations and an ongoing international disarmament conference, but then
followed this up by signing a non-aggression pact in 1934 with Poland, a
country reviled by millions of Germans who saw it as occupying much of
the easternmost territory of the German Reich. Similarly, in March 1935
Hitler announced the introduction of general conscription and declared
that Germany would no longer respect the military stipulations of the
Treaty of Versailles. In response, Britain, France, and Italy, in a meeting at Stresa in northern Italy, declared their commitment to protect the
integrity of Austria. Hitler responded to the creation of this so-called
Stresa Front by reaching out to Britain to negotiate an agreement placing
limits on German naval expansion. The Anglo-German Naval Agreement of June 1935 drove a wedge between Britain, on the one hand, and
France and Italy, on the other.

The Stresa Front was dealt an even more fatal blow as the result of
Mussolini's decision to invade Abyssinia (Ethiopia) in October 1935 in
a bid to expand Italy's empire in North Africa. Mussolini felt betrayed
when Britain used its influence in the League of Nations to impose sanc-
tions on Italy. Until this point, the ideological affinities between Fascist
Italy and Nazi Germany had been overridden by Mussolini's concerns
about Hitler's intentions for South Tyrol. But the Abyssinian affair
proved to be a turning point, and henceforth the foreign policies of the
two countries became increasingly aligned in the so-called Axis. In the
Spanish Civil War (1936–39), for example, both countries intervened
on the side of the right-wing Nationalists. A further indication of the
emerging alignment between the two countries was the decision by the
Fascist regime in Rome to promulgate its first antisemitic racial laws in
late 1938. The convergence reached its culmination in May 1939 with
the formation of a formal alliance, the so-called Pact of Steel.

Hitler undertook a particularly bold action in March 1936 when, in
violation of Versailles and other agreements, he sent German troops into
the Rhineland, the region between the Rhine River and Germany's borders with France and the Low Countries. Hitler followed up this unilateral and shocking move with the usual claims of peaceful intentions,
appeals for fair treatment of Germany, and suggestions of new forms
of international cooperation, but the remilitarization of the Rhineland
represented Hitler's most audacious step in the international arena to
date. He had been emboldened by several factors. He had succeeded at
undermining the Stresa Front, and the rearmament program had made
significant progress.[7] Unemployment inside Germany had been largely

eliminated, in large part because of the militarization of the economy and the siphoning off of young men into the military. The winter Olympic Games had been held in Garmisch-Partenkirchen in February, while the preparations for the summer games, to be held in Berlin, included major infrastructure projects like new train tunnels under the center of the Reich capital. These successes encouraged Hitler to become more aggressive in pursuit of his foreign policy aims.

While 1937 did not see a dramatic event on the international stage comparable to the remilitarization of the Rhineland, Germany made dramatic progress in its rearmament program, spurred in part by the initiation of the Four Year Plan during the previous year. Progress in the production of military aircraft and naval vessels was especially significant.[8] The most important development in German foreign policy during 1937 was a secret meeting between Hitler and several top officials on November 5. The record of this meeting was first made known after World War II. The document in question is a summary of the meeting made by Colonel Friedrich Hossbach, Hitler's military adjutant, and is therefore known to historians as the Hossbach Memorandum. It is a key document reflecting Hitler's intentions for war and conquest.[9] Aside from Hitler, the attendees at the meeting were Field Marshall Werner von Blomberg, the minister of war; General Werner von Fritsch, the commander-in-chief of the army; Admiral Erich Raeder, the commander-in-chief of the navy; Hermann Göring, the commander-in-chief of the air force and the head of the Four Year Plan; and Konstantin von Neurath, the German foreign minister. The meeting was occasioned by a crisis in naval construction stemming from a steel shortage, and much of the discussion dealt with issues of the short term, such as the prospects for British and French military intervention against Germany in the event of a German attack on Czechoslovakia, which Hitler preferred to launch sooner rather than later. But Hitler opened the meeting with a number of general observations, emphasizing to his listeners that these comments should be taken as reflections of his fundamental beliefs about Germany's current and future situation, and therefore should be regarded as a last will and testament in the event of his early death.

Hitler stated that the highest priority should be given to safeguarding the "racial mass" (*Volksmasse*) of the German people. He considered German dependence on trade and imports to be not acceptable, and therefore posited autarky as a necessity. But autarky was not achievable, given Germany's agricultural capacity, its raw materials base, and the standard of living to be expected by and for the German people. The solution to this dilemma, he claimed, was "the acquisition of living space," for the German people, a project that would require "one to three generations." He described living space as "agriculturally use-ful space" and pointed to the need for Germany to gain control of new "raw materials regions in Europe." The conquest of the new space, he said, should be achieved by 1943–45, while Germany still enjoyed the advantages of its head start in rearmament over its rivals. Other countries would eventually catch up, he believed, and Germany's new weapons would become obsolete over time.

Three of Hitler's interlocutors at the meeting – Blomberg, Fritsch, and Neurath – were alarmed by Hitler's aggressive vision and pushed back, expressing concern about the potential dangers of a war. Within less than three months, all three had been removed from their positions and replaced by figures who were in greater ideological synch with Hit-ler, or who were at least more deferential to him. Blomberg was forced out of his position in January 1938 after evidence of his new wife's per-sonal scandals emerged. Fritsch was then dismissed on a trumped-up accusation of homosexuality. Both generals were replaced by more pli-ant figures. Just as important, Hitler reorganized the military command structure, appointing himself commander-in-chief.[10] At the same time, Foreign Minister Neurath, a career diplomat and conservative (he had first joined the NSDAP in 1937), was demoted and replaced by Joachim von Ribbentrop, a Hitler loyalist and Nazi Party member since 1932. The replacement of these three officials within a few weeks marked a dramatic shift in the balance between Nazis and conservatives in the "governing compromise" that had formed the original basis for Hitler's rule in 1933, helping to pave the way for a more aggressive stance in foreign policy starting in 1938.

In fact, historians of Nazi Germany have called 1938 a "Fateful Year." German expansionism set Europe on a course toward war, while inter-nal repression and exclusionary racial policies intensified. The parallel developments in foreign and domestic policy reflected an increased level of confidence and boldness on the part of the Nazi leadership, which sought to accelerate progress toward the realization of its ideological goals. On March 12, 1938, German troops crossed the border with Aus-tria and occupied the country, resulting in its annexation (*Anschluss*) to the German Reich. The takeover marked the culmination of a prolonged campaign of pressure directed by Hitler at the Austrian chancellor, Kurt von Schuschnigg, in collusion with Austrian National Socialists. Much of the world was shocked by the audacity and unilateral character of the move. But criticism was dampened by the fact that Austrians were widely seen as Germans, and it also appeared that the annexation was popular within Austria. Britain and France were not prepared to wage war to prevent Germany from extending its control over other Germans.

For its part, Italy had resigned itself to the likely outcome of an enlarged Germany on its northern border. Mussolini's fears regarding South Tyrol were assuaged by German assurances that, rather than the Reich pursuing the annexation of that German-speaking region, the German-speaking inhabitants could eventually be relocated to the Reich.

Having taken Austria, Hitler's attention naturally turned toward Czechoslovakia, a country whose very existence he resented viscerally. The Anschluss of Austria fueled his confidence and strengthened his resolve to destroy Czechoslovakia. As Hitler had laid out at the Hossbach meeting in November 1937, the grievances of the German ethnic minority in the Sudetenland could be used as a pretext for a German attack that would dismantle the Czechoslovak state. Months of international tensions ensued as Hitler ratcheted up pressure on the Czechoslovak government to make concessions to the ethnic German minority. He simultaneously encouraged the representatives of that minority to reject compromise offers from the government. The goal was not to settle the dispute amicably but rather to create a pretext for German military intervention. In May 1938, a misinterpretation of some German troop movements caused the British government to believe that a German invasion of Czechoslovakia might be imminent. This war scare, known as the May Crisis, quickly subsided, but after several months of military preparations, Hitler launched a coordinated propaganda and diplomatic campaign targeting Czechoslovakia.

These developments culminated in a major international crisis in late September 1938. At a conference in Munich, the leaders of Germany, Britain, France, and Italy agreed to cede to Germany the Sudetenland, a region in western Czechoslovakia bordering the German Reich and containing a large population of ethnic Germans. The Czechoslovak government, which was not represented at the meeting, was left with no choice but to comply. This so-called Munich Agreement has gone down in history as a notorious example of the futility of appeasement, the label given to the strategy employed by British Prime Minister Neville Chamberlain to avoid a new European war. What is often overlooked is that Hitler regarded Munich as a defeat because he had been determined to destroy Czechoslovakia by means of war, a goal he believed had been thwarted by Chamberlain.

Prior to the Munich conference, during the build-up to the planned military operation against Czechoslovakia, differences of opinion had emerged between Hitler and several of his generals, most notably Ludwig Beck, the chief of the army's general staff. Beck did not object to Hitler's aim of dismantling Czechoslovakia but believed that Germany was not yet prepared to deal militarily with the likely intervention of Britain and

France. He predicted a catastrophic outcome for Germany. After failing to dissuade Hitler from moving forward with plans for the attack, Beck resigned from his post, and retired from the army a couple of months later. His departure reflected the limits of the military's ability and inclination to oppose Hitler during the lead-up to World War II. The same can be said of the coup d'état contemplated but inadequately prepared by General Franz Halder, Beck's successor and former deputy, during the Sudeten crisis in September. The plot was abandoned when the crisis was settled peacefully at Munich, thus leaving Hitler in power to plan the next aggression. Halder was involved in another anti-Hitler plot prior to the German Western offensive of 1940 (see below), but, despite his antipathy toward Hitler, helped to plan the German attacks against Poland, France, and the Soviet Union. Beck and Halder were representative of much of the German military elite during the 1930s. Nationalist, conservative, and traditional, they despised Hitler and other leading Nazis, whom they saw as plebian upstarts, if not as criminals. But they also recognized in the Nazi regime an opportunity to demolish the Treaty of Versailles and return Germany to great-power status. At some point it became clear to them that Hitler's expansionist ambitions would pose a mortal danger to Germany, but their sense of duty to the Fatherland and their commonality of purpose with Hitler prevented them from taking action, and this at a time when the military was the single institution in German society that could have taken Hitler out. In Beck's case, at least it can be said that, although retired from the military, he became a central figure in the plot against Hitler that culminated in the unsuccessful coup and assassination attempt of July 20, 1944, for which he paid with his life.[11]

After Munich, Hitler resolved immediately to destroy Czechoslovakia at the first available opportunity. At the core of his strategy was the exploitation of tensions between the Czech and Slovak halves of the country. Hitler encouraged the Hungarians and the Poles to participate in the partition of the country by seizing territories that they coveted, an example of his shrewd and cynical exploitation of nationalist rivalries and territorial claims among the European states. Hitler pressured the Slovak politician Jozef Tiso to declare independence. Hitler threatened a German invasion, justified by the need to stabilize the very situation that German actions had intentionally destabilized. On March 15, 1939, the German army occupied the Czech Lands, which were now redesignated as the "Reich Protectorate of Bohemia and Moravia" and governed directly from Berlin. Slovakia came into existence as a formally independent state, but in its foreign and military affairs (and later in its policies toward its Jewish citizens) was really a German satellite.

Germany's destruction of Czechoslovak statehood was a successful application of Hitler's strategy for isolating the targets of his expansionism. But it also constituted a flagrant violation of the Munich Agreement and served as dramatic proof that Hitler could not be taken at his word. The mood in Europe darkened, and many ordinary Germans now resigned themselves to the inevitability of war. Britain and France, having been disabused of any remaining illusions about Hitler's good will, issued a guarantee of Poland's independence, knowing that country would be Germany's next target. To nobody's surprise, Hitler intensified pressure on Poland using grievances of ethnic Germans, as well as the situation in and around the city of Danzig, a German city surrounded by Polish territory, as pretexts for an attack.

A major question mark was the position to be taken by the Soviet Union in any coming war. In the event of a German attack on Poland, any successful intervention by the Western powers would be contingent on Soviet support for their side. But the distrust of the Soviet Union ran high in the West, and British Prime Minister Neville Chamberlain was loath to cooperate with the Soviet leader, Joseph Stalin. In late August 1939, Germany and the Soviet Union announced that they had agreed to a non-aggression pact. In a secret annex to the agreement, the two countries agreed to divide Poland and other parts of Eastern Europe between them. The announcement of a treaty between the fervently anti-Communist Nazi regime and the homeland of Communism was shocking to many, but also seemed to make sense on a geopolitical level to the two countries, both of which had lost territory to the newly restored Polish state in 1918. From Hitler's perspective, the pact was a cynical and opportunistic move. He would have a free hand in Poland in the short term, deal with Britain and France, and then, at the appropriate moment, tear up his agreement with Stalin and launch his desired war of conquest against the Soviet Union. Stalin's reasons for cooperating with Nazi Germany are more difficult to explain. He may well have been playing for time in the knowledge that a confrontation with Nazi Germany would occur eventually. It is also possible, however, that Marxist-Leninist ideological blinders prevented Stalin from taking seriously the Nazi doctrine of race and space as it applied to Eastern Europe. The Communist leader may well have genuinely believed that he could keep the Soviet Union out of internecine disputes among the capitalist powers.[12] Whatever the case, the Hitler–Stalin pact paved the way for a German attack on Poland, which commenced on September 1, 1939, the date usually cited as the beginning of World War II in Europe.

Military Events, 1939–41

When one considers the years-long stalemate that had characterized much of World War I, the speed with which Germany established hegemony over a huge portion of Europe during the opening phase of World War II is striking. In the short term, the strategy of isolating countries and fighting them one at a time, while avoiding a two-front war, proved effective. Taking full advantage of Germany's industrial and technological prowess, the German military brought to bear an overwhelming concentration of force, coordinating air power, armor, and motorized infantry in waging a "lightning war" (*Blitzkrieg*) against its targets.

The Hitler–Stalin Pact had isolated Poland, and while the Polish army fought valiantly, the far more modern German forces advanced rapidly. On September 17, the Red Army (as the Soviet army was known at the time) invaded Poland from the east. After Poland's capitulation on October 6, the country was divided between Germany and the Soviet Union according to the stipulations of the Hitler–Stalin Pact. Germany subsequently annexed much of western Poland, formally integrating it into the German Reich, while placing the south-central part of the country under an occupation regime called the General Government.

After Germany attacked Poland, France and Britain honored their commitment to defend it by declaring war on Germany, but they did not attempt to intervene militarily, except for a token and quickly aborted French offensive against the Saarland region of southwest Germany. Because virtually no fighting took place on land in Europe, the period between Poland's surrender in October 1939 and the launching of the German offensive against the West in April 1940 has come to be known as the Phony War. The Western powers did, however, impose a naval blockade on Germany in an attempt to damage it economically, while British and German naval forces engaged each other in the opening skirmishes of what eventually came to be known as the Battle of the Atlantic.

Hitler understood that he would have to wage war against France eventually, and while he hoped that Britain would sue for peace and acknowledge Germany's supremacy on the European continent, he was under no illusion that this would happen. Thus, he ordered his military commanders to prepare a campaign against the Western powers. The offensive was at first supposed to occur in the fall of 1939 but was postponed on account of weather, and perhaps also because members of the Wehrmacht high command harbored serious doubts about Germany's readiness to take on France and Britain so soon. Hitler therefore postponed the Western offensive until spring 1940. In the meantime, in order to secure Germany's northern flank, in April 1940 Hitler ordered the invasion of Denmark and Norway. Denmark was defeated and occupied within hours. The victory in Norway took several weeks, owing in part to the participation of a British expeditionary force in the fighting. Eventually the British withdrew, and Norway was subordinated under Nazi Germany's growing European hegemony.

Germany launched its Western offensive on May 10. The pact with Stalin enabled it to concentrate the entirety of its military power in the West. The "lightning war" methods of the Germans, who enjoyed a substantial airpower advantage, proved too much for the inadequately coordinated French, British, Dutch, and Belgian forces. Almost 350,000 Allied troops were evacuated from the French port of Dunkirk to Britain over ten days in late May and early June. On June 22, France and Germany signed an armistice, and, two days later, Hitler paid a visit to German-occupied Paris to gloat (see Figure 7.1). The armistice provided for German forces to occupy the strategically important northern and western regions of the country. Humiliating as the defeat was for France, the arrangement was moderated by German fears that the French, if treated too harshly, would place their considerable navy at the disposal of the British. The government of France was entrusted to a conservative authoritarian regime, led by Marshal Philippe Pétain, a hero of World War I, which used the town of Vichy in unoccupied France as its capital.

Hitler hoped that the defeat and occupation of France would force Britain to accept the new status quo on the continent and seek peace with Germany. Britain, however, now under the leadership of Winston Churchill, who had become prime minister on the day that Germany invaded the West, remained resolute. Hitler decided that Britain would have to be dealt with militarily before Germany could turn eastward and pursue its war for living space against the Soviet Union. Britain would, ideally, be defeated or at least be pushed out of the war while it was isolated. German air power could be used to pummel Britain from the sky and persuade it to capitulate. If necessary, Germany could invade Britain, an eventuality for which the British had already begun to prepare.

The German aerial assault on Britain began in July 1940. At first it focused on military targets and on achieving air superiority, but in late August Hitler shifted the focus onto terror bombing targeted at the British population – as the Germans had done previously in Warsaw and Rotterdam. When German bombers attacked London, the British retaliated against Berlin. In September, the Germans launched a massive series of bombing raids on London over the course of several weeks. Dubbed "the Blitz" by the British press, these attacks were intended to break the will of the British public and, if necessary, soften British defenses in advance of a German invasion. That particular strategy failed, but Hitler had

Figure 7.1 Hitler in Paris, June 1940 (Photo by Heinrich Hoffmann/ Roger Viollet via Getty Images).

unleashed a modern form of warfare that would eventually result in the destruction of Germany's own major cities by the British and American air forces.

Britain by itself could do little to dislodge Germany from its dominant position in Central Europe, but it continued to challenge Germany at the periphery. In connection with a botched Italian invasion of Greece in the fall of 1940, the British established a military presence in the latter country. As this would have presented a danger to Germany's southern flank during the planned offensive against the USSR, Germany invaded the Balkans in April 1941. Italy, Bulgaria, and Hungary joined Germany in dividing up Yugoslavia among themselves and creating a puppet regime in Croatia. In Greece, German forces captured several thousand British soldiers and forced many more to evacuate. British forces were also fighting the Germans in North Africa, aiming to protect their strategically important position in Egypt and Palestine from both the Italians and the Germans.[13] All the while, German plans for Operation Barbarossa – the invasion of the Soviet Union – went forward.

German Popular Responses to Foreign Policy and War

The early foreign policy achievements of the Nazi regime were applauded by the majority of Germans. Before 1933, there had been a very widely held belief that Germany had been treated unfairly after World War I. Germans therefore welcomed Hitler's abandonment of the Treaty of Versailles and the restrictions on German freedom associated with it. Measures such as the reintroduction of military conscription, rearmament, and the remilitarization of the Rhineland found widespread approval domestically. These actions helped many Germans to overcome feelings of humiliation and national impotence, and to believe that Germany had once again joined the ranks of the great nations.[14] When German troops entered the Rhineland in March 1936 after Hitler's unilateral abrogation of international agreements, the local population greeted them with jubilation. Writing in her diary, Lore Walb, a 16-year-old girl in the Rhineland town of Alzey, described the day as one of great historical significance, adding, "what courage our Führer has!"[15] The annexation of Austria in March 1938 reinforced such sentiments but also generated anxiety that Hitler might be pushing things too far and unleash a war. Germans who had been hoping that the Western powers would put a brake on Hitler's ambitions were once more disappointed. Anti-Nazi Germans feared that the success of the Anschluss had validated in the eyes of their countrymen a foreign policy based on unilateral force rather than on international cooperation.[16]

The series of crises over first Czechoslovakia and then Poland during the years 1938 and 1939 resulted in an increasingly widespread perception among the German people that war was inevitable. Not a small number of Germans harbored doubts that Germany could prevail over a hostile coalition including Britain, France, and possibly the Soviet Union. Even many enthusiastic supporters of the Nazi regime feared the consequences of a war.[17] A war, they thought, would jeopardize many of the gains that Germany had made since 1933, especially economically.[18] Many ordinary Germans obviously failed to recognize the link between the country's economic recovery, the militarization of its economy, and the expansionistic thrust of its foreign policy.

Hitler, himself, recognized the anxiety of his own people at the prospect of war. On November 10, 1938, several weeks after the Munich conference (and on the evening after the Kristallnacht pogrom), Hitler offered some extraordinarily candid remarks to an audience of 400 publishers and editors gathered in Munich. He summarized his own strategy for conducting foreign policy as one of deception. While preparing his country for war, he had placed the emphasis of his rhetoric on peace. This strategy, he said, had succeeded inasmuch as it had provided cover for a series of foreign policy accomplishments that had restored Germany to great-power status and had expanded German territory. But the strategy, Hitler admitted, had also produced an unfortunate byproduct: the German people had not been psychologically prepared for war. The widespread fear of war on display in the German public at the time of the Sudeten crisis had driven this point home. It was necessary, Hitler said, "gradually to convert the German people psychologically, and slowly to make it clear to them, that there are things which, when they cannot be implemented by peaceful means, must be implemented by means of violence."[19]

Once the war began, German popular opinion reflected differing attitudes toward Poland, on the one hand, and the Western powers, on the other. Based on reporting from sources inside Germany, the exiled German Social Democratic Party concluded that "the action against Poland has found approval among wide circles of the German people." But what applied to Poland did not apply to Britain and France, as large numbers of Germans were fearful of a war against those countries.[20] While Poland was generally neither feared nor admired in German society, Britain and France had proved themselves worthy adversaries in World War I and were generally perceived to embody a higher level of civilization. But Germans also expressed resentment toward the Western powers for not letting Germany pursue its interests on the European continent, for wanting to keep Germany down, or for actually forcing Germany into the war in the first place.[21] Writing in her diary, Lore Walb from Alzey, now a young woman of 19, blamed France and Britain for "Polish shamelessness" and for "the Polish terror" against ethnic Germans.[22] But there were also many Germans who took a less self-righteous view of the international situation, expressing anger at their own government for taking Europe into another war.[23]

While Germans were nervous about the prospect of war against Britain and France, they were generally confident in an ultimate German victory.[24] Many hoped that France and Britain would not have the courage to fight, or would not risk their own safety for the sake of the Poles.[25] Some engaged in wishful thinking, embracing a false rumor that the British king had abdicated, the British government had resigned, and an armistice between Germany and Britain was in the offing. This fantasy was fueled by Hitler's public offering of a peace agreement with Britain.[26]

On November 8, 1939, just a month after Poland's capitulation, a spectacular but unsuccessful attempt to assassinate Hitler added to the sense of uncertainty. The would-be assassin was Georg Elser, a cabinetmaker by occupation, and a leftist who was not affiliated with the organized Communist or socialist resistance (see Figure 7.2). Elser constructed a time bomb and planted it inside a column in a Munich beer hall where Hitler had been scheduled to speak on the anniversary of the 1923 Beer Hall Putsch. The bomb exploded as planned, killing seven people, but Hitler had stepped down from the speaker's podium and departed from the beer hall thirteen minutes ahead of schedule. Elser was captured while attempting to flee into Switzerland. Although he confessed to the act and proved to investigators that he had acted alone, the authorities withheld this information from the public. Germans therefore quickly integrated the failed assassination into pre-existing political and ideological narratives. Militant German antisemites responded to news of the assassination attempt with attacks on Jews. The regime's propagandists blamed the explosion on a sprawling conspiracy among the British secret service and anti-Hitler German émigrés. Many supporters of Hitler assumed that renegade Wehrmacht officers were behind the attack. Meanwhile, many anti-Nazi Germans suspected that the bomb had been orchestrated by Hitler himself in order to justify intensified domestic repression, much as they believed that the Reichstag Fire of 1933 had been. None of these explanations lent credence to the possibility that Elser, an ordinary German, had acted alone, a fact that became established only on the basis of historical research in later decades. In his interrogation by the Gestapo, the transcript of which was unearthed in a German archive in the 1960s, Elser explained that his deed had been motivated primarily by his belief that Hitler had taken the country into

Figure 7.2 Georg Elser in Gestapo custody, November 1939 (Keystone-France/Gamma-Keystone via Getty Images).

a war that would ultimately prove ruinous. Elser's conduct thus stood in stark contrast to that of the German generals who had opposed Hitler's war plans but failed in the end to take decisive action.[27]

From the spring of 1940 onward, the German people rode an emotional roller coaster, buffeted by propaganda from their own government and by the reality of the war. During the Phony War, Germans were lulled into a false sense of security about what the costs of war would be for them. No bombs had yet fallen on the country, and a certain sense of invincibility set in. Meanwhile, propaganda had created a widespread belief that the British desired the break-up of Germany.[28] The beginning of the Western offensive in May 1940 was accompanied by great apprehension. Germany was now at war not with Poland but with Britain and France (in addition to the Netherlands and Belgium), and many sensed that a moment of truth had arrived. News of the rapid German advance brought relief and inspired confidence in a victorious outcome, faith in the national leadership, and pride in the armed forces. The occupation of Paris was celebrated on the streets of Germany, and the French capitulation generated widespread satisfaction that the defeat of 1918 had been avenged. But with France out of the war, many Germans became impatient for the campaign against Britain to begin. Emotions were a complex combination of anxiety, impatience, confidence, and confusion. Many Germans looked forward to a reckoning with Britain, while others feared it.[29]

Anxiety deepened in July 1940, when British bombs began to fall on Germany. Apprehension was especially pronounced in places where people had to go down into bomb shelters. On the other hand, the bombings made some Germans even more impatient for a major offensive against Britain, which they hoped would bring it to its knees. As more bombs fell, the desire for revenge intensified. The late summer brought satisfaction and hopes for a quick victory as the German air force intensified its own raids on Britain. But the German people were hostages to the propaganda of their own government. The incessant reports of good news on the military front created expectations for a quick victory that never came.[30]

In early September, Germans were flabbergasted when British bombers were able to penetrate to Berlin and drop bombs on the city. They had been led to believe that such a thing could never happen. The desire for revenge against Britain grew stronger, and there was widespread popular support for the intensive German aerial assault on Britain, both to avenge the bombing of German cities and to bring the war to a victorious conclusion. What the Luftwaffe could achieve in Warsaw and Rotterdam, people believed, it could also achieve in London and Manchester. German propaganda depicted the British airmen as "pirates." The hypocrisy was not lost on Friedrich Kellner, the previously mentioned anti-Nazi civil servant, who wrote in his diary: "When English pilots fly to Berlin, it is piracy. When German pilots bomb London, it is heroism."[31]

Disappointment set in during the autumn. "Only a few Volk comrades still believe that the war will end soon," the Security Service concluded in a report on the public mood in October 1940. Germans began to prepare themselves mentally for the possibility of a long war. As the Blitz against Britain continued, frustration over the British refusal to capitulate led many Germans to hope that the Luftwaffe would intensify its attacks on British cities even more.[32] They were seemingly oblivious to the possibility that continued escalation of the air war could eventually lead to the destruction of their own cities. In January 1941, Anne Haag, an anti-Nazi living in Stuttgart, wrote the following in her private diary: "What makes me sick is the fact that it has occurred to so few people in this country that we could actually lose the war."[33]

8   The Nazi Empire

By the end of 1940, Germany had established itself as the hegemon in Europe west of the Soviet Union. It had conquered Poland, France, the Low Countries, Norway, and Denmark, annexing some territories, while militarily occupying others. The ascendant Reich could also command deference, if not obedience, from the remaining independent states in its orbit, such as Italy, Hungary, Romania, and Slovakia. Germany now used its power to initiate a profound transformation of the areas under its influence. This New Order, as it was called, had economic, political, and racial dimensions. German hegemony on the continent created an opportunity to realize the vison of the "large area economy" and the goal of economic autarky. A German economic empire conceived on this basis began to emerge to serve first and foremost the economic interest of the German Reich and its people. The blockade of Germany initiated by the Western powers in September 1939 seemed to validate the wisdom of autarky all the more. In practice, however, the large area economy actually implemented after September 1939 deviated from the theory. The long-term sustainability of the economic area required that the needs of the non-German regions not be overexploited. In practice, this principle was breached, and simple rapaciousness prevailed as Germany tried to address short-term needs for raw materials and labor. German praxis was more confiscatory than the theorists of the large area economy had envisaged. One historian has estimated that about one-third of all the resources expended by Germany on all fronts during the war had been extracted from the economies of the countries it had conquered.[1] The extent to which Germany would go to exploit the areas under its domination depended on a variety of geographic, strategic, and economic factors. It was very much influenced by the Nazi ideological-racial perception of the nation or population group in question. It was not coincidental that the most ruthless forms of exploitation were imposed on Jews, Poles, and Ukrainians, peoples whom Nazi racial ideology held in particularly low regard.[2]

Additionally, the political systems and policies of the European states were brought into line to one degree or another with the authoritarian and antisemitic principles of Nazism. France, which had been the birthplace of the egalitarian spirit in Europe, offers a particularly tragic case study of how this form of subjugation could function. France retained its formal independence, but many of its policies were brought into alignment with German interests and priorities. Soon after its creation, for example, the right-wing government of Marshall Pétain issued a powerful gesture of its readiness to cooperate with Germany. During the summer and fall of 1940, in the first months of its existence, the Vichy government issued a series of anti-Jewish laws on its own initiative, which is to say that it did not do so in response to a demand from the Germans. The antisemitic legislation implemented by France during this period created a foundation for the deportation of Jews from France to Nazi death camps later in the war.[3]

Substantial parts of the Nazi empire were subject to racial colonization by Germany by means of forced population transfers and support for German settlers. At the same time, racial policies inside Germany were radicalized. German Jews were subjected to intensified stigmatization, physical segregation, and forced labor. "Racial hygiene," which previously had depended on forced sterilization, now escalated to a program of mass murder targeted at disabled Germans. All of the above-mentioned developments unfolded simultaneously. This occurred not because they were elements of a master plan for empire – which did not exist as such – but because they sprang from a worldview at the core of which lay the welfare of the German race.

The extent to which European overseas colonialism in general, and Germany's pre-1918 colonial practices in Africa in particular, influenced Nazi Germany's actions within its short-lived European empire in the early 1940s has been a matter of some debate. On the one hand, few Germans who had acquired experience in the country's colonial possessions in Africa participated in the German imperial project in Europe during World War II. On the other hand, there was an undeniable continuity of mentalities and practices rooted in pre-World War I colonialism, which involved the exploitation by one society of the resources and labor of another, the racialization of ethnic and national groups, colonization through resettlement, and genocide. The manner in which antisemitism and antipathy toward Slavic peoples, which were both deeply rooted in Germany as either religious or cultural attitudes, became racialized during the zenith of European colonial expansion in the late nineteenth century serves as a compelling example of how a particular colonial mentality was transferred from Africans and Asians onto Europeans. Nazi leaders sometimes referred to the British Empire and the American frontier when speaking about their own expansionist aspirations. Moreover, Nazi

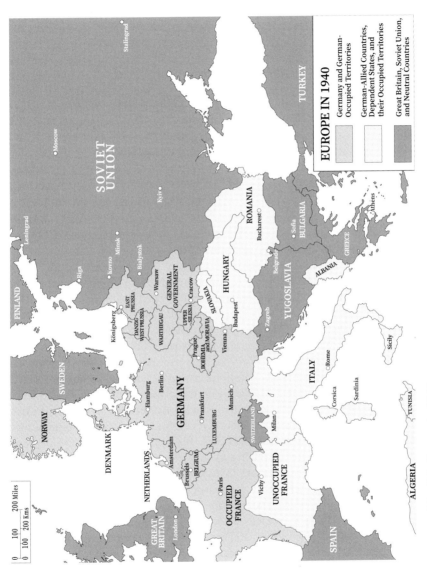

EUROPE IN 1940

Germany and German-Occupied Territories

German-Allied Countries, Dependent States, and their Occupied Territories

Great Britain, Soviet Union, and Neutral Countries

GREAT BRITAIN
London

NETHERLANDS
Amsterdam
BELGIUM
Brussels
LUXEMBURG
OCCUPIED FRANCE
Paris
Vichy
UNOCCUPIED FRANCE
SWITZERLAND

DENMARK
NORWAY
SWEDEN
FINLAND

GERMANY
Hamburg
Berlin
Frankfurt
Munich

Königsberg
EAST PRUSSIA
DANZIG-WEST PRUSSIA
WARTHEGAU
GENERAL GOVERNMENT
Warsaw
UPPER SILESIA
Cracow
SLOVAKIA
BOHEMIA and MORAVIA
Prague
Vienna
HUNGARY
Budapest

Leningrad
Riga
Kovno
Minsk
Bialystok
Kyiv

SOVIET UNION
Moscow
Stalingrad

ROMANIA
Bucharest
YUGOSLAVIA
Zagreb
Belgrade
BULGARIA
Sofia
ALBANIA
GREECE
Athens

TURKEY

ITALY
Rome
Milan
Corsica
Sardinia
Sicily

SPAIN

ALGERIA
TUNISIA

0   100   200 Miles
0   100   200 Kms

Map 8.1 Europe in 1940.

theorists of *Lebensraum* drew from an intellectual tradition that included, for example, Frederick Jackson Turner, the originator of the American "frontier thesis," according to which societies draw vitality from the ability of pioneers to expand into new territory.[4] It is, however, also important to remember that fantasies of hegemony in Central Europe and expansion into Eastern Europe had a long history of their own in Germany, independent of the history of the American West or European overseas colonialism. The Teutonic Knights, who fought against the Poles in the fourteenth century, played at least as large a role in the Nazi historical imagination as did British colonial officers in India or pioneers in the American West. Moreover, the Nazi empire was shaped not only by mentalities inherited from the past, but also by needs and opportunities arising out of the immediate circumstances of World War II.[5]

Foreign Labor in the Nazi Empire

Significant numbers of foreign workers had come to Germany already before the advent of the Nazi regime, a pattern that continued after 1933 and even expanded on account of labor shortages. By 1939, there were 435,000 foreign workers in Germany.[6] The need for foreign labor increased during the war, which drained even more German men out of the labor market and increased pressure on both industrial and agricultural production. By summer 1940, 300,000 Polish men and women had been deported to Germany as forced laborers, in addition to 400,000 Polish POWs who were compelled to work in the Reich before being sent home. By the spring of 1941, the number of foreign workers in the country had risen to 1.3 million civilians, who were mostly Polish. These were in addition to 1.2 million, mostly French, POWs, who were compelled to provide labor for the Reich.[7] An additional million Polish workers soon arrived. Foreign labor recruitment expanded significantly starting in 1942, when Fritz Sauckel, the Gauleiter of Thuringia, was placed in charge of it. According to the calculations of one historian, by late 1944 the German economy was exploiting the labor of 8.4 million foreign civilian laborers (both voluntary and forced), 4.6 million POWs, and 1.7 million concentration camp inmates and Jews. These workers constituted about one-quarter of the total labor force inside Germany. Foreign workers were especially numerous in agriculture, where they comprised 46 percent of the workforce, and were also highly utilized in mining (34 percent of the workforce), and construction (33 percent). These figures, it should be emphasized, do not include the as many as 10 million foreign workers who labored for the German army and other German agencies in German-occupied Europe (see Figure 8.1).[8]

Figure 8.1 Foreign workers in a German factory during the war (ullstein bild/ullstein bild via Getty Images).

The foreign workers performed their labor in factories, on farms, on construction projects, and for the Wehrmacht. The Organization Todt, which was responsible for large construction projects such as motorways, railways, and fortifications, was one of the major exploiters of foreign labor.[9] Many of the foreign workers can accurately be described as "forced" or "slave" laborers, while others had been recruited to work in Germany. But even those in the latter category were treated poorly, subject to harsh disciplinary measures at work and prohibited from socializing with Germans or visiting cinemas, bars, or theaters.[10] Early in the war, Hitler had stipulated the death penalty for any Polish worker caught having sex with a German. More generally, the experiences of the millions of foreign workers differed based on their nationalities, the nature and location of their work, and the conditions under which they were recruited or impressed into their jobs. Workers from Eastern Europe tended to live and work under harsher conditions than those from Western Europe. In the final phase of the war, foreign workers, especially those from Eastern Europe, frequently fell victim to atrocities. An estimated 170,000 laborers from Eastern Europe died inside the Reich during the war, a figure that does not include Jews or Soviet POWs, who were killed in far greater numbers.[11] For most Jews, inside Germany and elsewhere, forced labor eventually proved to be a step on the path to murder.

Some influential Nazis and police officials concerned with questions of internal security and racial purity objected to the importation of so many non-Germans, especially the ones from Poland and elsewhere in Eastern Europe. The labor was needed, however, so a certain tension developed between economic necessity and ideology. Propaganda adjusted to this contradictory situation by emphasizing the dangers posed to Germans by socializing with foreign workers, and, especially in the case of the Eastern workers, by driving home the message about their racial and cultural inferiority. Germans were instructed to show no solidarity with the foreigners, who, rather than being part of the People's Community, were there to serve it.[12]

The German Occupation of Poland

In surveying the Nazi empire, special attention must be given to Poland, which was subjected to a ruthless occupation starting with the German invasion in September 1939.[13] Measures targeted at Polish Jews will be examined in more detail in the following section, but they must be seen as having been part and parcel of a racial reordering of Poland. The German attack on Poland involved extreme violence employed with premeditation against non-combatants. Operation Tannenberg was the codename for a German plan to decapitate Polish society and neutralize centers of potential Polish resistance. Special task forces (*Einsatzgruppen*) formed by the SS were sent into Poland with orders to kill thousands of members of the Polish elite in the intelligentsia, the clergy, the aristocracy, the military officer corps, and the Jewish community.[14] The German army lent support to Tannenberg, thus implicating it in a massive premeditated war crime at the very outset of the conflict.[15]

After its conquest by Germany and the Soviet Union in 1939, Poland was partitioned into three regions. The eastern section of the country was integrated into the Soviet Union, while the western part became part of the German Reich. The south-central section of Poland was transformed into a zone of German colonial rule called the General Government. The areas in the west that were annexed by Germany had held significant populations of ethnic Germans living among the Polish majority. The largest of these areas, now designated as the Gau Wartheland, was placed under the leadership of Arthur Greiser, who intended to transform the region into a "model Gau" and "a parade ground for National Socialism."[16] Greiser pushed an uncompromising policy of

Germanization in his Gau, suppressing Polish political activity and cultural life. Under Greiser, the persecution of the Polish Catholic church, traditionally a vessel of Polish national identity, was particularly severe, and hundreds of priests were murdered.[17]

Greiser also pushed for forced population transfers of both Poles and Jews as part of the larger Germanization project. By March 1940, tens of thousands of Poles had been deported from the Gau Wartheland into the General Government. The deportation of Jews out of the region could not be completed over the short term for logistical reasons, and thus it became necessary to erect a ghetto in the city of Łódź. Another region annexed by the Reich was located around the city of Katowice in the East Upper Silesian mining and industrial region. Here the deportation of the Polish population could not occur immediately because it was needed for labor. In order to deal with Polish resistance and opposition in the region, the Germans established a concentration camp at Oświęcim (the German name for which is Auschwitz), which eventually developed into a key site of mass murder.[18]

The total number of Poles deported from the annexed territories into the General Government during the war is estimated to have been 365,000. This number does not include Poles who remained in the annexed territories but were forced from their homes to make room for ethnic German settlers. It has been estimated that about three-quarters of a million Poles in the annexed territories were forcibly relocated during the war – not including Jews.[19] The transfer of the Polish population was a traumatic and often violent undertaking. Poles who refused to go along were beaten or killed. The deportation procedure often involved forcing the deported Poles into overcrowded rail freight cars, without food, water, or heat.[20]

About 350,000 ethnic Germans from Germany and elsewhere in Europe had been resettled into the annexed areas of Poland by 1944. Germanization included a systematic sorting through of the population to separate Germans from Poles, a task sometimes made difficult by the presence of families of mixed ancestry. An elaborate set of criteria applied, including but not limited to biological ancestry. Pure-blooded Germans and those of mixed ancestry who were judged as acceptable for inclusion in the German nation were included in the so-called German Ethnic Register (*Deutsche Volksliste*).[21]

The Germanization effort was the responsibility of multiple agencies, but a special role was given to the SS under Heinrich Himmler, who in October 1939 was appointed Reich Commissioner for the Strengthening of Germandom, thus adding to his already considerable list of offices. Academic experts were hired to help plan the German colonization, addressing issues of agriculture, transportation, and infrastructure. The planning began with the annexed territories and was eventually extended into the General Government. After the attack on the Soviet Union in June 1941, planning for the extension of the Nazi empire into the East took place on an ever more megalomaniacal scale. A central figure in this endeavor was Professor Konrad Meyer, an expert in agricultural sociology at the University of Berlin. The term *Generalplan-Ost* came into use as a shorthand for the many different proposals that were in circulation. The work included proposals for the extension of the Nazi empire into Russian territory, and the deportation, enslavement, or extermination of tens of millions of Slavs over a period of decades. The war turned against Germany before the most ambitious of these plans could be operationalized. The so-called "Final Solution of the Jewish Question" was linked ideologically to these monstrous visions for a racially transformed Europe, although it was planned separately and treated as a more urgent and immediate priority. It is not knowable what would have happened to the Slavic peoples of Eastern Europe over the long term had the Nazis won the war, but their fate would likely not have been a pleasant one.[22]

Although planning for the Germanization of conquered regions occurred in various SS agencies, a much broader circle of Germans saw themselves as the beneficiaries of the colonization project. Many German women, for example, willingly and even enthusiastically participated as settlers in Poland. Some saw themselves as pursuing a womanly mission to secure Germandom against the threat posed by Slavs ad Jews. The German colonial project, as they saw it, required their expertise as homemakers and mothers. For some, the colonial project was considered a patriotic adventure, while for others, such as young female teachers, the East offered new professional opportunities.[23]

While Germanization efforts in occupied Poland focused on the annexed territories, they also extended into the General Government. About 100,000 Germans from the Reich and an additional 9,000 ethnic Germans from other parts of Europe settled in the General Government by 1944.[24] Under the direction of Hans Frank, a Nazi "old fighter" who had been appointed governor general by Hitler, the region at first served as a dumping ground for unwanted populations, a staging area for future German military operations in the East, and a source of raw materials and labor for exploitation by the German economy. It attracted German business enterprises and war profiteers seeking to exploit Polish (including Jewish) labor, as well as national resources. As initially conceived, the Poles in the General Government were to be denied an autonomous national existence permanently. Later in the war, however, when the tide turned against Germany, Frank gave some thought to the prospect of setting up the region as a rump Polish nation within the German sphere of influence, but he never acted on the idea.[25]

There were also forced resettlements in the West. After the defeat of France, the provinces of Alsace and Lorraine, long objects of dispute between Germany and France, were annexed to the Reich. The regions, which had been French since 1918, were now subjected to political "coordination" and Germanization. German authorities engaged in the suppression of the French language and cultural life, and undertook purges of French-speaking people from influential positions. In October 1940, about 6,500 Jews were deported from Alsace into unoccupied France. In late 1940 and early 1941, over 100,000 French-speaking inhabitants of Alsace were either deported into unoccupied France or prevented from returning to Alsace after having fled during the fighting. Indicative of the mentality underlying the Germanization effort in Alsace was a legal prohibition on the wearing of French berets.[26]

Germanization efforts in the Czech Lands – the so-called Reich Protectorate of Bohemia and Moravia – offer an instructive example of the interplay between ideology and pragmatism. Despite the Nazis' general contempt for Slavs, they had a higher opinion of the Czechs, who had, it was believed, undergone extensive racial mixing with Germans on account of their longtime domination by Austria within the Habsburg Empire. In essence, as Nazis saw it, the level of Czech racial stock had been raised by this mixing. Czech blood was considered, according to one expert, "some of the best in the Slavic area." As part of the Germanization of the Czech Lands, therefore, Czechs deemed capable of Germanization would be allowed to stay; the remainder would be expelled. The Czech nation would no longer exist in the end.

An elaborate system of racial selection and testing was set up in the Protectorate. Racial experts from the SS Race and Settlement Main Office examined people from various segments of society, focusing largely on school children, who would be the central objects of long-term Germanization. The experts examined the shapes and sizes of heads, the roundness of chins, and other physical features. Many Czechs were certified for Germanization in this manner. The others, however, could not be deported immediately because they were needed as workers. The Protectorate had been integrated into the German economy since 1939, and, for practical reasons, the Germanization process would have to take place over an extended period. Plans for dealing with the non-Germanizable segments of the Czech population shifted over time. If expulsion could not be done for economic reasons, then perhaps mass sterilization could be achieved through systematic exposure to x-rays.[27]

The Persecution of the Jews, 1939–41: Segregation and Forced Labor in Germany and Beyond

Prior to the war, Jews had been defined racially, deprived of their jobs and property, socially isolated, and physically terrorized.[28] Until September 1939, 247,000 Jews had emigrated from the German Reich, not including Austria, while tens of thousands more had departed from post-Anschluss Austria. Slightly over 200,000 Jews remained in the Reich by the end of 1939. Between the beginning of the war and October 1941, when emigration was cut off for Jews, only an additional 30,000–35,000 were able to leave.[29] As it had become exceedingly difficult for Jews to emigrate to Britain, France, the United States, or Palestine, many German Jews undertook arduous journeys to safety, passing through places like Shanghai and Iran.[30] In Germany, organizing emigration was the responsibility of Jewish organizations, most notably the Reich Association of German Jews, the representatives of which faced diminishing resources, lack of cooperation from German officials, and harassment and chicanery from the Gestapo. The obstacles thrown up by the German bureaucracy were counterproductive to the stated goals of driving the Jews out of the country, but disdain for Jews tended to supersede the logic of cooperation.[31]

The Jews still in the country were concentrated in larger municipalities, where they were subjected to closer surveillance and control. They were largely impoverished, socially marginalized, and severely restricted in their movements and actions. In late 1939, about 25 percent of German Jews were receiving financial support of some kind from the Reich Association. They were singled out for reduced food and clothing rations and limited to shopping in specific stores. In January 1940 in Berlin, Jews were allowed to shop for groceries only during a specified two-hour period in the middle of the day. In July, Jews were prohibited from having telephone lines in their homes. In August, the time window for shopping was reduced to a single hour between 4:00 and 5:00 pm. They were also subject to an 8:00 pm curfew.[32]

While some "Aryans" helped their Jewish friends and neighbors, others believed that the Jews were not suffering enough. Authorities received complaints about Jews supposedly hoarding food and other provisions, or purchasing milk and poultry illegally directly from farmers. Some Germans demanded that Jews be banned from buses, trams, and other forms of mass transportation. People even denounced their neighbors for not breaking off friendships with Jews.[33]

The number of Jews in German concentration camps increased significantly after the beginning of the war. Although most of the Jews who had been arrested and put in camps after the Kristallnacht pogrom in

November 1938 had been released after a few weeks, some of them were still there when the war started. On September 7, 1939, the police were ordered to arrest all male Jews over the age of 16 who possessed Polish citizenship. A few weeks later, Heinrich Himmler announced that Jews engaging in "behavior hostile to the state" would be sent to camps. After April 1940, Jews were released from camps only if they could prove that they could emigrate in the immediate future. Otherwise, they would remain in the camps until the end of the war.[34]

The first wartime deportations of Jews from Nazi Germany were undertaken in late 1939 and early 1940 as part and parcel of the broader ethnic reorganization of Central Europe envisaged by the Nazi leadership. Initial deportations were organized by Adolf Eichmann, the Gestapo's point man for Jewish issues, with the approval of Reinhard Heydrich, the head of the Reich Security Main Office, and Hitler himself. The idea was to relocate a large number of Jews from the Reich into the General Government in Poland in order to make room inside the Reich for the settlement of ethnic Germans from South Tyrol in Italy and from the Soviet-occupied regions of Poland and the Baltic states. An additional reason for the deportation of Jews from Vienna was the desire of the city government to de-Judaize the city and move Aryans into much sought-after urban dwellings.[35]

In October 1939, over 5,000 Jews were deported from Vienna, Moravská Ostrava in the Protectorate, and Katowice in annexed Poland. Most were sent to Nisko, near Lublin, in the General Government. For good measure, train cars carrying deported Roma and Sinti were coupled to a train carrying deported Jews from Vienna to Poland. As these transports were organized and implemented hastily, the passengers were subjected to harsh conditions during travel. In December, officials in the Reich Security Main Office began to discuss the possibility of using these deportations as an opportunity to establish a Jewish reservation in the General Government, potentially under Jewish self-administration. A memorandum regarding this possibility referred to the proposal as a "Final Solution" of the Jewish question in Germany, showing that this phrase, which ultimately came to be associated with mass murder, had a different connotation at this earlier moment. Ultimately the prospect of a Jewish reservation in the General Government was nixed by Hans Frank, the governor general, because he did not want additional Jews brought into the region under his control.[36]

To justify the cruel treatment of Jews, and to prepare Germans psychologically for even harsher measures to come, the government pursued a concerted propaganda campaign designed to lay the responsibility for the war at the feet of "World Jewry." In a speech delivered on July 19,

1940, Hitler blamed the war on "Jewish-capitalist warmongers." During the initial phase of the war, the Jews were linked to Britain and France; later they were tied to the Soviet Union and the United States. The propaganda portrayed the governing classes and social elites of Britain and France as having been infiltrated by Jewish money and, through intermarriage, by Jewish blood. By extension, the Jews still living in Germany represented a fifth column and a national security threat merely by virtue of their racial affiliation.[37]

While it is impossible to ascertain how widely these accusations were believed in German society, they most certainly did resonate in some segments of the population. In September 1939, the Security Service and police officials recorded reports from informers claiming that "the realization that the Jew alone bears the guilt for the war has penetrated everywhere." One citizen expressed the opinion that the death of every German soldier should be avenged by the killing of ten Jews. Many people were convinced that German Jews were conducting espionage for Britain and France. A resident of the city of Münster concluded that German-Jewish emigrants were helping the English to guide their bombs onto targets in German cities. How else could one explain why a bomb landed directly in front of the local headquarters of the air force? A second resident of Münster doubted that peace with Britain would be possible, because war with Germany was desired by "World Jewry" and the "Jewified English Government." Similarly, an audience of women in Munich warmly received a lecture sponsored by the National Socialist Women's League in which they learned how the entire upper crust of French society had become saturated with Jews.[38]

At the same time, the intensifying antisemitic persecution and propaganda of the early phase of the war generated sympathy for Jews in some quarters. There were German shopkeepers who persisted in their normal friendly interactions with Jews, a transgression that resulted in denunciation to the authorities. Some religious Christians saw the war not as the fault of the Jews, but as God's punishment for Germany's unjust treatment of his chosen people. In a report on German public attitudes prepared in 1940, the Social Democratic Party in exile noted a disproportionately high degree of buy-in to antisemitic propaganda among young Germans who had been socialized after 1933, while older Germans were more resistant to it.[39]

The abandonment of the scheme for a Jewish reservation in the General Government compelled the German leadership to devise interim measures to address the continued presence of Jews in the German Reich. These measures took two basic forms: segregation and forced labor, both of which had already been imposed on Jews in the months before the beginning of the war. These approaches also mirrored actions taken against the Jews in German-occupied Poland, which will be discussed below.

In many, but not all, German cities, Jews were forced out of their residences and crowded into apartment buildings that were designated as "Jew Houses" (*Judenhäuser*). Physically concentrating Jews in this way fulfilled several goals simultaneously. It simplified the surveillance and control of the Jews, streamlined the eventual process of emigration or deportation, and freed up the homes and apartments previously inhabited by the Jews for deserving Aryan families. By segregating Jewish living quarters from those of the rest of German society, the Jew Houses also validated the stigmatization of Jews as dangerous. The Jew Houses were instituted more thoroughly in some cities than in others. They were established, for example, in Vienna and Berlin, but less so in Munich, where many of the remaining Jews were housed in a camp in the Milbertshofen district on the edge of the city. Some cities, like Dresden, employed combinations of Jew Houses and camps.[40] The Jew Houses tended to suffer from overcrowding, poor ventilation, bedbugs, inadequate cooking and eating facilities, bad plumbing, and unhygienic toilets.[41] Victor Klemperer, a literary scholar whose diary from the Nazi years has become an important document for historians, described the Jew House in Dresden where he lived as a "superior concentration camp."[42]

The imposition of forced labor on German Jews was partially a response to the ongoing national labor shortage and partially a method for humiliating Jews, who were accused by Nazis and other antisemites of harboring an aversion to honest, physical labor. Unemployed Jews had already been subject to forced labor assignments since 1938, but the practice was adopted more broadly after the outbreak of war. It was then expanded in the spring of 1940 once it became clear that the Jews of Germany would not be deported immediately. All Jewish men between 18 and 55, and women between 18 and 50, were required to register for labor assignments, including industrial and agricultural jobs.

The Jews were assigned to jobs in armaments factories but also performed street cleaning and snow shoveling for municipalities, and worked on public infrastructure projects, such as road-building. Some worked in forestry and gardening jobs. Many of the Jewish women were given jobs in textile production. The Jewish forced laborers lived in segregated Jewish housing in German cities, but also in labor camps set up near work sites. Working conditions were often harsh and humiliating, although they varied by employer. Wages were a good deal lower than for other workers in the same firm or organization. A total of 54,000 German Jews performed forced labor inside the Reich, representing roughly one-quarter of the Jews who remained after the beginning of the war.[43]

In German-occupied Poland, like in Germany, concentrating and seg-regating Jews, and subjecting them to forced labor, were not part of a grand plan prepared in advance, but rather an improvisation to address the immediate problem of the presence of an unwanted group of people. With the creation of Jewish ghettoes in Poland, the Germans intended to contain, control, and economically exploit Jews until a more permanent solution could be devised. Starting in late 1939, hundreds of ghettoes were created on occupied Polish territory (including, after June 1941, Polish territory that the Soviets had seized at the beginning of the war). The largest ghettoes were in Warsaw and Cracow, both in the General Government, and in Łódź, in the Gau Wartheland. The administration of daily life in the ghettoes was placed in the hands of Jewish councils, although the ultimate authority lay with German occupation officials. A byproduct of the creation of the ghettoes welcomed by the Germans in 1939 and 1940 was that about 300,000 Jews fled further into the East, crossing over into the Soviet-occupied part of Poland. The Jewish ghet-toes faced profound challenges when it came to housing, feeding, and caring for the medical needs of their inhabitants. Eventually, the Nazis closed the ghettoes, sending most of their residents to be murdered in death camps. But even before the dissolution of the ghettoes, hundreds of thousands of Jews perished inside them as a consequence of starvation and disease.[44]

The inhabitants of the ghettoes formed a pool of workers for the Nazi forced labor program. Many worked for German business enterprises and war profiteers who descended on Poland after the German con-quest. In addition, tens of thousands of Polish Jews were deported from the annexed territories of Poland to the "Old Reich" to work there.[45] In the General Government, the treatment of Jewish laborers eventually became the focus of a disagreement between German economic officials, whose main priority was productivity, and ideologues in the SS, who preferred to see the Jewish population reduced through attrition. This disagreement continued even after the mass murder of Jews began in the General Government in 1942. Thus, for Jews in Poland during the war, serving as a forced laborer could be lifesaving, a situation dramatized in the well-known Holocaust film *Schindler's List*.[46]

After the German victory over France in June 1940, a new possibility for solving the "Jewish Question" seemed to present itself in the form of the French colony of Madagascar, a large island in the Indian Ocean. The "Madagascar Plan," as it is known to historians, might seem pre-posterous from today's perspective, but was taken seriously in Berlin in 1940. Shipping European Jews to Madagascar had been discussed in both antisemitic and Jewish circles going back to the 1920s. The idea was embraced by antisemites in Poland in the 1930s. As a colonial possession of France, Madagascar became relevant after the signing of the armistice. The possibility of using the island as a Jewish reservation attracted considerable interest in the German Foreign Office and the Reich Security Main Office, generating numerous memoranda and planning documents. One of Germany's preeminent statisticians submitted an expert report testifying to the feasibility of relocating 6.5 million Jews to the island and sustaining them there over the long term. The plan seemed to hold much promise during the summer of 1940, when the German leadership was still hoping for a rapid conclusion to the war, but gradually faded from the agenda when the war continued on account of Britain's perseverance. By late 1940, as the attention of Hitler and others in the German leadership shifted to an attack on the Soviet Union, which was planned for the following spring, Madagascar had disappeared from the agenda as a matter of serious discussion.[47]

In August 1940, when Hitler informed the Foreign Office that he wished to deport all Jews out of Europe after the war, he was not expecting the war to last very much longer. The forced transfer of Europe's Jews to some overseas location was still the subject of high-level discussion at the end of the year. Hitler made no secret of his desire to clear Europe of Jews. In a speech in the Reichstag in January 1941 on the eighth anniversary of his coming to power, he referred to the "prophecy" he had uttered publicly two years earlier, threatening to exterminate the Jews of Europe in the event of a war for which they were to blame.[48] With schemes for the forced relocation of the Jews to the General Government and Madagascar having been abandoned in 1940, the German leadership seemed no closer to achieving its goal of a territorial Final Solution. This discrepancy between the intensions of the Nazi regime and its means for realizing them formed the background for later decisions to solve the "Jewish Question" by means of mass murder.

The German invasion of the Soviet Union in June 1941 opened the genocidal phase of the Nazi campaign against the Jews. In the autumn of that year, the Jews of Germany were marked for deportation and eventual murder. Jewish emigration had slowed to a trickle during the war, and about 170,000 Jews lived in the German Reich at the time of the attack on the Soviet Union. They were impoverished, segregated, subjected to forced labor, and socially isolated. But before their *en masse* deportation began in October 1941, the Nazi regime heaped one additional collective humiliation on them. On September 1, 1941, the government ordered that all Jews in the Reich would have to wear a yellow Jewish star on the outside of their clothing, on their left breast, when appearing in public. Victor Klemperer, writing in his diary, described how the stigma of the yellow star was "the worst blow so far" for Jews whom he knew.[49] Many Germans welcomed the marking of Jews, whom they regarded as deserving of such public degradation. But other Germans had sympathy for the Jews, and still others were simply embarrassed.[50]

The Escalation of Racial Policy inside Germany: The Mass Murder of the Disabled

Germany was by no means the only country to pursue a program of compulsory eugenic sterilization. When compared with the United States, for example, where such policies were implemented on a state-by-state basis, Germany was a relative latecomer – the first sterilization law in the United States had been passed in Indiana in 1907. But while Germany was not the first, it implemented the sterilizations centrally and far more efficiently than other countries. We can say, therefore, that, with regard to sterilizations, Germany had been exceptional only in its thoroughness. In contrast, Germany was entirely exceptional in a different respect: it was the only country in which eugenically motivated policy escalated to the systematic murder of disabled persons.[51]

This special status of Germany among the countries that practiced eugenics is attributable to several factors. First, the Nazi eugenics program was coupled to a broader policy of racial purification, or "racial hygiene," which was at the very core of Nazi ideology. Second, Hitler, who was personally very interested in the killing project, was uncommonly unscrupulous in pursuit of his ideological goals, having previously resorted to murder and other extreme measures. Third, the beginning of World War II in Europe in September 1939 offered the Nazi leadership an opportunity to implement a maximalist version of its eugenics program under the cover of war, a condition during which populations normally show greater deference to the authority of their governments. And fourth, the Nazi regime saw the murder of disabled people not merely as a eugenic measure, but as a way to remove what it saw as the economic burden of having to care for "unproductive" persons at a time of national sacrifice.

The last-mentioned of these factors had a history in Germany going back to the period immediately following World War I. In 1920, two prominent German scholars, Karl Binding, a professor of law at the University of Leipzig, and Alfred Hoche, a professor of psychiatry at the University of Freiburg, had published a book titled *Permission for the Killing of Lives Unworthy of Living*. The volume appeared during a time of economic upheaval and shortages in the immediate wake of the war. The authors criticized the allocation of precious economic resources to maintaining the lives of institutionalized patients with severe mental disabilities. They painted the following picture for their readers:

If one imagines a battlefield strewn with thousands of dead young men, or a mine in which methane explosions have trapped hundreds of industrious workers, and if, at the same time, one juxtaposes that image with our mental asylums, with their care for their living inmates – one is deeply shaken by the shocking discordance between the sacrifice of the finest examples of humanity on the largest scale, on the one hand, and by the greatest care that is devoted to lives that are not only absolutely worthless, but even of negative value, on the other hand.[52]

The argument posited by Binding and Hoche in favor of allowing the killing of certain mentally-ill patients drew equally from eugenical thinking and a hyper-utilitarian conception of a society emphasizing the productivity of its members. Neither Binding nor Hoche were Nazis; Binding died in 1920, and while Hoche lived to 1943, he was critical of the Nazi regime. Nevertheless, the two men laid out what essentially became the rationale for the Nazi program for the murder of disabled Germans during World War II.[53]

In some of the older literature, the Nazi program for the mass murder of the disabled is described as a "euthanasia program," but this phrase is now avoided by many historians. The word euthanasia, generally defined as the painless killing of a patient suffering from an incurable painful disease, connotes an act performed on behalf of the suffering patient. The Nazi program under discussion here, however, was carried out not for the benefit of suffering patients, but rather, as its protagonists saw it, for the benefit of the German Volk. Historians, therefore, tend to refer to this particular Nazi crime as the "murder of the disabled" (in German, *Krankenmord*).

The killings began soon after the outbreak of the war, about one and a half years before the Nazi regime initiated the mass murder of Europe's Jews. The immediate catalyst for the introduction of the program was the case of a severely disabled infant in a children's clinic in Leipzig, whose Nazi parents wanted it killed. As such a killing would have been illegal, the parents appealed to Hitler through his personal chancellery. Hitler granted his permission, although the authorization to kill a hospitalized child was contrary to German law. On a practical level, Hitler's will counted for more than the law. Hitler, who had been personally very interested in implementing such a program, granted his permission over the objections of several high-level subordinates, most notably Hans Heinrich Lammers, the chief of the Reich Chancellery. Hitler charged Karl Brandt, one of his personal physicians, and Philipp Bouhler, the chief of staff of the Chancellery of the Führer, with planning and leading the project.

The agency built by Brandt and Bouhler to coordinate the killing of the disabled was headquartered at Tiergartenstrasse 4 in Berlin, and therefore came to be known by the abbreviation T4. As the killings were

Figure 8.2 Patients being transferred from a psychiatric hospital to a killing center, 1941 (Pressestelle der Diakonie Neuendettelsau).

to be kept secret, T4 operated a network of cover organizations, such as the "Reich Working Committee for Cure and Nursing Homes," and engaged in massive forgery of documents to cover its tracks. The killings began with children, but from the very beginning the intention was to expand the program to adolescents and adults. T4 operated from September 1939 through the late summer of 1941.

Unlike the sterilization program, T4 targeted Germans who lived in institutions dedicated to the care of people with disabilities so severe as to make life in normal society impossible. The T4 office in Berlin required hospitals and sanitaria to submit information about each patient institutionalized on account of a serious disability. The information submitted to T4 was then examined in Berlin by a panel of doctors, who decided on the life and death of each patient. Those patients who had been selected for killing were then transferred to one of several medical facilities around Germany that had been retrofitted to kill patients, sometimes with poison injections, but more usually by carbon monoxide gas (see Figure 8.2). The corpses of the victims were then transferred to a crematorium for disposal. While the vast majority of those killed in T4 were "Aryan," a "special operation" aimed at Jewish patients inside Germany claimed about 1,000 lives.[54]

Three important points should be emphasized about the process described above. First, the killing process was administered by medical personnel, including doctors, nurses, and administrators of hospitals and sanitoria. Although much attention has been given to Nazi doctors who performed gruesome medical experiments on concentration camp prisoners during World War II, the magnitude of the involvement of medical professionals in T4 was actually a good deal greater. Second, it was with T4 that the Nazi regime broke through the moral and psychological barrier to mass murder. The T4 killings proceeded through 1940 and early 1941, at precisely the time that the Nazi leadership was trying to decide what to do with the dramatically expanded number of Jews who had been brought under its control. The decision to murder a population of highly vulnerable victims inside Germany, the vast majority of whom were "Aryans," thus helped pave the way for the decision to murder the Jews. Third, the basic outline of the killing process in T4 provided a model for the mass murder of Jews in German-occupied Europe. The process involved, first, the identification of the victims; second, their transfer to a centralized killing facility; third, their killing with poison gas; and fourth, and finally, the cremation of their bodies. In fact, many of the officials who had set up this killing process for T4 were later transferred over to agencies charged with the mass murder of the Jews, where they applied the experience gained through the murder of the disabled to the larger genocidal project.

Unlike the sterilization program, which was open and legal, the T4 operation was illegal and secret. But it proved impossible to keep a murder program of such scale, carried out domestically, under cover. Knowledge of the killings was widespread among employees at the hospitals and sanitoriums, and some of them objected to it. They shared the information with others, including their priests or pastors. In addition, many of the families of the victims developed suspicions. The standard operating procedure of T4 was to generate counterfeit death notices to be sent to the families. When such forgeries numbered in the tens of thousands, it was inevitable that clues about the truth would filter through. Sometimes the system generated duplicate death notices for one patient, listing different causes of death.

As knowledge of the killings spread, objections multiplied and percolated up to the national leadership. There were critical views in the civil service, the judiciary, and especially the churches. In July 1940, Theophil Wurm, the Protestant bishop of Württemberg, protested the killings to the ministers of the interior and justice. A few weeks later, a group of Catholic bishops lodged a formal objection with Lammers at the Reich Chancellery. Michael Faulhaber, the archbishop of Munich, arguably Germany's most prominent Catholic official, submitted his own protest to the minister of justice. In September 1940, Anna Haag confided to her diary that "everywhere here there is outrage over the murder of the insane and the mentally ill. What incredible barbarity!"[55] In December 1940, Pope Pius XII condemned the killing of the disabled in Germany in a public statement. This criticism culminated with a series of Sunday sermons by Clemens von Galen, the Catholic bishop of Münster, a city in northwest Germany. Galen's sermons, which condemned the killings in fire-and-brimstone terms, were published as a brochure and distributed around the country. Most historians of T4 agree that it was Galen's protest that prompted the regime to close down the program.

The impact of Galen's sermons must be understood in the context of the chronology of World War II. On June 22, 1941, Germany attacked the Soviet Union, dramatically expanding the magnitude of the war in Europe. Galen delivered his sermons in the weeks immediately following this event. The German leadership was very conscious of the need to maintain domestic morale and public support as the war expanded. A phasing out of T4 would thus remove a source of dissent within the population.

Historians disagree about one possible additional factor explaining the end of T4, namely that the leaders of T4 could claim that the program had essentially met its goals. The total number of patients killed had reached 70,000, roughly one-tenth of 1 percent of the German population. This number corresponded to the one-in-ten-thousand kill rate calculated as desirable by racial hygiene experts at T4. Some of the older scholarship on T4 cites this number as evidence that T4 believed its mission to have been accomplished. But more recent research shows that the leadership and medical staff at T4 were surprised by the stop order and hoped to continue the killing beyond 1941.[56]

The termination of T4 did not, in any event, put an end to the systematic killing of persons who were considered "unproductive." In an operation codenamed 14f13, prisoners at concentration camps who were old, sick, and no longer able to work were selected to be killed. Like T4, this was not a eugenics measure per se, as the victims were not selected based on disability, but rather according to a cold-bloodedly efficient rationing of resources. Historians estimate that 15,000 to 20,000 prisoners were killed as part of this operation. Moreover, many thousands more were murdered as the result of initiatives that, starting in 1942, continued the practices of T4 on a regional level. The rationale for these killings was to more efficiently husband the resources of a medical system that was coming under increasing strain as the result of mounting civilian and military casualties during the war. These decentralized programs of mass killing show that the fundamental assumptions that had undergirded T4 had become anchored in many parts of the German health care system even after T4 had been dissolved.[57]

9   The War of Annihilation

For Hitler, a war against the Soviet Union was never a question of if, but rather one of when and under what circumstances. While the timing and strategy of a German attack might be determined based on military contingencies, the necessity of war against the Soviet Union was the result of Hitler's fundamental ideological commitments. The war would allow Germany to attain two goals simultaneously, acquiring living space (*Lebensraum*) for the German Volk in the form of agriculturally useful territory, and destroying the Communist state, which Hitler regarded as an outpost of "World Jewry." Because of the nature of the enemy, as Hitler and many other Nazis saw it, this would be a war of annihilation in which the normal rules of warfare and treatment of civilian populations would not apply.

By late 1941, German power over the continent of Europe extended from the Pyrenees to deep inside the Soviet Union. The German conquests, undertaken by a large, modern military, backed by a technologically and industrially modern economy, and wedded to an ideology of expansion and domination, unleashed violence on a previously unimaginable scale. Tens of millions were killed throughout Europe as the result of combat between armies, war waged against civilians, and genocide.

After providing a summary of the major military developments from 1941 to 1944, this chapter will focus on Nazi crimes in German-occupied Europe resulting from the attempt to impose German domination and the racist vision of Nazism. The Final Solution, a distinct program of mass murder targeted at Europe's Jews, and a top priority among the highest levels of the Nazi leadership, must be understood within this broader context of the attempted racial reordering within the Nazi empire.

Chronology of the War, 1941–44

Hitler had begun to discuss a campaign against the Soviet Union already in late May 1940, while the fighting in France was still ongoing.[1] At the end of July 1940, his decision became firm, and he ordered his military assistants to plan an attack for the spring of 1941. As the planning proceeded, some military advisors urged Hitler to delay the reckoning with the Soviets until the victory over Britain had been attained. Hitler was not dissuaded, however, arguing that, if Britain were still in the conflict, a quick victory over the Soviets would convince Britain to agree to German demands. Removing the Soviet Union from the conflict would also kill British hopes for American intervention, as a Soviet collapse would strengthen Japan's position and keep the Americans focused on the Pacific. Consistent with this thinking, Germany forged a Tripartite Pact with Italy and Japan in September 1940. Japan recognized the leadership roles of Germany and Italy in Europe's "New Order," and the European powers reciprocated by recognizing Japan's hegemonic role in East Asia. The three countries agreed to come to one another's assistance in the event of an attack by another country; the pact was clearly targeted at the United States.

Hitler did not expect the campaign against the Soviet Union, which was governed, as he saw it, by racially degenerate Judeo-Bolshevists, to be especially long or difficult. Germany would win in a matter of weeks, and then be able to refocus its efforts with a strengthened hand against Britain, if necessary. Hitler's ideologically determined underestimation of Soviet military potential proved fateful, as it led to precisely the kind of two-front war that his strategy had been designed to avoid, and therefore also eventually led to the defeat and destruction of his country.

Germany invaded the Soviet Union on June 22, 1941, in an operation dubbed "Barbarossa." German troops were joined by those from Romania, Hungary, Slovakia, and Italy, countries with anti-Communist, Fascist, or right-wing authoritarian governments, and all of which hoped to share in the spoils of the expected victory, in terms of territory, status, or Germany's favor. Finland joined the conflict on Germany's side a short time later, as did units of volunteers from Spain, the Netherlands, Denmark, Belgium, France, and Norway.[2] The responses of ordinary Germans ranged from apprehension to hubris. Friedrich Kellner, who closely observed life in the small community of Laubach in north-central Germany, kept a detailed diary in which he recorded comments from the local townspeople. The bailiff of the court where Kellner worked warned that "we will not have an easy task with Russia." But a local military man predicted that "Russia will be finished soon." In a doctor's waiting room, Kellner's interlocutors boasted about the initial German victories, leading Kellner to angrily confide to his diary, "a mania for victory rules the nation."[3]

Surprise, tactical advantage, and superiority in arms did, in fact, allow the forces of Germany and its allies to quickly drive eastward into the Soviet Union, occupying huge swaths of land, killing hundreds of thousands of Soviet troops, and taking hundreds of thousands more prisoner, all within the initial weeks of the invasion. Following behind the German army, special task forces (*Einsatzgruppen*) initiated systematic murder targeted at political officials and Jews. The Germans moved quickly toward Moscow and laid siege to Leningrad (now St. Petersburg), as the result of which a million Soviet citizens would eventually die of starvation. In November 1941, German forces were poised to take Moscow.

The Red Army launched a major counterattack in early December 1941. The German army, suffering from attrition and an overextension of supply lines, had to retreat. The battle of Moscow was the first major defeat for the German army since the start of the war in September 1939. But a Soviet counteroffensive along the entirety of the front stalled, and the Red Army, for its part, suffered massive casualties. The Germans, however, had also suffered over a million casualties (killed and wounded) by the end of 1941 and were plagued by equipment shortages. Food was not a problem for the German forces, as they had taken control of food production in Ukraine, but oil was in short supply, especially as the motorized units of the German army depended on it (as did the German air force and navy). Hitler tried to compensate for this shortage by ordering his forces to push further in the southeast toward Soviet oil fields in the Caucasus and by developing synthetic oil production. At the same time, the Soviet armed forces and Soviet society held up much better under the German assault than the Nazis, who operated according to racist stereotypes of inferior Slavs, had expected, and Soviet industry proved capable of producing quality weapons in large numbers, particularly the T-34 tank.

On December 7, 1941, Japanese forces attacked the American naval base at Pearl Harbor in Hawaii. This attempt to neutralize the American Pacific fleet marked the culmination of tensions between the two countries after the United States had been pushing back against Japanese expansionism in East Asia. Germany's pact with Japan did not require it to join in the conflict against the United States, as Japan had been the aggressor, but Germany declared war on the US on December 11 in any case. Hitler had psychological, strategic, and ideological reasons for taking this step. The United States had been providing material and military assistance to Britain since the beginning of the war, so entering an actual state of war with the US produced a sense of clarity. Hitler saw the US as a Jew-dominated, racially mongrelized plutocracy. Having just recently, in the fall of 1941, ordered the murder of all European Jews, Hitler saw a military reckoning with the United States as fitting neatly into his ideological understanding of the conflict. Better that the reckoning take place now, while Japan was fighting the US at the same time, than later. Now was also better than later because the US would need time to rearm. Hitler's ideological blinders also prevented him from recognizing that the entry of the US into World War I in April 1917 had led directly to Germany's defeat in that conflict. He was convinced that a "stab in the back" by domestic traitors, rather than the arrival of fresh American troops, had caused Germany's defeat in 1918. As it had done in 1917, now in 1941 the United States, with its entry into the war, would bring to bear its large population and enormous industrial capacity in the form of ships, planes, and troops.[4]

On the German–Soviet front, momentum shifted back to the Germans during the summer of 1942, but the push to the oil fields in the southeast continued to overextend German supply lines. In August 1942, the German Sixth Army and other Axis troops reached Stalingrad, a strategically important city on the Volga River. One of the momentous battles of World War II unfolded here over the following five months. The German air force reduced Stalingrad to rubble, but the German army subsequently suffered horrendous losses in street fighting inside the city. After the Red Army crushed two Romanian armies operating to the north and south, by late November it had encircled and trapped 300,000 German troops inside the city. Attempts by other German armies to come to their assistance having failed, most of them eventually perished, in combat or by starving or freezing to death. About 90,000 German troops finally surrendered on February 2, 1943. Although the Soviets continued to suffer setbacks in other places, Stalingrad marked the turning point in the German–Soviet theater of war. The defeat dealt a blow to German morale and undermined the confidence of Germany's Axis partners in an eventual German victory.

With the Red Army bearing the brunt of the fighting on the ground in Europe, Stalin had been pushing the Western Allies to establish a second front in the West. An Allied invasion of German-occupied France would require lengthy preparation, but, in the meantime, Britain and the United States intensified the air war against Germany elsewhere. In November 1942, an Allied landing in Morocco and Algeria was timed to support a British offensive in Egypt designed to keep German forces from reaching the Middle East. German and Italian troops in North Africa now faced Anglo-American forces in the west and British forces in the east. In July 1943, the Allies invaded Sicily from North Africa, prompting, first, Mussolini's overthrow, and then, in turn, Germany's invasion and occupation of Italy, accompanied by the reinstallation of Mussolini as a German puppet based in the north of the country. In September 1943, the Allies invaded the Italian peninsula and began to fight their way north. Allied forces eventually entered Rome on June 4, 1944.

The air war between Germany and Britain, which had begun in 1940, escalated through 1941 and 1942, with the Americans joining in as well.

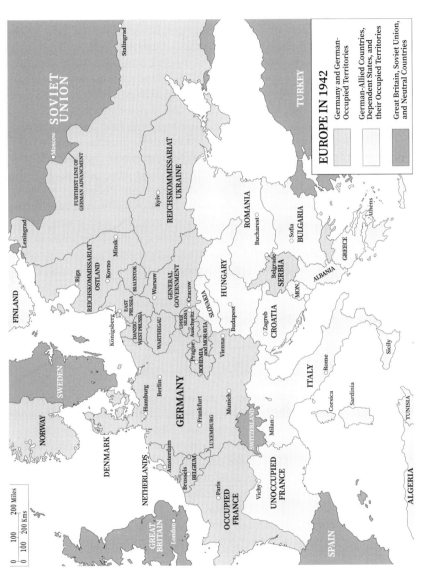

Map 9.1 Europe in 1942.

The Allied air raids helped the Soviets by forcing Germany to divert resources to defending its cities and industrial targets against attack from the air.[5] There was also the hope that the bombing campaign would break the will of the German people. British air raids on German cities increased in frequency and destructiveness during 1942. In July 1943, the first major combined Anglo-American bombing raid on Hamburg created a firestorm in the city that resulted in around 40,000 German deaths. Further major attacks on Frankfurt, Hanover, and other German cities followed in the fall of 1943. Attacks on Berlin, which lay considerably further to the east, also increased in frequency and intensity.

On the Soviet front, the Germans launched their final major offensive in July 1943 at Kursk, initiating one of history's greatest tank battles. The Soviets held their ground, and from this point onward, the momentum remained with them. By June 1944, the Red Army had pushed the Germans back into Ukraine and soon advanced into Poland.

The Allies launched their long-awaited invasion of France on June 6, 1944 (known popularly as D-Day), when a massive amphibian operation placed Allied forces and their equipment on the Normandy coast. Nazi Germany now faced opposing armies approaching from the west, east, and south, and was being pummeled from the air. The prospect of defeat prompted an unsuccessful attempt by military officers to assassinate Hitler on July 20, 1944, and led to an escalation of internal violence inside Germany as both the Nazi elite and ordinary Germans mentally and psychologically confronted the prospect of defeat.

German Atrocities in the Soviet Union

With the imposition of German hegemony on the continent of Europe, Nazi notions of race and racial hierarchy shaped or influenced a broad range of German policies and practices. These included the German treatment of Soviet prisoners of war, the recruitment and impressment of foreign labor, so-called Germanization measures, which included the forced resettlements of hundreds of thousands of people (in addition to the planned forced resettlement of millions more), and the methods used to counter resistance activity in regions occupied by German forces. The genocidal campaign against the Jews must be understood as part and parcel of this broader effort by Nazi Germany to create a new order in Europe.

On March 30, 1941, while the German military was preparing for Barbarossa, Hitler spoke before 250 high-ranking military officers. He characterized the impending conflict with the Soviet Union as a "struggle between two ideologies." He characterized Communism as a form of "social criminality" that posed a "monstrous danger for the future." Therefore, he explained, traditional notions of soldierly comradeship should not apply in the war against the Soviet Union. "The Communist was and is not a comrade," he continued, and the war should be seen as a "war of extermination" (*Vernichtungskampf*). Referring to Communist political officers, Hitler instructed that "commissars are criminals and should be dealt with as such."[6]

Based on the Führer's instructions, the German army implemented the so-called Commissar Order, according to which the political officers embedded in Red Army units were to be identified, sorted out, and executed. There would be a division of labor between the army and the SS. The military would identify and execute Soviet military commissars, but civilian commissars would be turned over to the SS. This policy, which constituted an egregious violation of the laws of war regarding POWs, was justified by a bit of tortured reasoning. On account of their "barbaric Asiatic methods of combat," Soviet political officers were automatically classified as war criminals without legal protection.[7] The order was worked out by the military high command and issued on June 6, 1941, sixteen days prior to the invasion. The order was carried out on a widescale basis (although not universally) within the Wehrmacht, even though professionally trained German officers were clearly aware of its illegality. They carried it out nonetheless, whether out of a sense of military discipline, in pursuit of a deeply ingrained anti-Bolshevism, or some combination of both. The minority of officers who objected or avoided executing the order did so on moral grounds or for reasons of military professionalism. There is no reliable estimate of the number of executions carried out by the Wehrmacht, although 4,000 executions have been verified for 1941/42.[8] This number, however, does not include the much larger number of Communist political officers executed by the SS.

The vast majority of these executions were carried out in occupied Polish and Soviet territory, but large numbers of Soviet POWs were also sent to Germany and killed there. The pace at which Soviet soldiers fell into German hands made it impossible to identify the political officers in the field, so much of that process took place inside Germany proper. After the start of Barbarossa, the Reich became dotted by prisoner-of-war camps for Soviet soldiers, who were held in contempt by much of the local German population. "One generally hears that the Russians are not like humans," was how Karl Dürkefälden described the dominant sentiment in and around Hanover.[9] Units of the Gestapo and other German police formations entered the POW camps to interrogate the prisoners. They separated out the suspected political officers, who were sent to concentration camps, where they were eventually shot. About 38,000

Figure 9.1 SS leader Heinrich Himmler inspecting Soviet POWs (Corbis via Getty Images).

Soviet prisoners of war were killed in this way between the summer of 1941 and the summer of 1942. Many of the victims were not political officers at all but were simply Jews whom the Gestapo automatically red-flagged as potential Communist officials.[10]

The mass killing of Soviet prisoners was by no means limited to the political officers. About 3 million Soviet POWs died in German hands during the war (see Figure 9.1). From the very beginning of the war in the East, the fighting saw killings of POWs on both sides. But the Germans took far more prisoners. The mass death among Soviet POWs in German captivity is attributable to several causes: insufficient food and medicine allocated to the maintenance of the POWs; the impro-vised nature of the accommodations for prisoners, which, for example, provided no heat during the winter; and German disdain for the Soviet soldiers, many of whom were not of European origin and therefore quali-fied as dreaded and despised "Asiatics." The deaths of these prisoners of war, it should be emphasized, were an intentional result of German policy and not simply an unfortunate byproduct of war. After a huge number of POWs had come under German control during a brief period after June 1941, the Wehrmacht officials in charge of their imprisonment understood that the food rations allocated to them would lead to mass starvation and death, and they did not change the policy while the dying was happening, mainly in late 1941 and early 1942. There was a conscious decision to undernourish the Soviet POWs to the point of dying. In addition to the food shortages, many of the POW camps lacked heating or even roofs, exposing the undernourished prisoners to the bitterly cold temperatures.[11]

German atrocities in the occupied regions of the Soviet Union also extended to the general population. German measures targeted at Soviet partisans took an enormous toll on unarmed civilians. Soviet citizens were also subjected to mass starvation, forced labor, and forced relocation. The convergence of these policies proved especially lethal in the region of Ukraine. In planning for the invasion of the Soviet Union, German agricultural experts planned to exploit Ukraine as a source of food, specifically grain, to feed the Wehrmacht and to bolster grain supplies in Germany and the areas it controlled. Already before the war, Germany had had to import a significant portion of its food supply, a problem made worse since the war began because of the British blockade. The German plan for Ukraine projected a transfer of grain that would create severe food shortages in the Soviet Union. High-level officials in the SS noted that such a famine would be consistent with Himmler's goal of "the decimation of the Soviet population by thirty million." The plan was not implemented as its originators had envisaged, but starvation did become a weapon used against the Soviet population.[12]

After German setbacks in the East in late 1941, military conscription was broadened to expand the size of the German army. This, in turn, exacerbated the labor shortage. Labor recruitment in German-dominated Europe became more aggressive, and the line between voluntary and forced labor was gradually erased. Workers in Poland and the Soviet Union were pressed into labor by German police and the Wehrmacht. Tens of thousands of workers were essentially kidnapped and sent to Germany or elsewhere in German-occupied Europe. Ukraine was an especially important source of workers "recruited" in this fashion starting in 1942.[13]

Parts of Ukraine were also earmarked for Germanization. One of Heinrich Himmler's pet projects envisaged housing for 10,000 Volhynian Germans in the Zhytomyr region. The project, centered on Hegewald, a former Soviet airbase, consisted of a cluster of ethnic-German agricultural settlements and SS garrisons along a line that would help protect German-controlled Europe from the "Asiatic hordes" further to the east. In 1941/42 the area was cleared of Jews, Ukrainians, and a small number of Roma. The new communities were populated by ethnic Germans from the Volhynia region, these being the descendants of Germans who had migrated to Ukraine in the nineteenth century when it had been part of the Russian Empire. The resettlement of the ethnic Germans began in October 1942. Over 10,000 non-Germans were deported from the area abruptly, and then about 6,000 ethnic Germans were moved in to replace them. Agriculture specialists in the SS Race and Settlement Main Office allotted land. The resettlements continued through March 1943, by which time Hegewald's population had grown to 9,000. The SS organized occupational training so that the community would be properly served by artisans and technicians. In the end, the project failed because it proved difficult in wartime, especially after the war turned against Germany in 1943. But the Hegewald settlement shows that Germanization plans involved more than just Nazi fantasies.[14]

War Crimes in Occupied Europe

As the Soviet Union had been unprepared for the German invasion, resistance to the German occupation in general, and armed partisan activity in particular, were initially fragmented and relatively ineffective. But partisan warfare coalesced into a coordinated campaign during 1942, and then took on greater military significance in 1943 and especially during the Red Army's summer offensive in June 1944. The occupied Soviet territories contained considerable potential for armed resistance. The size of the region was immense, the German supply lines were under stress, and there were Soviet soldiers whose units had been smashed but who had avoided capture. The partisans were often pitiless in their treatment of German troops and Soviet civilians suspected of collaboration. The Soviet secret police (NKVD), which coordinated much of the partisan effort, encouraged an unforgiving approach toward the Nazi invaders. German occupation officials, both civilian and military, tended to treat the partisans as illegitimate "bandits," even though they were defending their country against an invading army prosecuting a war of annihilation. Thus, German methods of anti-partisan warfare were ruthless.

In 1942, the partisans intensified their attacks on German troops and supply lines in White Russia (Belarus). In response, the Wehrmacht developed an anti-partisan plan designed to exterminate resistance using overwhelming force. In late March and early April, a coordinated effort by German army and police units combed through the region southeast of Minsk, destroying villages and massacring civilians. This was the first major anti-partisan operation among many that would cost the lives of thousands upon thousands of unarmed Soviet civilians. In the summer of 1942, German commanders decided that it would be wise to abandon indiscriminate killing and to distinguish instead between civilians who supported the partisans and those who did not, and to treat the two categories accordingly. The concern was that the indiscriminate violence was driving civilians into the arms of the partisans, thus strengthening their hand. But such a distinction proved impossible to translate into practice. Moreover, SS and police units, who were more ideological than army units, tended to care less about winning the sympathies of the local population. As the tide of the fighting turned against Germany increasingly in 1943 and 1944, the partisans intensified their attacks, and the Germans reciprocated with increasingly violent retaliation. We do not have a precise number for Soviet citizens killed by the Germans specifically in anti-partisan operations, but one prominent expert on the subject has posited an estimate of over 200,000, the majority of whom were unarmed civilians.[15]

In Poland, the emergence of effective resistance had been at first preempted by the systematic liquidations of the Polish elite during Operation Tannenberg in 1939. But a resistance movement did ultimately develop, especially after 1942. The German Security Police responded with mass shootings of civilians suspected of harboring resistance members. At times, the German police employed kangaroo courts to administer speedy justice, often in the form of death penalties. Sometimes they dispensed with the *pro forma* trials entirely, carrying out summary executions instead. Around 20,000 Poles were killed in this manner by the Germans. As part of the anti-resistance operation, the Germans partially or entirely destroyed an estimated 800 Polish villages.

These atrocities were, however, dwarfed by the German response to the Warsaw Uprising, which took place from August to October 1944. The uprising was organized by the Polish Home Army, a nationalist resistance organization. Two questions about which historians have debated – whether the Red Army, which had reached the outskirts of Warsaw, paused its advance intentionally to let the Germans liquidate the Polish resistance, and whether the leaders of the Home Army unnecessarily invited German retaliation by launching the uprising in the first place – have generated heated debate among specialists in Polish history. The suppression of the uprising was undertaken mainly by German SS and police units (as opposed to Wehrmacht). On direct orders from Hitler, these units shot Polish citizens indiscriminately. An estimated 200,000 Poles were killed in the uprising, the majority in mass executions. The Germans then intentionally destroyed much of the city, putting a large part of the surviving population in camps and forced labor.[16]

German reprisals for partisan activity were also especially severe in the Balkans. The German and Italian occupation and the creation of the puppet state of Croatia unleashed ethno-nationalist passions in what had been a diverse, multi-cultural state. As part of the partition of Yugoslavia in April 1941, the Germans had taken northern Slovenia (which was adjacent to Austria), and 6,700 Slovenes had been deported to German-occupied Serbia. This had been part of a complex ethno-national transfer of peoples among the various regimes in power in the Balkans in 1941. A large number of Serbs had also been forced out of Croatia.[17]

The partisan movement in Yugoslavia was relatively large. The rugged, mountainous terrain gave it space to operate and to hide. Soon after the occupation of Yugoslavia in April 1941, two resistance movements emerged: the Communists, led by the future president of the country, Josip Broz Tito, and the Chetniks, who consisted of Serbian nationalists under Draža Mihailović. The two groups fought the Germans but also each other. German anti-resistance efforts were aided by the Ustaše, which was composed of Croatian nationalists. In September 1941, Hitler ordered the execution of 100 hostages for each German soldier killed by the resistance. The German army carried out the reprisals, often using Jews as the hostages.

The harshness of German anti-resistance methods in Yugoslavia is explainable in part as a reflex response of German commanders to disruptions to their operations. Severe treatment of resistors was part of their training and tradition. In Yugoslavia, however (as elsewhere in the Slavic regions of Eastern Europe), their response was also conditioned by anti-Slavic sentiment and antisemitism, the latter of which was reflected in the fact that Jews were so often chosen as the hostages. The counterinsurgency strategy was based primarily on terror. The German army's readiness to resort to these methods was also in part the result of being overstretched. The effectiveness of the partisans, in Serbia especially, prompted the German commanders to crack down even more.[18] By the end of 1941, about 30,000 civilians had been murdered by the Wehrmacht. This number does not include resistance fighters killed by the Croatian Ustaše.

In December 1942, Field Marshall Keitel, on Hitler's instructions, ordered the Wehrmacht to proceed against partisans in the Balkans "with the most brutal means," to ignore the Geneva Conventions, and to not hesitate to harm women and children while pursuing partisans. In Greece, the implementation of this policy led to the destruction of over a thousand villages, the massive obliteration of homes, churches, and farms, and the killing or maiming of over 20,000 Greek civilians (in addition to 70,000 Greek Jews who were deported and murdered).

The Germans practiced hostage-taking on a massive scale, taking prominent members of villages, such as doctors and priests, into custody and threatening to kill them in reprisal for attacks on German troops. Probably the most notorious massacre in Greece took place in October 1943, when, in retaliation for the killing of 78 German soldiers by partisans, the entire male population of the town of Kalavryta, about 500 persons, was shot *en masse*.[19]

In the Czech Lands – the so-called Protectorate of Bohemia and Moravia – the intention to Germanize a substantial segment of the population and the importance of the region to the German economy had at first led the Germans to pursue a relatively mild form of occupation when compared, for example, to Poland. The Czech resistance nevertheless intensified its actions in late 1941, expanding its use of boycotts, strikes, and pamphleteering. No less a figure than Reinhard Heydrich, head of the Reich Security Main Office, was sent to the Protectorate to quell the resistance. Heydrich intensified the use of terror, declaring martial law and presiding over mass arrests. About 400 executions were carried out in the first 20 days of Heydrich's presence in Prague. In response, the Czech resistance escalated its own activities, culminating on May 27, 1942, when it assassinated Heydrich. After the assassination, 3,000 additional members of the German Order Police were sent to the Protectorate to conduct searches and interrogations. They carried out multiple executions. The climax of this operation was the massacre at Lidice on June 9–10, 1942. Order Police entered the town of 500 inhabitants, where, they believed, the assassins were in hiding. The German policemen did not find the assassins, but they shot the entire adult male population, sent the remainder of the inhabitants to concentration camps, and then burned the entire town to the ground.[20]

Italy had been an ally of Germany through the fall of 1943, collaborating with its conquest of much of Europe. After Mussolini was overthrown in July of that year, Germany invaded and occupied much of the country, placing Mussolini in charge of a puppet "Italian Socialist Republic" based at Salò in the north. The Germans demanded the surrender of all units of the Italian army to German troops. Those that did not do so were subjected to harsh punishments. There were multiple massacres of Italian soldiers, the largest of which was the execution of 5,000 unarmed Italian POWs on the Greek island of Cephalonia in September 1943. Many of the Italian soldiers who were taken into captivity were sent to Germany or elsewhere in German-occupied Europe to serve as forced laborers. Germany interned a total of 750,000 Italian soldiers, 46,000 of whom died in German captivity. These were in addition to another approximately 50,000 civilians, including partisans and Jews, who were killed during the German occupation. The brutality of the German measures in Italy was driven by a German sense of having been betrayed by their erstwhile Italian allies. It was also a response to a very spirited anti-Nazi and anti-Fascist resistance that sprang up in the country after Mussolini's fall.[21]

The armistice arrangement with France in June 1940 allowed the Germans to place their security apparatus in France. The focus of German anti-partisan warfare was the Communist resistance. In the spring of 1941, French police (not German ones) arrested over 2,000 people alleged to be members of the resistance. The resistance nevertheless increased attacks on German soldiers and installations. The Germans, in turn, retaliated with increased hostage shootings. Initially, hostage shootings in reprisal for the of killing German soldiers had been ordered by local German commanders, but, in September 1941, the order for the shooting of 100 hostages in retaliation for every German soldier killed arrived from Berlin. During the war, about 30,000 French hostages were shot by German occupation forces. About 5,000 French citizens fell victim to the "Night and Fog" decree, which provided for the arrest and deportation of suspected resisters without notification to their families. Some 20,000 residents of France who were not Jewish died in concentration camps and prisons, where they had been sent for real and suspected resistance activity.[22] In addition, 75,000 Jews were deported from France as part of the Final Solution, and most of them were killed.

The single most notorious instance of a German reprisal in occupied France took place at Oradour, a village in west-central France, in June 1944. The D-Day landings at Normandy had taken place just a few days previously, and German commanders were concerned about resistance aiding the Allied forces. On June 10, about 120 members of the "Das Reich" division of the Armed SS (Waffen SS) entered the town, suspecting that munitions and arms for the resistance had been hidden there. The SS soldiers rounded up the population, locked the women and children in the church, and demanded that the men disclose the location of the weapons. When no information was forthcoming, the SS divided the men into groups, took them to the surrounding buildings, and slaughtered them with machine guns. The SS then killed the women and children by detonating a smoke bomb in the church, suffocating many, and shooting those who managed to get out. The SS then set the church aflame, and then the rest of the town. The total number killed in this way was 642.[23] To this day, the burned ruins of Oradour stand as a memorial to the civilians murdered there.

The magnitude of the criminality perpetrated by Nazi Germany in combatting local resistance to its rule in occupied Europe is astonishing, even as it often remains obscured by the out-and-out genocide it committed at the same time. In trying to understand the ferociousness of the anti-partisan methods and the crimes against civilians, it is worth distinguishing between military and non-military perpetrators, as well as between ideological causes and situational factors. The Wehrmacht was a military organization in which there was a substantial degree of residual military professionalism and an awareness of the laws of war. On the other hand, it had undergone a good deal of Nazification since 1933, both in its officer corps and among its rank and file. Millions of young men had been exposed to Nazism as teenagers before the war, in school, in the Hitler Youth, and more generally in German society. Many of them never internalized Nazi ideology, or even rejected it. But the Wehrmacht was based on universal male conscription, thus young men of all ideological stripes were drafted into it. Many brought an ideological commitment to Nazism with them onto the battlefield. Young soldiers arrived in Poland and the Soviet Union harboring feelings of superiority over Slavs and feelings of resentment and disgust toward seemingly exotic, caftan-wearing East European Jews.[24]

Even among soldiers for whom ideological commitment was not at first paramount, it became increasingly important over time in some situations. After their units (their "primary groups," in the jargon of military sociology) were severely eroded by the fierce fighting in the Soviet Union, soldiers fell back on an ideological understanding of the conflict. For many, the war devolved into a primitive, tribal struggle for survival, and the worldview into which they had been indoctrinated came to play a dominant role in shaping their conduct.[25] But this explanation can by no means be applied to all crimes of the Wehrmacht. The mass starvation of Soviet prisoners of war, for example, was set in motion while the war was still going well for Germany. It resulted from the intersection of a limited food supply with an ideologically and culturally determined dismissal of the humanity of the captives. Similarly, the conduct of the Wehrmacht in its anti-partisan warfare in Yugoslavia stemmed from a combination of anti-Slavism, on the one hand, and the unenviable mission of combatting a potent partisan movement, on the other.

In contrast to the Wehrmacht, a professional military organization that had become infused with Nazism, the Waffen SS was much more purely a creature of the Nazi system, and the same can be said for much of the German police apparatus in occupied Europe. These units played an outsize role in many of the atrocities described above. The massacre at Oradour, for example, was the work of a Waffen SS division. The Waffen SS consisted of German men who had been recruited on the basis of unimpeachable Aryan ancestry, personal toughness, and loyalty to National Socialism. Once in, the men continued to undergo incessant ideological training. "Soldiers of the Führer" was the identity that was cultivated in the organization.[26] A similar ethos motivated members of the German Order Police unit that massacred the inhabitants of Lidice and countless other towns and villages across Europe.

The Final Solution: The Mass Murder of the Jews

While the systematic mass murder of the Jews, which began in 1941 during the German drive into the Soviet Union, must be understood as part and parcel of a broader Nazi project for the demographic transformation of Europe, the Holocaust, as it has come to be called, rightfully occupies a special place in the history and memory of Nazi persecution.[27] The worldview of Nazism assigned an especially menacing and destructive role to the Jews in world history and contemporary affairs. While Nazism cast other peoples, such as Slavs, Roma, and peoples of African origin, for example, as intellectually and culturally inferior, lazy, and dishonest, it framed the Jews as a far more sinister force. "World Jewry" allegedly stood behind capitalism, Bolshevism, organized crime, sexual degeneracy, and all the other forces that were seen as undermining European civilization. This demonization of the Jews was constitutive to Nazism in a way that cannot be said of the ideology's other racial, ethnic, or political prejudices. During the 1930s, antisemitism had been a constant and almost omnipresent feature of the regime's policies and propaganda. The advent of the Nazi empire dramatically increased the number of Jews living under German control, causing Nazi leaders to first entertain but then reject proposals involving the mass relocation of Jews to Poland and Madagascar.

The phrase "Final Solution of the Jewish Question" was the euphemism employed by Nazi leaders and German bureaucrats to refer to planning for the removal of Jews from Germany and German-dominated Europe. At first, the phrase implied the intention to relocate Jews on a massive scale; historians describe such intentions with the term "territorial Final Solution." In the summer and autumn of 1941, during the attempted conquest of the Soviet Union, the concept shifted, and the phrase "Final Solution" came to mean mass murder. This lethal escalation was the result of four factors: first, the uncompromising desire to rid German-dominated Europe of Jews; second, the absence of a desirable territorial solution; third, the feeling of invincibility induced in the Nazi leadership by German military successes in the Soviet Union in the summer and fall of 1941; and fourth, the fact that the psychological barrier to mass murder as the solution to a perceived demographic problem had already been breached in Germany by the T4 program between 1939 and 1941.

During German preparations for the invasion, the national police apparatus in the SS created four special task forces (*Einsatzgruppen*) to carry out ideologically motivated liquidations on a large scale. The units, which comprised a total of about 3,000 men, were motorized, enabling them to move quickly from one location to the next. The members of the task forces were drawn in large part from militarized police forces, for example, the Secret State Police (Gestapo), the Security Police (SD), and the Order Police (Orpo). Thus, the task forces consisted of men who had been selected based on their ideological dependability, their discipline and hardness, and their previous training in the use of armed force against civilian populations.

A precedent existed in Operation Tannenberg, in which Germany decapitated the Polish state in 1939 through mass murder of the Polish elite. In 1941, the task forces were to follow the German army into Soviet-occupied Poland and then into the Soviet Union proper and carry out the mass executions behind the front lines of the fighting. The commanders of the task forces did not receive an explicit order to murder all Jews, but the danger posed by Jews and by Jewish connections to the Communist leadership cadre was emphasized to them repeatedly.[28] Once the task forces began their operations in June 1941, they targeted officials of the Soviet Communist Party and other office holders. They also targeted adult, male Jews. In a matter of weeks, the victims expanded to include all Jews in the Soviet Union. Heinrich Himmler, the head of the SS, personally managed this expansion of the task forces' mission.[29] Eventually the task forces were deemed too small to carry out their mission on their own and were therefore reinforced by units of German Order Police and Reserve Order Police. In this way, "ordinary men" representing a broader cross-section of German society were drawn into the enterprise of mass murder.[30]

The main killing method employed by the task forces was mass shootings. Typically, an *Einsatzkommando* (sub-unit of an *Einsatzgruppe*) would arrive in a village or town, identify the Jewish residents, march them to the periphery of the community, and shoot them (see Figure 9.2). Often the Jewish victims were forced to dig the very ditches into which they were shot. One of the largest and most notorious of the massacres took place near the Ukrainian city of Kyiv. At a ravine called Babyn Yar, on the periphery of the city, about 34,000 Jews were murdered over two days at the end of September 1941. At Babyn Yar and elsewhere, German killing units benefitted from the active assistance of local collaborators who were motivated by antisemitism or a desire to curry favor with the occupying power.

It is important not to confuse the Wehrmacht, which was a war-fighting organization, with the *Einsatzgruppen*, whose mission focused on the liquidation of civilians. Nevertheless, the Wehrmacht did play a role in the massacres in several important ways. First, as an occupying military force, the Wehrmacht was responsible for respecting the laws of war, which included the protection of civilians, but it systematically looked the other way as large numbers of civilians were slaughtered under its nose. Army generals were

Figure 9.2 Mass shooting of Jews by an *Einsatzgruppe* in Ukraine, 1941 (Corbis via Getty Images).

informed in advance of the planning of the larger massacres, and in some cases high-ranking army officers were present. Second, the *Einsatzgruppen* depended on the Wehrmacht for logistical support, supplies, and communication. Third, Wehrmacht units were often drawn into committing massacres themselves, something they did under the pretext of anti-partisan warfare, murdering civilians while falsely claiming that the victims had been involved in armed resistance to the military occupation.[31] In numerous cases, army units became directly involved in massacres, with soldiers serving as the actual shooters. The complicity of Wehrmacht elements in such crimes differed significantly from one unit to the next depending to a large degree on the conduct of the commanding officer.[32] Thus, while the Wehrmacht was not a criminal organization on the level of the *Einstazgruppen*, neither was it the ethically clean military organization that many Germans made it out to be in the decades after World War II.[33] Antisemitism was certainly widespread among the troops. Letters written to family members by soldiers at the front sometimes expressed their antisemitism openly and sometimes in the crudest terms. From Siedlice in Poland, an army private described in 1940 how "the Jews lie in the street like pigs, worthy of a 'chosen people.'" Some of the soldiers made no attempt to hide their approval of mass murder. "There is only one thing we can do with Jewry," wrote a solder from the German-occupied Soviet Union in 1942, "extermination."[34] While a substantial number of letters expressing such antisemitism survived the war, it is impossible to conclude with any degree of statistical precision how typical they were of the sentiments of the millions of young German men who served in the Wehrmacht.[35]

During the fall of 1941, as the mass executions of Jews in the Soviet Union was in full swing, Hitler decided to expand the systematic murder of Jews to the rest of Europe. This decision was made when Germany seemed invincible, and the long-fantasized destruction of Jewry seemed within reach. In their research about this decision, historians have found no written order or authorization from Hitler like the T4 authorization he had signed in September 1939. But historians have found written, contemporaneous summaries of conversations that Hitler had with leading Nazis, such as Propaganda Minister Joseph Goebbels, and several foreign leaders, in which he shared his intention to expand the systematic murder of Jews from the Soviet Union to the remainder of Europe.[36]

The fundamental decision to murder all the Jews of Europe, then, was made by Hitler at some point during the autumn of 1941. But now the decision had to be implemented. Responsibility for overall coordination lay with the Reich Security Main Office under Reinhard Heydrich. But the project would require the participation of many government ministries and offices of the Nazi Party. To get all participating agencies on the same page, Heydrich organized a meeting in the Berlin suburb of Wannsee. The now-notorious Wannsee Conference took place on January 20, 1942, although it had originally been scheduled for the previous month and then delayed. The plan described at Wannsee involved the combing of Europe from west to east in a search for Jews. The Jews would be rounded up and sent to Eastern Europe, where they would be subjected to forced labor. The labor itself would kill many Jews, and those who survived would be murdered. The plan envisaged not 6 million Jewish victims, but rather 11 million – all the Jews of Europe, including those in countries that the Holocaust, in the event, did not reach, such as Great Britain, Ireland, Spain, Portugal, Finland, and the European part of Turkey. Although it was not mentioned at Wannsee, the Reich Security Main Office also later established an *Einsatzgruppe* for the murder of the Jews in Palestine, the German conquest of which was prevented by the British victory at the battle of El Alamein in Egypt in 1942.[37]

The expansion of the Final Solution from the Soviet Union to the remainder of Europe was accompanied by a shift in the methodology of genocide. In the Soviet Union, the Germans felt no need to move cautiously or worry about the reaction of the local population. The Germans also employed severe methods against the majority non-Jewish population of the region. Other areas of Europe, where the Final Solution would only begin in 1942, involved a different kind of challenge. Some countries, like France, Belgium, and the Netherlands, were under German occupation, but the German strategy was to keep fewer German troops on the ground there, as they were needed on the Soviet front. In these places, the German occupation relied on a lighter touch. Other countries with significant Jewish populations, such as Hungary and Romania, were not occupied by Germany but rather allied with it. Sending German murder commandos into these places to kill Jews where they lived would not be acceptable to the governments of those countries.

A second reason for the shift had to do with psychological problems faced by the hands-on killers during the mass shootings. Even for those killers who believed in the righteousness of what they were doing, it had often proved psychologically difficult to carry out murder on such a vast scale. Alcoholism and breakdowns were common, and there were some suicides. By shifting from mass shootings to a more industrial system of murder, one could introduce a division of labor in which very few Germans would have to carry out the actual killing. While the majority would engage in support functions, such as transporting the Jewish victims to the extermination camps, only a small minority would be needed to operate gassing facilities and crematoria. Much of the dirty work, such as the burning of corpses, could also be forced onto Jewish prisoners.

Thus, after the Wannsee Conference, the Germans began to build facilities in German-occupied Poland designed for the mass murder of Jews by means of poison gas, implementing the killing model of T4 but on a far vaster scale. In some cases, existing camps were converted to a genocidal purpose, while in other cases, entirely new camps dedicated solely to mass murder were constructed. There were six such camps in all: Chelmno, Maidanek, Belzec, Sobibor, Treblinka, and Auschwitz. Several of these camps were improvised, technologically primitive installations used primarily for the killing of Polish Jews. The more technologically sophisticated Auschwitz-Birkenau camp included modern facilities for the gassing of thousands of people at a time, and for the cremation of their corpses. Auschwitz-Birkenau became the destination of Jews deported to Poland from many places in Nazi-dominated Europe between 1942 and 1944. About a million Jews were murdered there, while the total number of Jews killed in all the extermination camps erected by the Germans in occupied Poland was about 3 million.[38] Looking beyond the camps, a large percentage of Jewish deaths in the Holocaust was attributable to relatively simple forms of killing, such as shootings and death-by-privation in the ghettoes.[39] Thus, although the Holocaust is often associated in the popular imagination with the modern, industrial methods of murder employed at Auschwitz-Birkenau, that camp was not necessarily typical of the manner in which most Jewish victims of the Nazis perished.

The mass round-ups and deportations of Jews envisioned at the Wannsee Conference would be straightforward enough in German-occupied Poland and in Germany itself, where little resistance was to be expected. But the situation would be more challenging elsewhere, in a region described by Raul Hilberg as "a vast semi-circular arc, extending counterclockwise from Norway to Romania." Several of the countries in this arc – Norway, Denmark, the Low Countries, and France – were occupied, wholly or partially, by Germany. But in these places, unlike in Poland or the Soviet Union, the German occupation strategy was to allow for a semblance of normal life and to avoid basing large numbers of German troops. These were also countries in which the Jewish minority was socially, culturally, and economically well integrated. Removing the Jews might, therefore, generate resentment and possibly resistance to the German occupation. The deportations would have to be organized carefully, and with some regard given to public opinion. The Holocaust played out differently in all these countries. The small Jewish community of Denmark, for example, was rescued by an overnight boat convoy to Sweden. In contrast, the Vichy government in France adopted a strategy of sacrificing Jews who had arrived recently to save those whose families were long-established in the country, claiming that the deportation of the latter group would be deeply unpopular and therefore potentially destabilizing to the Vichy regime.

The remainder of the countries in the semi-circular arc – Italy, Croatia, Hungary, and Romania – were not occupied by Germany, but were rather *allies* of Germany. Italy was a Fascist dictatorship that had been allied with Germany since the late 1930s. Croatia, previously a region within the Kingdom of Yugoslavia, was set up as a state of its own when

Figure 9.3 Deportation of Jews from Würzburg, Germany, November 1941 (Galerie Bilderwelt/Getty Images).

Germany invaded Yugoslavia in 1941. While nominally independent, it was a satellite of Germany. Hungary and Romania, two authoritarian countries that were economically dependent on Germany, participated alongside Germany in the attack against the Soviet Union in 1941. Although Germany was the dominant partner in its relationships with all these countries, it could not dictate to them when it came to the question of what to do with their Jewish populations. Organizing the deportations required diplomacy, pressure, and cajoling. Here, too, the Holocaust unfolded very differently in each country. The government of the Croatian puppet state proved quite forthcoming to German requests for the deportation of its Jews. Hungary and Italy balked, even though both countries had implemented their own antisemitic legislation. Only when Germany invaded those countries – Italy in 1943 and Hungary in 1944 – did the deportation of their Jewish populations to Auschwitz commence. Romania also refused to allow the deportation of its Jews, even though the Romanian army had carried out massacres of Jews in Transnistria, a region it had seized from the Soviet Union in 1941.

As for Germany itself, the systematic deportation of Jews began in October 1941 (see Figure 9.3). Many Jews in the initial transports were sent to German-occupied Lithuania, where they were shot by

Einsatzgruppen. Others were sent to ghettoes in Poland or directly to Auschwitz, where they were murdered. To preserve the cover story that the deported Jews were being resettled somewhere in Eastern Europe, where they would live and work, the regime set up a ghetto at Terezín (called Theresienstadt in German) in Bohemia for German Jews who were too old to work. After a time, once the ghetto had outlived its value as a tool of propaganda, Jews there were transferred to Auschwitz to be killed. By the end of 1942 the Jews left in Germany were mainly forced laborers whose work was considered essential and Jews living in mixed marriages, the deportation of whom was considered as potentially damaging to the morale of the population.

The Germans who planned and carried out the Final Solution came from many different corners of German society. The leadership corps of the Reich Security Main Office, which was at the center of the genocide, forced resettlements, and other ideologically motivated crimes, consisted of a relatively well-educated cadre of young men, the vast majority born after 1900. Having grown up amidst the insecurity of World War I, the political and economic vicissitudes of the Weimar Republic, and the Depression, they gravitated to Nazism, which gave them politically meaningful employment and an ideological framework for understanding the world in which they had felt buffeted. They were drawn from a wide variety of occupational and educational backgrounds, such as law, pharmacy, agronomy, engineering, and education. Two-thirds of them held a university degree, and half of those had earned doctorates. One of the *Einsatzgruppen* commanders, Otto Ohlendorf, possessed two doctorates.[40]

The Final Solution required hands-on killers, people on the ground who pulled triggers or operated gas chambers, but it also needed people to organize the genocide at a variety of levels. In German, this category of managers and bureaucrats is known as "perpetrators of the desk" (*Schreibtischtäter*). A central figure in organizing the deportation of Jews was Adolf Eichmann, the head of the Office for Jewish Affairs (Office IVb4) in the Reich Security Main Office. Eichmann was not well known either inside or outside of Germany during the Nazi era because he was a mid-level official rather than a top-level figure. It was only after 1945 that war crimes investigators and historians figured out that he had played a key role in coordinating the deportations. Eichmann was not a policymaker but rather a functionary who implemented policies and decisions passed down by others. He has, however, become a notorious historical figure for reasons having to do with his post-war fate. Eichmann escaped justice after the war and fled to Argentina, where he lived under an assumed identity until 1960, when he was captured by Israeli agents, taken to Jerusalem, and placed on trial. The German-Jewish philosopher Hannah Arendt, who had fled Germany in 1933 and eventually landed in the United States, was present for part of the trial and wrote about it. In her book, *Eichmann in Jerusalem: A Study in the Banality of Evil*, Arendt argued that Eichmann had been no evil or diabolical genius, but rather an ordinary, or banal, bureaucrat.[41] The "banality thesis" is often cited when trying to explain the conduct of bureaucratic perpetrators in the Holocaust and other atrocities. These are not sadists, but rather people who facilitate wrongdoing by holding meetings or processing paperwork. They are just doing their jobs, not serving a cause or working toward the realization of an ideology. Arendt's thesis remains useful even though the specific case study on which she originally based it, that of Adolf Eichmann, has been invalidated by historians. Eichmann, we now know, was a highly motivated, ideologically committed antisemite.[42]

After the war, when challenged about knowledge of the mass murder of the Jews, a response common among Germans was "we didn't know anything about it" (*davon haben wir nichts gewußt*). Historians have assessed such assertions based on research in private diaries, secret government reports, and other sources. There is little doubt that knowledge was widespread inside Germany about the mass shootings of Jews in the East in 1941 and 1942. Soldiers who witnessed massacres described what they had seen to family members and clergymen while on furlough. The stories circulated and were occasionally written down. For example, on October 28, 1941, Friedrich Kellner recorded the following remark in his private diary:

A soldier on leave reports to have been an eyewitness to horrible atrocities in the occupied region of Poland. He watched as naked Jewish men and women, who were lined up in front of a long, deep ditch, were shot at the base of their skulls by Ukrainians at the order of the SS and fell into the ditch. The ditch was then shoveled closed. Screams still came out of the ditch![43]

Other private diaries of Germans kept during the Nazi period contain similar entries. Writing in her diary in Stuttgart in July 1942, Anna Haag complained how "there are still people in Germany who claim not to have heard of the massacres of Jews or of the persecution of the Jews altogether. It's hard to fathom."[44] In December 1942, after Allied governments issued a joint declaration denouncing Germany's mass murder of Jews, the BBC broadcast a report about the atrocities in Germany. Karl Dürkefälden later recalled listening to the report, from which he learned that "Poland was the largest slaughterhouse" for the Jews, the majority of whom had been murdered on order of the German government by the end of 1942.[45]

While awareness of the mass shootings of Jews was common, evidence of knowledge among ordinary Germans of the mass murder operations at Auschwitz and other camps, though present, was rarer. The discrepancy can be explained by a couple of factors. The mass shootings occurred relatively early during the Soviet campaign, when Germans were less distracted by bad news about the war and by Allied air raids than they were just a year or eighteen months later. Moreover, although the deportation of German Jews was not a secret, there were fewer German witnesses to actual killings in the camps, making it easier for Germans to buy in to the official cover story about Jews being resettled in the East.[46] But for those who paid close attention, like Victor Klemperer, the truth about Auschwitz was clear. "The most horrible of the camps" was how he referred to it in his diary.[47]

Based on the understanding that news about the mass murder was circulating in German society, the Nazi regime engaged in domestic propaganda campaigns to justify the barbaric treatment of the Jews. The message was that the war itself, and therefore the suffering of the German people, had been caused by the Jews, therefore the Jews deserved what had been happening to them.[48] This message was also repeatedly communicated openly by top Nazi leaders throughout the war. In numerous speeches, Hitler reminded his listeners about his prophecy of January 30, 1939, according to which a world war caused by Jewry would result in the "annihilation of the Jewish race in Europe." One can interpret such statements as exploiting the Jews as hostages to threaten the Allies, or, alternatively, as attempts to draw the German people into the circle of complicity and, by doing so, strengthen their will to fight to the bitter end. It is equally, if not more, likely, however, that Hitler was simply looking for a way to brag about an achievement of which he was proud.

10   The Destruction of Nazi Germany

The Nazi leadership preferred to insulate the German home front from the war as much as possible. This desire was based to a significant degree on Hitler's understanding of how Germany had been defeated in 1918, when, according to him, a civilian population weakened by scarcity became vulnerable to the treasonous machinations of Marxists and Jews. His strategy for fighting short wars against isolated enemies, which required limited domestic mobilization, had worked well before June 1941, with the exception of Britain. But the failure to defeat the Soviet Union quickly, as had been the plan, combined with the entry of the United States into the war, compelled the German leadership to alter its approach. After the fighting began to shift against the Germans decisively at Stalingrad, the government announced the transition to a "Total War" footing, extending the mobilization to ever more segments of the civilian population. But the war against Germany continued to intensify as well, as its enemies increasingly brought their combined military and industrial potential to bear on the conflict. Between 1942 and 1944, German cities and economic targets were subjected to ever-intensifying bombardment from the air. The Allies invaded Italy in 1943 and France in 1944, and the Red Army, after halting the Germans at Stalingrad, began to push back and eventually began to rout the Wehrmacht. The prospect of defeat prompted an attempt by Germans in the military and civilian resistance to assassinate Hitler and unseat the Nazis in July 1944. The failure of the plot magnified the extremism of the Nazi leadership and its fanatical followers, strengthening their determination to fight to the bitter end, and producing convulsions of internally directed violence. By the end of the war, Germany was defeated and occupied, its cities in ruins. Rarely in history had a single country descended from the heights of power to the depths of defeat so thoroughly and so quickly.

Mobilizing German Society for Total War

In December 1942, Hitler placed Joseph Goebbels in charge of totalizing the German war effort. In practical terms this meant, first, a broader

216

Figure 10.1 German POWs near Stalingrad (Hulton Archive/Getty Images).

mobilization of women in the German economy; second, the suspension of nonessential industrial production; and third, the activation of several hundred thousand Germans who had received draft deferments for essential non-military activity. In addition to economic measures, a major propaganda campaign intended to make the German people aware of the gravity of the situation, impress upon them the sacrifices that would be necessary to win the war, and motivate them with warnings about how defeat would deliver Germany to its mortal enemies. "Now the bosses and the propagandists are filled with bluster, attempting with arrogant tirades to cover up the shame called Stalingrad," was how Friedrich Kellner described the rhetoric in his diary (see Figure 10.1).[1]

On February 3, 1943, German radio officially announced the defeat at Stalingrad. The war had not been going well for some time, but Stalingrad forced the regime to finally acknowledge the existence of the problem. A couple of weeks later, on February 18, Goebbels gave a major speech at the Berlin Sport Palace, in which he emphasized the threat posed by Bolshevism and Jewry. Only Germany, he said, could prevent the Bolshevik tide from sweeping across Europe. He described Jewry as "an immediate danger to every country." Rather than bow to these threats, Germany would fight them, using "the most radical measures" if necessary. The numerous references in the speech to the Jews and the necessity of adopting decisive measures against them can be understood as veiled references to the Final Solution, knowledge of which existed among many ordinary Germans. The audience at the Sport Palace speech consisted of state and party officials, soldiers, and party members from Berlin. Goebbels posed ten questions to them, to which they all responded, in unison, positively and enthusiastically. They expressed their approval for a "total war" even if it were to become "more total and more radical than we can today imagine." The loudest chorus of affirmation came in response to the question of whether the audience had "trust in the Führer" (see Figure 10.2).[2]

"Total war" was not simply a slogan invented on the spot in 1943, but rather a theory of war developed during the 1920s and 1930s. It was in part a reaction to the "stab in the back" myth, the belief that the German army had won World War 1 but had been betrayed by Jews and leftists who had been able to exploit a war-weary population. The lesson drawn from this episode of history was that the psychological mobilization of the entire population was the key to success in modern warfare.[3]

While Goebbels dominated the propaganda campaign for total war, responsibility for mobilizing much of the German economy was entrusted to Albert Speer, formerly Hitler's favorite architect, who had been appointed minister of armaments in early 1942. Speer intended to increase the productivity of the German armaments industry to enhance Germany's war-fighting capacity. The drive for greater efficiency affected not only German workers in civilian industry but also foreign forced workers and concentration camp inmates. Together with Goebbels, Speer boasted publicly how German armaments production dramatically outpaced that of Germany's enemies. Speer claimed to have brought about an armaments miracle, but, in reality, increases in German armament production trailed those in the Soviet Union, and were certainly not sufficient to turn the war around. Moreover, the increasing frequency and scale of Western air raids on German cities caused many Germans to question official claims about the superiority of German weaponry.[4]

Efforts to mobilize German women for the war effort yielded mixed results. At the beginning of the war, the Nazi regime had promulgated a law allowing for the drafting of women into the economy, but Hitler decided not to compel women into the workforce. Nevertheless, in 1943 the government and the Women's League implemented a propaganda campaign to encourage more women into the workforce. While it achieved some success, many women chose not to seek work, due at least partially to an adherence to traditional sex roles, which Nazi ideology and propaganda had encouraged all along. The "total war" registration drive to attract women into the workforce produced about 1.5

Figure 10.2 Audience members cheering during Goebbels' "Total War" speech, February 18, 1943 (ullstein bild/ullstein bild via Getty Images).

million additional female workers, which was hardly enough to cover the shortage of male labor. German women accounted for about one-third of the German workforce during the war. They were based disproportionately in agriculture, on small, family-owned farms. Relatively few German women worked in industry, in contrast to women in Britain or the United States. The German economy therefore remained highly dependent on foreign and forced labor.[5]

German women did serve in important roles in defense against air raids, specifically in educating the public about emergency procedures, as nurses, and managing bunkers or underground shelters. Many took pride in this activity, seeing themselves as integral participants in the "war community" (*Kampfgemeinschaft*).[6] About half-a-million women served in support roles for the German armed forces, attending to wounded soldiers, in clerical roles, or as communications specialists. Another 400,000 worked for the German Red Cross, which was active inside the Reich and in theaters of combat. Women also worked for the police, the Gestapo, and the SS. While some had simply landed in such positions, others shared the ideological commitment of their male colleagues.[7] For many German women, the war was a time of opportunity in traditionally male-dominated spheres. For example, Liselotte Purper, a photographer in her twenties, received commissions from Nazi organizations to undertake photographic documentations of their activities in German-occupied Eastern Europe. For Purper, the combination of a labor shortage among males and the Germanization projects of the Nazi regime resulted in attractive professional possibilities. Many of her photographic projects documented the experiences of other German women who served the Reich as pioneers in Eastern Europe as workers, scientists, and mothers.[8]

A specific set of mobilization efforts had been targeted at university students even before the transition to total war. Many male students had been drafted into the armed forces. Starting in the summer of 1941, students still in civilian life were obliged to work for the war effort in one manner or another. Many took jobs in armaments factories, in the railroad system, or in agriculture. Female students were often put to work caring for evacuated children in rural areas and cleaning up rubble after bombing raids. While some students resented being assigned to menial jobs that were beneath their abilities and self-image, others valued the opportunity to help their Fatherland in its hour of need. A couple of thousand students were sent to jobs in the conquered areas of Poland to encourage them to settle there permanently after the war. Some were given tasks that made use of their intellectual skills, for example, conducting research that could be used by government agencies.[9]

The war transformed the composition of student bodies at German universities, which consisted increasingly of women, disabled war veterans, and students of medicine. Whereas, in 1939, 14 percent of university students had been female, by 1944 the percentage had climbed to 46. (At the technical academies, the percentage of female students rose from 2 to 17 percent during this same period.) The percentage of students in medicine rose from 49 percent in 1939 to 61 percent in 1944, and the percentage of all medical students who were women rose to 38 percent by 1943, almost double what that figure had been ten years earlier. One thing that did not change was the class origins of German university students. Only a tiny percentage of them came from working-class families. The women who enjoyed greater educational opportunity during the war came from the same classes as the male students who had dominated the student bodies all along.

Early in the war, medical students were given furloughs by the army to return to the universities to complete or to continue their studies. The military needed medical personnel, and German society faced a shortage of physicians more generally. Beginning in 1941, medical students were organized into medical companies that would allow them to remain in the army but stay at the university and study simultaneously. They wore uniforms to class and around the university. There were also special companies for students in fields such as engineering, pharmacy, veterinary medicine, and meteorology. The members of the student companies were paid as soldiers, underwent training, had to appear for roll calls, and at some universities shared common living quarters. The members of the student companies were a privileged group, as they could continue their education for elite professions while others of the same age group were serving at the front. Between semesters and upon graduation, however, they also had to participate in the war.

As before the war, the National Socialist Student League attempted to politicize student life at German universities. But many students, also as before the war, pushed back. They were busy with their studies, or with the military requirements of the student companies, and did not want to attend political education sessions. On the other hand, feelings of patriotism and national responsibility ran high among students. During the war, many felt the need to serve their country even while they resented attempts at Nazi indoctrination. For them, the cause was Germany and not Nazism. Political skepticism was widespread, but did not translate into rejection of the war, and most students celebrated news of victories and lamented news of defeat just like most other Germans.[10]

In March 1939, membership in the Hitler Youth had been made compulsory for all Germans aged 10–18. When the war began, the Hitler

Youth had no plan in place for how its millions of members would be mobilized. It had not been integrated into any aspect of war planning. Thus, the Hitler Youth improvised its way through the first phase of the war somewhat chaotically, and only gradually became integrated into the operations of the army, the SS, and civilian agencies. Hitler Youth members were given jobs as street cleaners, in railroad stations, in anti-aircraft (FLAK) units, in the postal system, in agriculture, in grocery stores, and in factories. They were also assigned as helpers to police and firefighting units. Some girls were trained to watch the sky and spot Allied aircraft. As most members of the Hitler Youth remained in school for much of the war, their work assignments were mostly for a few hours a week.

The Hitler Youth was also involved in the German colonial project in the East. Ethnic German children in the conquered territories that were subjected to Germanization were integrated into newly founded Hitler Youth chapters. In the annexed areas of Poland, the Hitler Youth welcomed 168,000 new members in 1940. The new members were subjected to Nazi indoctrination, with a special emphasis on the inferiority of the neighboring Slavic peoples. New Hitler Youth members, attached to local units of the SS Race and Resettlement Head Office, helped with the relocation of newly arrived ethnic Germans and with the expulsion of Poles and Jews. The enlistment of children as agents of Germanization extended also to Ukraine and other parts of the Soviet Union.[11]

Allied bombing of German cities increasingly disrupted the lives of German children, forcing the closure or repurposing of many school buildings. School buildings that had not been destroyed were used as quarters for troops, hospitals, police stations, and housing for bombed-out citizens. Starting in 1943, the evacuation of children to the countryside from cities was implemented on a broad basis. By war's end, about 5 million children had been evacuated from their home cities. Most of them lived in special camps set up in rural areas inside the Reich and in some German-occupied areas, while others lived with rural familes.[12] This mass relocation of children was one of many profound consequences of the air war on German society.

German Society and the Air War

The air war brought the war home to ordinary Germans like no other aspect of World War II.[13] It resulted in the destruction of homes, schools, churches, places of work, and shops where people bought their life essentials. It caused the deaths of friends and relatives far from the front. It led to nights spent in fear in air-raid shelters. It forced

Germans to live in crowded temporary housing and to become dependent on community kitchens for meals. Inhabitants of cities not yet hit by air raids lived in fear that theirs might be next. Rumors of imminent raids, often false, caused panic. Allied planes dropped not only bombs but also leaflets by the hundreds of thousands, intending to undermine German morale and turn German citizens against their government. Possession of such a leaflet could bring a stiff penalty or even a death sentence. City governments, Nazi Party agencies, and emergency service organizations struggled to respond to the destruction, but were often overwhelmed, especially after 1943. The air raids disrupted food supplies, medical services, and hospital operations. Even the operation of mortuaries and crematoria were affected, and cities started using mass graves in defiance of an official prohibition. The mass organizations of the Nazi movement – the SA, the Hitler Youth, the Women's League – were mobilized to clean up and tend to the killed and wounded. Foreign workers were also used in large numbers to clear rubble and repair damage. Many foreign workers also died in the bombing raids.

The system used for protecting the population from bombardment reflected Nazi ideological priorities. German cities constructed numerous underground bomb shelters and above-ground bunkers, but there was still a shortage of space inside them. Access to the shelters and bunkers was therefore restricted. Foreign workers from Eastern Europe and Jews were excluded as a matter of principle, leaving them more vulnerable. Foreign workers from Western Europe or citizens of countries allied with Germany could be granted access at the discretion of the individual shelter or bunker wardens. The apartments and possessions of deported Jews were given to "deserving" German families that had been bombed out of their homes.

The plunder of bombed-out shops and homes forced the police and the court system to deal with increasing numbers of cases under the "Enemies of the People Decree" of (*Volksschädlings-Verordnung*) of September 1939. That law was one among many wartime measures designed to enforce discipline and punish nonconformity. Another law, which prohibited listening to foreign radio broadcasts, led to many arrests and prosecutions. The vast wartime increase in the number of such prosecutions led to pressure on the court system, in which speedy justice increasingly took precedence over procedural protections. Between 1939 and 1945 German courts passed down thousands of death penalties for dissent, defeatism, and other acts deemed as detrimental to the war effort.[14] The brief official record of one such case, that of Ernst Schmidtseifer, reads as follows:

Schmidtseifer was arrested on December 16, 1943. He was accused of having subverted the national defense by having made "comments of a grave nature" in an "occupied passenger train." In July 1944, the senior Reich prosecutor of the People's Court transferred the investigation to the chief prosecutor at the Higher Regional Court in Kassel. The Higher Regional Court condemned Schmidtseifer to death on October 7, 1944. After the rejection of his plea for clemency on November 3, he was executed by beheading on November 21, 1944 in the prison of Frankfurt/Main-Preungesheim.

In 1944, multiple similar death sentences were passed down by the same court for Germans convicted of "continued grave comments about a negative outcome of the war," refusing to give the Hitler salute, and listening to foreign radio broadcasts.[15]

The Allied air raids, which increased in frequency and intensity as the war progressed, posed a special challenge to the propaganda machine under Joseph Goebbels. The intensification of the air war in 1943 generated calls for revenge attacks against England, but the German air force was no longer able to wage a major air campaign against Britain. Goebbels spoke in vague terms about miracle weapons still in development that would ultimately turn the tide. He was referring to the V-1 and V-2 rockets, which were launched against Western targets starting in the fall of 1944. The gap between the rhetoric about the coming revenge and the lack of real action to back it up produced criticism in the population, but not defeatism, and many Germans remained hopeful.

German propaganda heaped scorn on the American airmen carrying out bombing missions over Germany. It compared them to gangsters, and claimed that respect for historical and architectural treasures could not be expected from people who celebrated "cheating boxers," a racist reference to African American boxer Joe Louis. Consistent with the broader strategy of blaming the entire war on "World Jewry," German propaganda held the Jews specifically responsible for the bombing of German cities. Official opinion reports about the public mood showed that such propaganda did have resonance in some circles of the population. A good number of Germans subscribed to one or another version of the story that Jews, including émigré German Jews, were choosing targets for the Allies. Some believed that the air raids were Jewish revenge for the November 1938 pogrom. Others, who lived in cities that had not been bombed, assumed that they had been spared because some local Jewish residents had not yet been deported. A variation of the same delusion held that certain cities had been spared because their former Jewish residents were planning to return and reclaim their properties. In cities that had in fact been bombed, some supposed that Jewish émigrés,

knowing that they would never return, preferred to see their former properties and homes destroyed rather than let Aryan Germans live in them.[16]

Resistance inside Germany

During the war, resistance existed along a political spectrum ranging
from Communists on the far left to conservative nationalists (and even
disillusioned Nazis) on the far right, and included both liberals and people who identified strongly as Christian. It would, however, be difficult
to argue that domestic resistance among Germans played any significant
role in bringing about the end of the Nazi rule. The regime was ultimately
destroyed not from within but from without, by a military coalition possessing superior military and economic might. The German resistance
was ineffectual both because it was not extensive and because the regime
employed violence ruthlessly to crush it. It is nevertheless important to
study the resistance as a means for understanding the spectrum of German responses to Nazism. As the emphasis of much recent scholarship
on German society during those years has tended to be on complicity in,
or passive acceptance of, Nazi rule, it becomes all the more important
to recognize and explain the actions of those who actively opposed the
regime.

   We have seen how the Nazi regime destroyed the power of the labor
movement through a combination of terror and cooptation. Nevertheless, during the war, the underground Communist movement attempted
to exploit dissatisfaction among German workers. Although the average
workweek in German industry remained fairly constant during the war
at about 50 hours, decreases in food rations led to discontent among
German workers, and there was widespread resentment that the more
affluent segments of society could acquire food via personal connections
or on the black market. During the spring of 1942, when shortages of
vegetables occurred, arguments broke out in queues of people waiting
to buy produce. Particularly problematic was a shortage of potatoes.
There was also a bread shortage. Working-class women complained that
women of the higher classes – such as the wives of businessmen and military officers – remained idle while they had to work.

   Morale reports prepared by the Security Service reported widespread
disillusionment with the war especially after Stalingrad. Criticism of the
leadership became more common as workers blamed it for plunging
Germany into a war that the country could not win. There was widespread skepticism regarding news reporting about the war. Many workers believed that the government was hiding or embellishing the bad
news. The morale of workers declined, leading to increased absenteeism

and dereliction of duty. This, in turn, led to more severe punishments by employers and authorities, often with the collusion of the German Labor Front.

In an attempt to mobilize working-class resentment, the Communist resistance organized cells in factories and working-class neighborhoods, and disseminated negative views of the regime in printed leaflets and underground newspapers. The Gestapo investigated these activities relentlessly and ruthlessly, conducting mass arrests that brought in hundreds of people who were subjected to harsh interrogation and torture. A wave of mass arrests of Communists in Berlin and other cities netted a large number of prisoners in early 1942. Thousands were put on expedited trial and then executed or sent to prison or concentration camps.[17]

In January 1942, the Moscow-based Communist International sent an agent into Germany to coordinate Communist resistance. Wilhelm Knöchel was a member of the central committee of the German Communist Party who in 1935 had gone into exile in the Soviet capital. Knöchel arrived in Germany via Amsterdam under a false identity. His goal was to undermine the regime's support among the working class in the hope of disrupting industrial production. He established new underground newspapers in which workers were urged to work more slowly or to abandon their factories for the countryside after air raids. Similarly, Knöchel published calls to farmers against dealing with official distributors, asking them instead to sell their produce directly to members of the working class. A series of pamphlets published by Knöchel was titled *The Patriotic SA-Man* (*Der Patriotische SA-Mann*) and attempted to appeal to the class consciousness of "left-wing" members of the Nazi Party, a naïve and futile strategy based on a hopelessly outdated understanding of the Stormtroopers. The pamphlets conveyed bad news from the Eastern front that official propaganda had been obfuscating. Operating within the framework of a Marxist ideology in which the working class was exalted, the Communist resistance underestimated the appeal of Nazism to members of the working class. Knöchel's organization was infiltrated and broken up by the Gestapo in January 1943.[18]

The left-wing resistance also included the "Red Orchestra" (Rote Kapelle), a designation coined by the Gestapo in 1942 to refer to a loose, sprawling network of resisters consisting of academics, artists, intellectuals, and some workers. The term "orchestra" was actually quite misleading, because the network had no central coordination. The central figures in the Red Orchestra included the economist Arvid Harnack and Harro Schulze-Boysen, an aviation specialist. Already during the Depression, Harnack had become convinced that Soviet-style central planning was preferable to the capitalist system. With poor prospects for an academic career, he landed a civil service job as a trade expert in the Reich Ministry of Economics. Schulze-Boysen, for his part, had started out as a conservative nationalist but drifted leftward. He had published *Der Gegner* (*The Opponent*), an anti-Nazi publication that was closed down in 1933. Neither Marxist nor Communist, his outlook can be best described as anti-bourgeois. He wanted to bridge the left and the right into an anti-capitalist, anti-materialist coalition for the sake of the younger generation. During the Nazi period, he was commissioned as an officer in the German air force and worked in the Ministry of Aviation as a specialist on foreign military aviation. A resistance network began to coalesce around Harnack and Schulze-Boysen in 1940. The two men cultivated contacts with a wide circle of actors, including the US embassy in Berlin, which continued until the break of relations in December 1941. The American connection was facilitated by Harnack's wife, Mildred, an American literary scholar whom Harnack had met while studying at the University of Wisconsin.

Harnack and Schulze-Boysen envisaged a post-Nazi socialist Germany engaged in a cooperative relationship with the Soviet Union. Their hostility to capitalism led them to idealize the Soviet Union and to overlook its more authoritarian and oppressive features. They regarded the Hitler–Stalin pact as a purely opportunistic maneuver, believing that war between the two countries was inevitable. They saw the Soviet Union as the key to the destruction of Nazi Germany and to the hoped-for transition away from capitalism. Neither man had a well-thought-out concept of how to bring the Nazi regime to an end. Their focus was on helping the Soviets to withstand a German attack. Their government positions in Berlin allowed them to see evidence of German preparations for the invasion of the Soviet Union in June 1941. Schulze-Boysen sent warnings to Moscow, with no apparent result. Harnack developed contacts with the Soviet trade mission in Berlin while working on a study of the Soviet economic system. He did not work for Soviet intelligence, as was often alleged during the Cold War, although he had contacts with it and attempted to convey information that he regarded as detrimental to the Nazi state. Harnack, his wife, and Schulze-Boysen were captured by the Gestapo as the result of some sloppy communication by Soviet intelligence. All three were executed in 1942.[19]

The group known as the White Rose consisted of six students in their early twenties at the University of Munich, in addition to one member of the faculty. The members of the group had complex motives for their resistance, including liberalism, Christianity, and moral outrage at war crimes and persecution. The stepmother of one member was of Jewish descent and thus suffered persecution. The students were also motivated by anger at the conformism demanded of them and people of their generation. Their opposition activity began as a discussion group.

Figure 10.3 Hans and Sophie Scholl (Authenticated News/Archive Photos/Getty Images).

During the summer of 1942, the group, having taken on the moniker White Rose, printed and distributed a total of six leaflets emphasizing the importance of individual freedom and the restoration of rationalism and decency to German society. This was very much in contrast to the Communist leaflets focusing on the welfare of the German working class. The White Rose leaflets emphasized the moral duty of every German to topple the National Socialist state. Printed in 1942, the second leaflet explicitly condemned the murder of 200,000 Jews in German-occupied Poland. This subject was not mentioned in the other leaflets, so it remains unclear how important this issue was among the motivations of members. The final leaflet was printed in February 1943 and emphasized the military catastrophe at Stalingrad. In addition to the leaflets, members of the group painted political graffiti with phrases such as "freedom" and "down with Hitler" on buildings around the university.

Two members of the White Rose, the siblings Hans and Sophie Scholl, were arrested on February 18, 1943 while distributing leaflets in the atrium of the main building of the University of Munich (see Figure 10.3). The Gestapo then tracked down the other members of the group.

In short order, all were given a perfunctory trial before the People's Court in Munich and executed. One of the executed was Kurt Huber, an adjunct professor of philosophy at the university. The White Rose has served as an inspiration, especially to young people, to take action in the face of injustice. But it was a small group of outliers whose actions had little, if any, tangible effect on the opinions or conduct of others in Munich or at the university.[20]

The most potentially consequential act of resistance within Germany was the July 20, 1944 attempt to assassinate Hitler and remove the Nazi movement from power. The chief figure in the plot was Colonel Claus von Stauffenberg, the chief of staff of the Replacement Army, which was responsible for training soldiers and units inside Germany prior to their stationing abroad. The Replacement Army was the largest element of the German armed forces stationed inside Germany itself. Part of its mission was to quell domestic unrest, which was feared especially, given the presence of so many foreign workers in the country. Among its contingency plans was Operation Valkyrie, which was designed to put down an insurrection or protect the homeland in the event of an invasion by foreign paratroopers. Stauffenberg and his co-conspirators intended to assassinate Hitler, blame the SS for it, and implement Valkyrie to seize the levers of power inside the country. The action would also involve arresting other members of the Nazi top leadership. While only the leaders of the plot were clued in about the true intention for invoking Operation Valkyrie, the vast majority of the soldiers required for the plot to work would simply follow orders, as they had been trained to do.

Stauffenberg, who was 37 years old, an intellectual and an aesthete, was not alone among German military officers who despised Hitler and wanted to get rid of him (see Figure 10.4). Neither was July 20, 1944 the first attempt by members of the military to eliminate Hitler. An attempt to explode a bomb on the Führer's airplane failed in 1943 when the device malfunctioned. Some officers objected to the atrocities of the Nazi regime, which they saw as immoral and besmirching of Germany's name. A larger number believed that Germany could not win the war and that Hitler was leading the country on a path to ruin. By July 1944, the German army was in retreat all along the Eastern front, and the Allies, having pulled off the D-Day invasion, were pouring troops into France.

By this time, a bridge had been created between the military opposition and a group of liberal and conservative critics of the regime in civilian society. Retired General Ludwig Beck, the former chief of the army general staff, who had clashed with Hitler in 1938, had been instrumental in connecting the diverse factions of the opposition. The most prominent

Figure 10.4 Claus von Stauffenberg (Gedenkstätte Deutscher Widerstand/ AFP via Getty Images).

figure on the civilian side was Carl Goerdeler, the former mayor of Leipzig and a conservative. On July 20, a bomb planted by Stauffenberg at a military briefing attended by Hitler at his military headquarters in East Prussia exploded, leaving the Führer injured. The plot fell apart when top generals, upon learning that Hitler was still alive, refused to go along. Stauffenberg and several of his co-conspirators were summarily executed. Others were prosecuted at show trials before the People's Court, which were staged to humiliate the plotters and to strike fear into the hearts of the regime's opponents. The Gestapo eventually identified a total of 132 participants in the plot drawn from many different sectors of German society. The roughly 100 people who were executed for their participation encompassed military officers, civil servants, diplomats, businessmen, clergymen, and figures from the labor movement, including Wilhelm Leuschner, a Social Democrat and former minister of the interior of the state of Hesse. Several were members of the Kreisau Circle (discussed in Chapter 6).[21]

The plot failed for a couple of reasons. Because of a stroke of bad luck, the bomb did not kill Hitler. The conspiracy was not deep, and the army generals either remained loyal to Hitler or were reluctant to overthrow him. One important consequence of the failed assassination was that Hitler came to rely more on Nazi Party loyalists, while his distrust in other institutions, especially the military, intensified. Trusted Nazi comrades such as Heinrich Himmler and Joseph Goebbels were granted additional powers. The Nazi Party regional leaders (Gauleiter) also came to play an enhanced role in running the country domestically after July 20. Some of them began to organize local militias, which would later form the basis for the party-controlled national militia, the Volkssturm. The failed July 20 plot, therefore, rather than putting an end to the Nazi regime, radicalized it further, strengthening the determination of Hitler and his loyalists to escalate violence against domestic opposition and to fight Germany's foreign enemies. In the eyes of true believers, Hitler's survival served as yet another sign that the Führer was "protected by providence."[22]

The End Phase of the Nazi Regime

The violence of war did not peter out during the final phase of the Nazi regime's existence between July 1944 and May 1945, but in many respects intensified. At a time when the prospect of a German victory became increasingly and obviously hopeless, Germans remained determined to fight on. Two factors were at the root of this refusal to accept a surrender that would have undoubtedly saved a great many German lives. First, Adolf Hitler, who saw the war as an apocalyptic struggle against Jewry and Bolshevism, ruled out any possibility of capitulation, and there was still no shortage of fanatical Nazis who took their signals from their Führer. Second, a profound fear of the consequences of defeat had taken hold of much of German society. This fear had been fueled by official propaganda that warned of the vengeance that "World Jewry" and "Asiatic Bolshevism" would wreak on a defeated Germany. It was also fueled by a general awareness in German society that the country had, in effect, burned its bridges by treating other countries barbarically and could therefore now expect a certain amount of reciprocation.

Some observers have identified the Allied insistence on Germany's unconditional surrender as an additional factor explaining the refusal to capitulate. That policy had been announced by Franklin Roosevelt at the Casablanca Conference in January 1943. Critics of unconditional surrender have criticized it for prolonging the war by ruling out a negotiated peace with Germany. But the Allied decision to adopt it is quite understandable in retrospect. By January 1943, the criminal nature of the Nazi regime had become abundantly clear. In December 1942, for example, the Allies had issued a statement confirming and condemning the mass murder of Jews in German-occupied Poland. The notion of a negotiated settlement with a Nazi regime that would potentially continue to exist was simply unacceptable to the leaders of the anti-Nazi alliance. They were also motivated by their understanding of the history of the "stab in the back" legend that had destabilized the Weimar Republic and helped bring Nazism to power. In 1918, they had concluded, too many Germans had been allowed to delude themselves into believing that Germany had not been defeated on the battlefield but rather had been betrayed by Jews, Marxists, and other anti-patriotic forces. In this new war, it would be important to make sure that Germans did not harbor any doubts that they had suffered a military defeat.[23]

During the second half of 1944 and the early months of 1945, enemy armies advanced on Germany from the west, the south, and the east. Meanwhile, the British and American air forces intensified their bombings of German cities and targets of military and economic importance. The Allies invaded France at Normandy on June 6, 1944 (D-Day), consolidated their positions for several weeks, and began their march eastward through France in late July. An Allied invasion of southern France followed on August 15. Paris was liberated in late August, and, by mid September, the Allies had brought most of Belgium and Luxembourg under their control. The fighting then moved into Germany itself. In December 1944, the Germans launched a major counteroffensive in the Ardennes Forest (known in the English-speaking world as the "Battle of the Bulge"). After some initial success, the offensive was halted by the Allies. The German army was now in permanent retreat in the West. By late March 1945, seven Allied armies had crossed the Rhine and had a clear path into the heart of the country.[24]

From January through April 1945, British and American bombers dropped more than twice as much explosive on German cities as they

Figure 10.5 Berlin, 1945 (PhotoQuest/Getty Images).

had during the entire year 1943 (see Figure 10.5).[25] Although much of the scholarship and discussion of the air war has focused on the ethics of bombing cities, on the experiences of citizens under the bombs, and on the measures taken by governments to deal with the damage, Allied strategic bombing did contribute to the ultimate military victory. The bombing of cities forced Germany to relocate labor and resources away from the front, while the bombing of industry and infrastructure severely damaged the German war economy. One key factor in the collapse of the German ability to wage war was the destruction of important parts of its railroad network.[26]

A combination of British air defenses and British–American attacks against German airfields severely eroded the ability of the Germans to retaliate against targets in the British Isles. After 1941, German bombers had focused on the Soviet Union, where they inflicted great destruction on cities such as Minsk and Stalingrad. But the intensifying British and American raids had provoked calls for revenge attacks among the German population. After months of rhetoric about the introduction of new "miracle weapons," the V-1 and V-2 rockets were deployed in 1944, the V-1 starting in June and the V-2 starting in September. The V-1s, which were essentially primitive cruise missiles, were produced and launched in much greater numbers. Even though about half of the V-1s that made it across the English Channel were shot down over Britain, almost 2,500 landed on London. The V-2s, which were ballistic missiles that traveled at far greater velocity, could not be shot down, but were not especially accurate. Nevertheless, over 500 V-2s hit London, and many hit cities in Belgium. All told, the V-weapons killed about 15,000 people, injured many more, and destroyed thousands of buildings.

The V-weapons did not, however, prove to be a militarily significant factor in the war. The total explosive power of all the V-weapons that landed on London over ten months was about the same as what the Royal Air Force dropped on the German city of Dortmund on the single day of March 12, 1945. The V-weapons also failed to produce the hoped-for psychological turnaround in the war. The rockets did not intimidate the British public, but rather reinforced its commitment to victory. Nor did the V-weapons convince many Germans that the war could be won.[27] While the "V" in the names of the weapons officially stood for *Vergeltung* (revenge), an acquaintance of Friedrich Kellner joked that it stood for *Verzweiflung* (desperation).[28]

In a series of offensives along the very broad front in the East in 1944 and 1945, Soviet forces pushed the Germans back, first expelling them from the Soviet Union proper and then forcing them to retreat from Poland. As the Soviets reached the Hungarian border, Germany sent troops into that country, leading to the deportation of a large percentage of the Hungarian Jewish population to Auschwitz in the late spring of 1944. At the same time further north, the Red Army stood poised to invade Germany in East Prussia. In January 1945, the Red Army launched an offensive from the west bank of the Vistula aimed at Berlin. By mid February, they were at the Oder River inside Germany. By mid April 1945, a Soviet offensive involving 2.5 million soldiers was launched against Berlin. The Germans put up a stiff defense, and the fighting was bitter, but the Red Army ground through the German forces.[29]

The German insistence on fighting to the bitter end exacted a high price. More Germans were killed between July 20, 1944 and May 1945 than in the entire war before July 1944. During the final 98 days of the war in 1945, 1.4 million German soldiers were killed, an average of 14,000 a day.[30] Moreover, as the invasion of Germany became imminent, the regime and its fanatical supporters attempted to mobilize the society to repel the invaders. In the process, they intensified the terror directed internally, targeting Jews, foreign workers, deserters, and Germans who were considered defeatist.

With the Wehrmacht no longer capable of protecting the country, the Nazi leadership created a compulsory national militia, the Volkssturm, in September 1944. As Hitler's trust in the Wehrmacht leadership had been shattered by the July 20, 1944 plot, he placed the Volkssturm under the authority of the Nazi Party rather than the military. While the military operations of the Volkssturm were coordinated by Heinrich Himmler, its political affairs were supervised by Martin Bormann, head of the NSDAP chancellery. The Nazi Party Regional Leaders (Gauleiter) also received substantial power over the Volkssturm within their regions. The Nazi leadership intended to draft into the Volkssturm all civilian males between the ages of 16 and 60, that is, those who were too young or too old for service in the Wehrmacht. Some 6 million men were eligible, but precisely how many actually served is not known. The creators of the Volkssturm did not envisage it primarily as a combat force. They hoped it would free up Wehrmacht soldiers for combat by relieving them of support functions. There was also a psychological strategy at work. The Volkssturm, it was hoped, would help stiffen the spine of the German population and prevent defeatism by demonstrating an uncompromising commitment to the defense of the Fatherland.

The members of the Volkssturm were charged with a wide range of duties. They monitored the skies, looking for Allied bombing raids and paratroopers. They hunted Allied airmen who had been shot down, in addition to Wehrmacht deserters, spies, and escaped concentration-camp prisoners. They performed guard duty at prisoner-of-war camps, and enforced rules and curfews on foreign workers. Some Volkssturm units supported the Wehrmacht directly in defensive combat operations. The Volkssturm pointedly avoided engaging in guerilla warfare against Allied soldiers, which would have placed its members at greater risk of retaliation. Members wore uniforms or clearly visible armbands. In contrast to the Werewolf (see below), the Volkssturm was intended as a legal militia that would enjoy the protection of the Geneva Conventions.

Military historians generally regard the Volkssturm to have been ineffective. It was hastily organized and poorly trained. Many if not most of its members understood that the war was lost. In the West, many willingly surrendered to British or American forces. Those in the East fought more fanatically to save themselves from capture and retribution, as they saw it, by the Soviet Asiatic hordes. Casualty rates were, not surprisingly, much higher in the East. After the war, the International Red Cross listed 31,000 members of the Volkssturm as missing in action, although the actual number killed was probably a good deal higher.[31]

Also created in September 1944, the Werewolf was conceived as a guerilla fighting organization that would inflict pain on the enemy and potentially promote a negotiated settlement favorable to Germany. It was set up by Heinrich Himmler and operated under the authority of the Higher SS and Police Leaders, who reported directly to him. It consisted of about 5,000–6,000 mainly young, fanatical Nazis, many of whom were drawn from the Hitler Youth. They blew up bridges, assassinated Allied and Soviet soldiers, and threated Germans with retaliation for collaboration. They also sabotaged communication systems and vandalized military vehicles. The Werewolf operated a transmitter to send out radio broadcasts encouraging Germans to resist the occupation of their country. All these actions were small in scale, posing more of a nuisance to the invading armies than a military threat. But the Werewolf did succeed in killing between 3,000 and 5,000 people. Among its victims were the Allied-appointed mayors of seven German towns and cities, including Aachen.

The Werewolf enjoyed little support in the population, unlike the Volkssturm. One historian estimates that 10 to 15 percent of Germans sympathized with the Werewolf. In the West, many Germans wanted to surrender to the Western Allies and bring about a clean transition to the post-Nazi phase. By the spring of 1945, most Germans understood that this period was over, but these did not include the fanatics of the Werewolf. There was greater popular support for the Werewolf in the East, where the ideological quality of the war was more pronounced, and the danger of a foreign occupation deemed more threatening.[32]

Crimes of the End Phase

The final months of the war inside Germany were characterized by chaos and struggles for survival. The future had become extremely uncertain in a way that it had not been earlier during the war and had really not been since 1933. Ideological group hatreds, desires for revenge, and the instinct of self-preservation resulted in spasms of violence.[33] This violence was not random. It was targeted at specific groups, defined racially, ethnically, and politically, that were deemed as threatening to the People's Community. These included foreign workers, real or imagined resisters or Allied collaborators, military deserters, and Jews. The perpetrators of these crimes belonged to the SS and the police apparatus, but also to institutions such as the army and the Hitler Youth, and finally to the newly established Volkssturm and Werewolf.

Foreign workers, especially those from Eastern Europe, were frequent targets of violence in late 1944 and early 1945. In October 1944, the regime placed them under intensified surveillance, fearing sabotage and other disruptive actions. The paranoia regarding the internal threat posed by the workers increased as the fronts closed in on Germany. More and more constraints were imposed on their freedom of movement, with draconian penalties threatened against those who broke the rules.

The intensified controls placed a heavy burden on foreign workers who, having been bombed out of their factories and living quarters, wandered through cities and the countryside, looking for food and shelter.

Killings of East European workers grew more frequent over time. On March 20, 1945, 208 East European workers were shot near Warstein in northwestern Germany. The town was located on a route through which columns of workers were marched away from the front. They were starving and begged for food. Some stole potatoes and turnips from a local storehouse. An SS division stationed nearby organized the massacre in the belief that the workers represented a threat to the local population. The 208 victims included men, women, and children.[34] At other locations, too, Security Police carried out summary executions of workers suspected of theft or preparing to assist invading forces. When foreign workers in bombed-out cities gathered in groups, the Security Police automatically feared the potential for an insurrection. The groups were labeled "terror gangs" or "resistance groups," although in most cases they were simply desperate people. Many were rounded up and shot. Plunder in bombed-out cities was also committed by desperate Germans, but the foreign workers were singled out for execution. The Security Police were especially suspicious of Soviet prisoners of war who had been impressed into forced labor. All of them were seen as potential carriers of Bolshevism and instruments of the approaching Red Army.

The Security Police also targeted specific groups of Germans. During evacuations from the front, many prison inmates who were considered untrustworthy were shot rather than relocated with the rest of the population. These killings were not localized eruptions of violence but were carried out in pursuance of a directive from the Reich Ministry of Justice in Berlin, which warned that certain categories of prisoners should not fall into enemy hands or go free. These included Jews, half-Jews, Poles, "Gypsies," and "asocial" prisoners.

The Wehrmacht, for its part, executed large numbers of soldiers for desertion. Fearing a repetition of 1918, when mutinies among members of the armed forces led to revolution and the alleged "stab in the back," the high command of the Wehrmacht, at Hitler's insistence, ordered draconian punishments for deserters and others guilty of breaking military discipline. These punishments were implemented within the existing system of military justice and applied with severity. Historians estimate the number of German soldiers who deserted in the final months of the war at between 100,000 and 300,000. About 15,000 of them were executed.[35]

The Wehrmacht also executed Germans who attempted to foil its scorched earth campaign in the spring of 1945. Hitler had ordered a scorched earth policy in March, according to which the retreating Germans would destroy infrastructure and material assets that might fall to the enemy. This would include motor vehicles, trains, and industrial installations. Albert Speer persuaded Hitler to revoke the policy.[36] But an order remained in place for the Wehrmacht to destroy bridges and transportation infrastructure during its retreat from the fronts. These measures led to clashes between Wehrmacht units and local residents who wished to preserve infrastructure and economic assets for the postwar period. The Wehrmacht and SS retaliated against civilians who mounted opposition, accusing them of insubordination and disrupting military operations. Shootings took place, often without the pretense of a trial.

Killings of Jews also continued into 1945, even though the systematic mass murder of the Final Solution had come to an end. The final major killing operation at Auschwitz – the murder of Slovakian Jews – had taken place in the fall of 1944. The camp was evacuated in January 1945 as the Red Army approached. Tens of thousands of prisoners were forcibly marched to the West on what survivors later called Death Marches. Many were killed along the way, or died from accidents, starvation, or illness. The prisoners were marched to camps inside Germany, where those who survived into April were liberated by Allied troops. The violence of the Death Marches resembled not so much the industrialized murder of the Final Solution as it did the violence of the end phase within Germany. Mass killings resulted from a combination of factors. First, the camp commandants and guards received orders not to let their prisoners fall into enemy hands. Second, the guards consciously employed terror as a method for controlling a large group of prisoners. Third, many of the guards acted on feelings of spite and vengeance directed at the prisoners, most of whom were Jews. The killing of prisoners in the Death Marches was not simply a product of a chaotic situation, but the result of ideologically conditioned hatred and paranoia, the cumulative dehumanization of certain categories of people, and a desensitization toward killing.

An estimated 113,000 prisoners embarked on Death Marches, about one-third of whom died. The Death Marches departed not only from Auschwitz, but also from forced-labor camps in the East. Among these was Stutthof, a camp just east of Danzig. About 7,000 Jewish slave laborers were marched from Stutthof and its subcamps to Königsberg, on the Baltic, where they were to be loaded onto ships and transported further west in the Reich. The plan proved impossible under the circumstances and was abandoned. The SS, however, was under strict orders not to leave prisoners behind. The Jews were massacred over several days at the end of January. The most notorious phase of the massacre occurred overnight from January 31 to February 1, when about 3,000 Jews were shot in the surf at the edge of the Baltic Sea in the town of Palmnicken.[37]

As the Death Marches proceeded, Nazi propaganda continued to blame the Jews for the war. In an article published in the newspaper *Das Reich* on January 21, Joseph Goebbels described "international Jewry" as "the motor behind all the perverse activity by which our united enemies lie to the world and attempt to control humanity from the shadows." The Jews, he wrote, "had mobilized the whole world against us" in retaliation for Nazism having recognized and broken the power of the Jews inside Germany. He labeled enemy soldiers – both British-American and Soviet – as agents of the "world conspiracy of a parasitic race." Goebbels also zeroed in on prominent Jews in enemy countries who had called for severe treatment of Germany, such as the Soviet writer and journalist Ilya Ehrenburg and the American secretary of the treasury, Henry Morgenthau, whose proposal for a "pastoralized" post-war Germany had been leaked in the fall of 1944 and widely presented in the German press as evidence of Jewish malevolence.[38] While propaganda of this sort was intended to instill the fear of defeat into the German people and thereby motivate them to continue the struggle, it also reflected the genuine worldview of the Nazi leadership.

The intensity of the fighting increased considerably as the Allied armies fought their way into Germany in early 1945. This was especially the case on the Eastern front, where the reciprocal demonization of the opposing forces motivated soldiers on both sides. The Red Army included former prisoners of war who had been treated atrociously by the Germans. The criminal nature of the German occupation of the Soviet Union during the preceding years was also no secret among the Soviet forces. Some Soviet soldiers gave vent to their rage by raping German civilian women.[39] Estimates of the number of rapes committed against German women at the end of the war vary from 100,000 to over 2 million. This sexual violence was part of a broader pillaging of towns and villages that included the beatings and killings of German men. Many of the rapes occurred in Berlin, where the fighting was especially intense. Rape – simultaneously an act of violence against women and one of humiliation toward men – has been committed by conquering armies through history, including, notably, the German army in the occupied Soviet Union. In many cases, German women reacted to their own rape by committing suicide. The shame traditionally accompanying rape was often deepened by the subhuman stigma that had been attached to the Soviet soldiers, especially those with central Asian origins, by German propaganda.[40]

More generally, many Germans chose the path of suicide when defeat was imminent, preferring to take their own lives rather than be taken captive by enemies from whom vengeance could be expected. This fear of revenge was not, under the circumstances, irrational, as some Red Army troops did behave viciously, but at times it reflected an ideologically determined or propagandistically induced hyper-paranoia about the Soviet Union. Such was the case in the town of Demmin, where 900 Germans killed themselves at the beginning of May 1945.[41] For Nazi fanatics, including members of the top leadership, suicide offered an escape from a future of imprisonment and prosecution, and also from a future without National Socialism. Hitler himself expressed this attitude in his final "political testament" in the following terms: "I do not wish to fall into the hands of the enemy, who is looking for a new spectacle organized by the Jews for the amusement of their hysterical masses."[42]

Hitler dictated this document in his bunker under the Reich Chancellery in Berlin on April 29, 1945. In one portion of the text, he appointed a successor government led by Admiral Karl Dönitz, whose loyalty to Hitler and whose determination to fight to the bitter end had never wavered. But much of the text consisted of a final tirade against the Jews, whom he blamed for the calamity that had befallen Germany and the world. "It is untrue," he contended, "that I or anyone else in Germany wanted the war in 1939. It was desired and instigated by those international statesmen who were either of Jewish descent or worked for Jewish interests." Britain, he claimed, had refused to let Germany deal with Poland as it wished because the British leadership had been "under the influence of propaganda organized by International Jewry." Hitler then, one final time, referred to his "prophecy" of January 30, 1933. He had, he claimed, "made it quite plain that, if the nations of Europe are again to be regarded as mere shares to be bought and sold by these international conspirators in money and finance, then Jewry, the race that is the real criminal in this murderous struggle, will be saddled with the responsibility." At the conclusion of his final testament, Hitler urged his successors to devote themselves to "scrupulous observance of the laws of race and to merciless opposition to the universal poisoner of all peoples, International Jewry." The next day, April 30, 1945, he killed himself.

Conclusion

The German armed forces surrendered unconditionally to the Western Allies and the Red Army in the early morning hours of May 9, 1945 in Berlin. The war that Hitler had fomented, unleashed, and prosecuted had produced a staggering death toll. The Soviet Union, which had been subjected to a merciless war of annihilation over a period of years, lost about 27 million people, equally divided between military and civilian deaths. Over 6 million Poles had lost their lives, about half of them Jews killed in the German-organized genocide. Germany itself had suffered over 5 million military and over 1 million civilian deaths. Almost 2 million people died in Yugoslavia, and about 1 million in Hungary. War-related deaths in Britain, France, the Netherlands, Italy, and Czechoslovakia numbered in the hundreds of thousands.[1] Germany was not alone responsible for the war, but the harnessing of that modern country's power by a movement committed to imposing by force a new racial and political order on Europe had been its primary cause. The chief legacy of National Socialism was not a People's Community but mass death across Europe.

Nazism had emerged as a synthesis of multiple historical developments: romantic nationalism, racism, antisemitism, eugenics, anti-liberalism, and anti-Communism. Its political attraction was attributable to a lost war, a young and unstable democracy, and a middle class that, during a global economic crisis, felt threatened by Communism. Nazism remained a marginalized political force until the Depression tore the Weimar Republic apart at its seams starting in 1929. Germans gravitated to National Socialism for many reasons. Chief among them were the desire to liberate Germany from the constraints of the Treaty of Versailles and restore its status as a great power; the hope to re-establish order and decisive political authority in a state that had proven itself ungovernable by a democratic system; the charisma of Adolf Hitler and the dynamism of the Nazi movement, which promised to break the logjam associated with parliamentary politics; a readiness to embrace antisemitism and employ Jews as a scapegoat for the country's problems;

and the perception that the Nazi movement could effectively stave off the threat to Germany's economic and social order posed by Communism. For many of its supporters, Nazism offered the promise of national integration in a society riven by ideological and class divisions. Although the Nazi movement drew its members and voters disproportionately from the middle and upper classes, it also attracted significant support from the working class. In this regard, the NSDAP was the first major political party in German history to appeal successfully to almost all sectors of the population.

Despite that particular political achievement, never did more than 37.5 percent of German voters cast their vote for the Nazi Party in a genuinely free election. Thus, even at the height of the party's electoral success in 1932, almost two-thirds of German voters preferred a different party. The NSDAP ultimately prevailed because of the fractiousness of the German party system, the conservative elite's contempt for democracy and readiness to enter a coalition with Hitler's party (which they expected they would control), and the lack of unity on the political left. While certain mechanisms of democracy resulted in Hitler's appointment to the chancellorship, it cannot be said that he or his party were thrust into power as the result of a genuinely democratic process. Many Germans and foreigners understood that Hitler's accession to power could lead to catastrophe, but few could imagine a country in ruins at the conclusion of a war costing tens of millions of lives. Even Hitler's own supporters could not foretell the magnitude of the disaster that lay a decade in the future.

Hitler and his movement were consistently underestimated by both their allies and their adversaries. The conservative nationalists, the liberal parties, the Catholic Center, and the parties on the left all underestimated the capacity of the Nazi movement to mobilize the passions and resentments of large numbers of Germans. They also underestimated the ruthlessness to which Hitler would resort to eliminate political opposition. This underestimation accounts not only for the Nazi rise to power but for its ability to establish a dictatorship in short order using emergency powers, the police, violence by Stormtroopers, physical intimidation, and concentration camps. Many Germans jumped on board, engaging in "self-coordination," while others resigned themselves to the dawn of a new era in German history. Others dissented and resisted, but the resistance was broken or at least contained by the regime's apparatus of terror. Many of those inclined to opposition became demoralized and ultimately went with the flow.

There was no Nazi consensus in German society in 1933 or 1934. But by September 1939 the situation had changed. Material life got better for most people in large part on account of the militarization of the German economy. Even many workers whose independent labor unions had been crushed were grateful or at least relieved by the economic recovery. In addition, Hitler's defiance of Germany's World War I enemies, his rejection of the Treaty of Versailles, and the rearmament of Germany met with widespread approval. This approval was not tantamount to endorsing a war of annihilation and continental conquest. But this is where Hitler led the country eventually.

The imposition of the Nazi vision of a People's Community was only partially successful. The attempted transformation of values and belief systems encountered considerable friction. Many Germans reacted negatively to the incessant politicization of their daily lives. Nevertheless, the extent of the transformation that had taken place by the outbreak of World War II was significant, especially when considering the compressed time frame in which it occurred. In 1939, most Germans believed the country to be in a much better place than it had been in 1933. Opponents of the Nazi regime could be found in the churches, the military, the civil service, and the working class, but not nearly to the extent that the dictatorship could be threatened. The rapid institutionalization of antisemitism, along with other measures of persecution, tended to meet with broad approval as long as they were implemented in a legal and orderly fashion. The distress unleashed in German society by the November 1938 Kristallnacht pogrom stood in stark contrast to the widespread consensus in favor of the legal and bureaucratic measures used to disenfranchise Jews since 1933. The program of mass eugenic sterilization, which was welcomed by much of the medical community and seen as scientifically state of the art, did not provoke significant pushback. The concentration camps and other organs of the "prerogative state" did instill fear in the population, but most ordinary Germans were not inclined to engage in acts of resistance in the first place.

The outbreak of war was not greeted by a swell of enthusiasm among Germans. Memories of the price of the previous war were still fresh, but government propaganda proved effective in the wake of Britain's refusal to acquiesce in Germany's continental hegemony, combined with British bombing raids on German cities. Many ordinary Germans were ready to participate in the country's colonization and exploitation of Poland, and otherwise to profit from Germany's newfound empire on the continent of Europe. The war provided cover for the escalation of eugenic sterilization into the mass murder of disabled persons. Insofar as this program was not well received in German society but deemed an important priority of the Nazi leadership, it established a precedent for the mass murder of Europe's Jews on a far larger scale starting in 1941.

German power in Europe reached its zenith in 1942, as the Wehrmacht drove deep inside the Soviet Union. Going to war against the

Soviet Union was a choice and not a necessity. Hitler made this choice in pursuit of ideological goals that were at the core of his worldview. He initiated the very two-front war he had previously wanted to avoid but assumed that the Soviet Union would collapse quickly. In the event, the Soviets did not fold as Hitler had expected, and a few months later he declared war against the United States, with which he desired a reckoning. Hitler's racism and antisemitism blinded him to the war-fighting capacities of both countries.

The eliminationist, racist logic of National Socialism, which judged the value of human lives according to ancestry, was linked to an apocalyptic understanding of the struggle against Communism and "World Jewry." The mass murder of Europe's Jews began as an element of this war of annihilation in the East and was soon expanded to encompass the rest of Nazi dominated Europe. As soldiers, producers of armaments, war profiteers, colonial pioneers, and members of commandos tasked with the liquidation of civilians, Germans participated in a barbaric war of territorial conquest. Internal resistance, which intensified as the war progressed and turned increasingly against Germany, produced numerous stories of courage and patriotism, but had little practical effect on the outcome of the conflict, which in the final analysis was decided by the superior military might of the anti-German alliance. In late 1944 and early 1945, as enemy armies closed in on the country from multiple directions, and as bombs rained down on its major cities, the violence unleashed by National Socialism focused increasingly on Germany itself. Fanatical Nazis lashed out at foreign laborers, Jewish survivors of the Final Solution, and Germans who preferred to end the war and cooperate with the Western Allies. In Eastern Germany and in Berlin, the population experienced retribution by Soviet forces, whose country and comrades had borne much of the brunt of Nazi Germany's war of annihilation.

An ideology and movement intending to regenerate the German nation and enable it to assert its presumed greatness, Nazism led instead to defeat, destruction, the loss of territory, and a decades-long division of the country. For many Germans, it produced an enduring sense of shame. We would all do well to study the lessons that they have taken to heart about the follies of racism, dictatorship, and national hubris.

Notes

Introduction

1 A good introduction to this question is Martina Steber and Bernhard Gotto, eds., *Visions of Community in Nazi Germany: Social Engineering and Private Lives* (Oxford: Oxford University Press, 2014).

2 Neil Gregor, "Nazism – A Political Religion? Rethinking the Voluntarist Turn," in Neil Gregor, ed., *Nazism, War and Genocide* (Exeter: University of Exeter Press, 2005), pp. 1–21.

3 Gavriel D. Rosenfeld, *Hi Hitler! How the Nazi Past Is Being Normalized in Contemporary Culture* (Cambridge: Cambridge University Press, 2015).

1 The Idea of Nazism

1 Franz Neumann, *Behemoth: The Structure and Practice of National Socialism* (Toronto; New York: Oxford University Press, 1942).

2 Alan Bullock, *Hitler: A Study in Tyranny* (New York: Harper & Row, 1962).

3 Alan E. Steinweis, *Studying the Jew: Scholarly Antisemitism in Nazi Germany* (Cambridge, MA: Harvard University Press, 2006).

4 Claudia Koonz, *The Nazi Conscience* (Cambridge, MA: Harvard University Press, 2003).

5 Michael D. Biddiss, *Father of Racist Ideology: The Social and Political Thought of Count Gobineau* (New York: Weybright and Talley, 1970).

6 Mark A. Weiner, *Richard Wagner and the Anti-Semitic Imagination* (Lincoln, NE: University of Nebraska Press, 1995); Jakob Katz, *The Darker Side of Genius: Richard Wagner's Anti-Semitism* (Hanover, NH: University Press of New England, 1986); Paul Lawrence Rose, *Wagner: Race and Revolution* (New Haven: Yale University Press, 1992).

7 Geoffrey G. Field, *Evangelist of Race: The Germanic Vision of Houston Stewart Chamberlain* (New York: Columbia University Press, 1981); Roderick Stackelberg, *Idealism Debased: From Völkisch Ideology to National Socialism* (Kent, OH: Kent State University Press, 1981).

8 Richard S. Levy, *The Downfall of the Anti-Semitic Political Parties in Imperial Germany* (New Haven: Yale University Press, 1975).

9 John W. Boyer, *Political Radicalism in Late Imperial Vienna: Origins of the Christian Social Movement, 1848–1897* (Chicago: University of Chicago

Press, 1981); Richard S. Geehr, *Karl Lueger: Mayor of Fin de Siècle Vienna* (Detroit, MI: Wayne State University Press, 1990).

10 Paul A. Hanebrink, *A Specter Haunting Europe: The Myth of Judeo-Bolshevism* (Cambridge, MA: Harvard University Press, 2018).

11 Michael Hawkins, *Social Darwinism in European and American Thought, 1860–1945: Nature as Model and Nature as Threat* (Cambridge: Cambridge University Press, 1997).

12 David Thomas Murphy, *The Heroic Earth: Geopolitical Thought in Weimar Germany* (Kent, OH: Kent State University Press, 1997).

13 Daniel J. Kevles, *In the Name of Eugenics: Genetics and the Uses of Human Heredity* (New York: Knopf, 1985); Alison Bashford and Philippa Levine, eds., *The Oxford Handbook of the History of Eugenics* (New York: Oxford University Press, 2010).

14 Dagmar Herzog, *Sex after Fascism: Memory and Morality in Twentieth-Century Germany* (Princeton: Princeton University Press, 2005).

15 Karl Dietrich Bracher, *The German Dictatorship: The Origins, Structure, and Effects of National Socialism*, trans. Jean Steinberg (New York: Praeger, 1970), p. 6.

16 Adolf Hitler, *Hitler's Second Book: The Unpublished Sequel to Mein Kampf*, ed. Gerhard L. Weinberg, trans. Krista Smith (New York: Enigma Books, 2003), p. 48.

2 The Triumph of Nazism

1 Jochen Hung, Godela Weiss-Sussex, and Geoff Wilkes, eds., *Beyond Glitter and Doom: The Contingency of the Weimar Republic* (Munich: Iudicium, 2012); Rüdiger Graf, *Die Zukunft der Weimarer Republik: Krisen und Zukunftsaneignungen in Deutschland 1918–1933* (Munich: Oldenbourg, 2008).

2 Hermann Beck and Larry Eugene Jones, eds., *From Weimar to Hitler: Studies in the Dissolution of the Weimar Republic and the Establishment of the Third Reich, 1932–1934* (New York: Berghahn, 2018).

3 Hans-Ulrich Wehler, *Das deutsche Kaiserreich, 1871–1918* (Göttingen: Vandenhoeck & Ruprecht, 1973).

4 David Blackbourn and Geoff Eley, *The Peculiarities of German History: Bourgeois Society and Politics in Nineteenth-Century Germany* (Oxford: Oxford University Press, 1984).

5 Helmut Walser Smith, "When the *Sonderweg* Debate Left Us," *German Studies Review* 31, no. 2 (2008): 225–40.

6 Roger Chickering, *Imperial Germany and the Great War, 1914–1918* (Cambridge: Cambridge University Press, 1998); Belinda Davis, *Home Fires Burning: Food, Politics, and Everyday Life in World War I Berlin* (Chapel Hill: University of North Carolina Press, 2000).

7 Walter A. McDougall, *France's Rhineland Diplomacy, 1914–1924: The Last Bid for a Balance of Power in Europe* (Princeton: Princeton University Press, 1978); Conan Fischer and Alan Sharp, *After the Versailles Treaty: Enforcement, Compliance, Contested Identities* (Hoboken, NJ: Taylor and Francis, 2013); Sally Marks, *The Illusion of Peace: International Relations in Europe, 1918–1933* (New York: Palgrave Macmillan, 2003).

8 Larry Eugene Jones, *German Liberalism and the Dissolution of the Weimar Party System, 1918–1933* (Chapel Hill: University of North Carolina Press, 1988).

9 Anna von der Goltz, *Hindenburg: Power, Myth, and the Rise of the Nazis* (Oxford: Oxford University Press, 2009).

10 Ian Kershaw, *Hitler: 1889–1936 Hubris* (New York: Norton, 1999); Peter Longerich, *Hitler: A Biography*, trans. Jeremy Noakes and Lesley Sharpe (Oxford: Oxford University Press, 2019); Volker Ullrich, *Hitler: Ascent, 1889–1939*, trans. Jefferson S. Chase (New York: Knopf, 2016).

11 Thomas Weber, *Hitler's First War: Adolf Hitler, the Men of the List Regiment, and the First World War* (Oxford: Oxford University Press, 2010); Richard S. Levy, "Political Antisemitism in Germany and Austria, 1848–1914," in Albert S. Lindemann and Richard S. Levy, eds., *Antisemitism: A History* (Oxford: Oxford University Press, 2010), pp. 121–35.

12 Max Weber, *Max Weber on Charisma and Institution Building: Selected Papers*, ed. S. N. Eisenstadt (Chicago: University of Chicago Press, 1968).

13 Wolfgang Schieder, *Adolf Hitler: Politischer Zauberlehrling Mussolinis* (Berlin: De Gruyter Oldenbourg, 2017).

14 Michael H. Kater, *The Nazi Party: A Social Profile of Members and Leaders, 1919–1945* (Cambridge, MA: Harvard University Press, 1983).

15 Longerich, *Hitler*, p. 111.

16 Kater, *The Nazi Party*.

17 Harold Gordon, *Hitler and the Beer Hall Putsch* (Princeton: Princeton University Press, 1972).

18 Jonathan Wright, *Gustav Stresemann: Weimar's Greatest Statesman* (Oxford: Oxford University Press, 2002.)

19 Detlev J. K. Peukert, *The Weimar Republic: The Crisis of Classical Modernity*, trans. Richard Deveson (New York: Hill and Wang, 1992).

20 Joan Clinefelter, *Artists for the Reich: Culture and Race from Weimar to Nazi Germany* (Oxford: Berg, 2005); Alan E. Steinweis, *Art, Ideology, Economics in Nazi Germany: The Reich Chambers of Music, Theater, and the Visual Arts* (Chapel Hill: University of North Carolina Press, 1993); Pamela Potter, *Art of Suppression: Confronting the Nazi Past in Histories of the Visual and Performing Arts* (Berkeley: University of California Press, 2016).

21 Larry Eugene Jones, *The German Right in the Weimar Republic: Studies in the History of German Conservatism, Nationalism, and Antisemitism* (New York: Berghahn, 2014).

22 Jeremy Noakes and Geoffrey Pridham, eds., *Nazism, 1919–1945: A Documentary Reader*, 4 vols. (Exeter: University of Exeter Press, 1998–2008), vol. 1, p. 45.

23 Dietrich Orlow, *The History of the Nazi Party*, 2 vols. (Pittsburgh: University of Pittsburgh Press, 1969–1973).

24 Geoffrey Giles, *Students and National Socialism in Germany* (Princeton: Princeton University Press, 1985).

25 Conan Fischer, *The Rise of National Socialism and the Working Classes in Weimar Germany* (Providence, RI: Berghahn, 1996); Max H. Kele, *Nazis and Workers: National Socialist Appeals to German Labor, 1919–1933* (Chapel Hill: University of North Carolina Press, 1972).

26 Jürgen Gimmel, *Die politische Organisation kulturellen Ressentiments: Der "Kampfbund für deutsche Kultur" und das bildungsbürgerliche Unbehagen an der Moderne* (Münster: LIT-Verlag, 2001); Alan E. Steinweis, "Weimar Culture and the Rise of National Socialism: The Kampfbund für deutsche Kultur," *Central European History* 24, no. 4 (December 1991): 402–23.

27 Michael H. Kater, *Doctors under Hitler* (Chapel Hill: University of North Carolina Press, 1989); Annette Eberle, *Die Ärzteschaft in Bayern und die Praxis der Medizin im Nationalsozialismus* (Berlin: Metropol, 2017).

28 Matthew Stibbe, *Women in the Third Reich* (London: Arnold, 2003).

29 Noakes and Pridham, *Nazism*, vol. 1, p. 58.

30 Dietmar Petzina, "Arbeitslosigkeit in der Weimarer Republik," in Werner Abelshauser, ed., *Die Weimarer Republik als Wohlfahrtsstaat* (Stuttgart: Franz Steiner Verlag, 1987), pp. 239–59.

31 Kater, *The Nazi Party*; Thomas Childers, *The Nazi Voter: The Foundations of Fascism in Germany, 1919–1933* (Chapel Hill: University of North Carolina Press, 1983); Jürgen W. Falter, *Hitlers Wähler* (Munich: Beck, 1991); Richard F. Hamilton, *Who Voted for Hitler?* (Princeton: Princeton University Press, 1982).

32 Konrad H. Jarausch, *The Unfree Professions: German Lawyers, Teachers, and Engineers, 1900–1950* (Oxford: Oxford University Press, 1990); Michael Wildt, *An Uncompromising Generation: The Nazi Leadership of the Reich Security Main Office*, trans. Tom Lampert (Madison: University of Wisconsin Press, 2009).

33 Theodore Abel, *Why Hitler Came into Power*, ed. Thomas Childers (Cambridge, MA: Harvard University Press, 1986); Peter H. Merkl, *The Making of a Stormtrooper* (Princeton: Princeton University Press, 1980).

34 Childers, *The Nazi Voter*.

35 Henry Ashby Turner, Jr., *German Big Business and the Rise of Hitler* (Oxford: Oxford University Press, 1985).

36 Larry Eugene Jones, *Hitler versus Hindenburg: The 1931 Presidential Elections and the End of the Weimar Republic* (Cambridge: Cambridge University Press, 2016).

37 Larry Eugene Jones, "Franz Von Papen, the German Center Party, and the Failure of Catholic Conservatism in the Weimar Republic," *Central European History* 38, no. 2 (2005): 191–217.

38 Henry Ashby Turner, Jr., *Hitler's Thirty Days to Power: January 1933* (Reading, MA: Addison-Wesley, 1996); Larry Eugene Jones, "Taming the Nazi Beast: Kurt von Schleicher and the End of the Weimar Republic," in Beck and Jones, eds., *From Weimar to Hitler*, pp. 23–51. Jones refutes the long-held belief that Schleicher intended to split the NSDAP.

39 Robert M. W. Kempner, *Der verpasste Nazi-Stopp: Die NSDAP als staats- und republikfeindliche, hochverräterische Verbindung: preussische Denkschrift von 1930* (Frankfurt: Ullstein, 1983).

40 Karl Dietrich Bracher, *The German Dictatorship: The Origins, Structure, and Effects of National Socialism*, trans. Jean Steinberg (New York: Praeger, 1970), p. 246.

3 The Nazi Dictatorship

1 Karl Dietrich Bracher, *The German Dictatorship: The Origins, Structure, and Effects of National Socialism*, trans. Jean Steinberg (New York: Praeger, 1970), p. 253.

2 Lawrence D. Stokes, *"Meine kleine Stadt steht für tausend andere …": Studien zur Geschichte von Eutin in Holstein, 1918–1945* (Eutin: Struve, 2004), pp. 388–89.

3 William S. Allen, *The Nazi Seizure of Power: The Experience of a Single German Town, 1922–1945* (New York: Franklin Watts, 1984), pp. 154–55.

4 Dirk Schumann, "Gewalt als Methode der nationalsozialistischen Machteroberung," in Andreas Wirsching, ed., *Das Jahr 1933: Die Nationalsozialistische Machteroberung und die deutsche Gesellschaft* (Göttingen: Wallstein, 2009), pp. 144–45.

5 Jeremey Noakes, "Nationalsozialismus in der Provinz: Kleine und mittlere Städte im Dritten Reich," in Horst Möller, Andreas Wirsching, and Walter Ziegler, eds., *Nationalsozialismus in der Region: Beiträge zur regionalen und lokalen Forschung und zum internationalen Vergleich* (Munich: Oldenbourg, 1996), pp. 237–52.

6 Ludolf Herbst, *Das Nationalsozialistische Deutschland 1933–1945: Die Entfesselung der Gewalt – Rassismus und Krieg* (Frankfurt: Suhrkamp, 1996), pp. 63–64.

7 Benjamin C. Hett, *Burning the Reichstag: An Investigation into the Third Reich's Enduring Mystery* (Oxford: Oxford University Press, 2014); Richard J. Evans, "The Conspiracists," review of Hett, *Burning the Reichstag*, *London Review of Books* 36, no. 9 (May 8, 2014).

8 Rainer Orth, *"Der Amtssitz der Opposition"? Politik und Staatsumbaupläne im Büro des Stellvertreters des Reichskanzlers in den Jahren 1933–1934* (Cologne: Böhlau, 2016), pp. 300–2.

9 Andreas Schwegel, *Der Polizeibegriff im NS-Staat: Polizeirecht, juristische Publizistik und Judikative 1931–1944* (Tübingen: Mohr Siebeck, 2005), pp. 41–43.

10 Karl Dietrich Bracher, Wolfgang Sauer, and Gerhard Schulz, *Die Nationalsozialistische Machtergreifung: Studien zur Errichtung des totalitären Herrschaftssystems in Deutschland 1933/34*, 2nd ed. (Cologne: Westdeutscher Verlag, 1962).

11 Douglas G. Morris, *Legal Sabotage: Ernst Fraenkel in Hitler's Germany* (Cambridge: Cambridge University Press, 2020); Ernst Fraenkel, *The Dual State: A Contribution to the Theory of Dictatorship* (New York: Oxford University Press, 1941).

12 Allen, *Nazi Seizure of Power*, p. 157.

13 Stokes, *"Meine kleine Stadt steht für tausend andere,"* p. 392.

14 Bracher, Sauer, Schulz, *Nationalsozialistische Machtergreifung*, pp. 152–53.

15 Wilhelm Hoegner, *Flucht vor Hitler: Erinnerungen an die Kapitulation der ersten deutschen Republik 1933* (Frankfurt: Fischer Taschenbuch Verlag, 1979).

16 Bracher, Sauer, Schulz, *Nationalsozialistische Machtergreifung*, p. 158.

17 Thomas Brechenmacher, *Das Reichskonkordat 1933: Forschungsstand, Kontroversen, Dokumente* (Paderborn: F. Schöningh, 2007).

18 Martin Broszat, *The Hitler State: The Foundation and Development of the Internal Structure of the Third Reich*, trans. John W. Hiden (London: Longman, 1982), pp. 104–7.
19 Bracher, Sauer, Schulz, *Nationalsozialistische Machtergreifung*, pp. 117–24.
20 Broszat, *Hitler State*, pp. 112–13.
21 Karl Dürkefälden, *"Schreiben, wie es wirklich war!": Aufzeichnungen Karl Dürkefäldens aus den Jahren 1933–1945*, ed. Herbert and Sybille Obenaus (Hanover: Fackelträger, 1985), p. 48.
22 Timothy W. Mason, *Arbeiterklasse und Volksgemeinschaft: Dokumente und Materialien zur deutschen Arbeiterpolitik 1936–1939* (Opladen: Westdeutscher Verlag, 1975), pp. 17–29.
23 Ibid., pp. 21–22; Timothy W. Mason, *Sozialpolitik im Dritten Reich: Arbeiterklasse und Volksgemeinschaft* (Opladen: Westdeutscher Verlag: 1977); Timothy W. Mason, *Nazism, Fascism and the Working Class*, ed. Jane Caplan (Cambridge: Cambridge University Press, 1995).
24 Bracher, Sauer, Schulz, *Nationalsozialistische Machtergreifung*, p. 180.
25 Ronald Smelser, *Robert Ley: Hitler's Labor Front Leader* (Oxford: Berg, 1988), pp. 128–33.
26 Rüdiger Hachtmann, *Das Wirtschaftsimperium der deutschen Arbeitsfront, 1933–1945* (Göttingen: Wallstein, 2012).
27 Brechenmacher, *Das Reichskonkordat 1933*.
28 Bracher, Sauer, Schulz, *Nationalsozialistische Machtergreifung*, p. 219.
29 *Völkischer Beobachter*, July 15, 1933, quoted in *Akten der Reichskanzlei, 1933/34*, vol. 1, part 1, ed. Karl-Heinz Minuth (Boppard am Rhein: Boldt, 1983), p. 659, note 1.
30 Henry Friedlander, *The Origins of Nazi Genocide: From Euthanasia to the Final Solution* (Chapel Hill: University of North Carolina Press, 1995), p. 27.
31 Anton Löffelmeier, "'Gleichschaltung' im Münchner Fussballsport 1933–1936," in Markwart Herzog, ed., *Die "Gleichschaltung" des Fussballsports im nationalsozialistischen Deutschland* (Stuttgart: Kohlhammer, 2016), pp. 54–56.
32 Michael Schwartz, "Schützenvereine im 'Dritten Reich'," *Archiv für Kulturgeschichte* 79 (1997): 444–46; Lorenz Peiffer and Henry Alexander Wahlig, *Juden im Sport während des Nationalsozialismus: Ein historisches Handbuch für Niedersachsen und Bremen* (Göttingen: Wallstein, 2012), p. 18.
33 Peter Hayes, *Industry and Ideology: IG Farben in the Nazi Era*, 2nd ed. (Cambridge: Cambridge University Press, 2000), pp. 87–99.
34 Annette Eberle, *Die Ärzteschaft in Bayern und die Praxis der Medizin im Nationalsozialismus* (Berlin: Metropol, 2017), pp. 49–58.
35 Alan E. Steinweis, *Art, Ideology, and Economics in Nazi Germany: The Reich Chambers of Music, Theater, and the Visual Arts* (Chapel Hill: University of North Carolina Press), pp. 37–38.
36 Gerhard L. Weinberg, *The Foreign Policy of Hitler's Germany: Diplomatic Revolution in Europe, 1933–36* (Chicago: University of Chicago Press, 1970), pp. 159–66.
37 Carole Fink, *Defending the Rights of Others: The Great Powers, the Jews, and International Minority Protection, 1878–1938* (Cambridge: Cambridge University Press, 2004), pp. 328–29.

38 Bracher, Sauer, Schulz, *Nationalsozialistische Machtergreifung*, pp. 355–58.

39 Ibid., pp. 351–68.

40 Adam Tooze, *The Wages of Destruction: The Making and Breaking of the Nazi Economy* (New York: Penguin Books, 2006), p. 43.

41 Gustavo Corni, *Hitler and the Peasants: The Agrarian Policy of the Third Reich*, trans. David Kerr (New York: Berg, 1990), ch. 4.

42 Steinweis, *Art, Ideology, and Economics*.

43 Norbert Frei and Johannes Schmitz, *Journalismus im dritten Reich* (Munich: Beck, 1999), pp. 27–29.

44 Mason, *Nazism, Fascism and the Working Class*, p. 80.

45 Ibid., ch. 3; Tooze, *Wages of Destruction*, p. 102.

46 Eleanor Hancock, *Ernst Röhm: Hitler's SA Chief of Staff* (Basingstoke: Palgrave Macmillan, 2008), ch. 14.

47 Orth, "*Der Amtssitz der Opposition*"?, p. 148.

48 Ibid., pp. 420–22.

49 Ibid., p. 424.

50 Ibid., pp. 451–53.

51 Hancock, *Ernst Röhm*, ch. 15.

52 Lothar Gruchmann, "Erlebnisbericht Werner Pünders über die Ermordung Klauseners am 30. Juni 1934 und ihre Folgen," *Vierteljahrshefte für Zeitgeschichte* 19, no. 4 (1971): 404–31.

53 Hett, *Burning the Reichstag*, pp. 195–96, 306, 319.

54 Burkhard Jellonnek, *Homosexuelle unter dem Hakenkreuz: Die Verfolgung von Homosexuellen im Dritten Reich* (Paderborn: Schöningh, 1990), pp. 95–110.

55 Joseph Bendersky, "Schmitt's Diaries," in Jens Meierhenrich and Oliver Simons, eds., *The Oxford Handbook of Carl Schmitt* (New York: Oxford University Press, 2016), pp. 117–46.

56 Daniel Siemens, *Stormtroopers: A New History of Hitler's Brownshirts* (New Haven: Yale University Press, 2017).

57 Bracher, Sauer, Schulz, *Nationalsozialistische Machtergreifung*, pp. 355–58.

4   The Nazi Economy, 1933–1939

1 Martina Steber and Bernhard Gotto, eds., *Visions of Community in Nazi Germany: Social Engineering and Private Lives* (Oxford: Oxford University Press, 2014).

2 *Hitler: Reden und Proklamationen, 1932–1945*, ed. Max Domarus, 4 vols. (Munich: Süddeutscher Verlag, 1965), vol. 1, pp. 229–37.

3 Ibid., pp. 259–64.

4 Ibid., pp. 349–51.

5 Robert Gellately, *Backing Hitler: Consent and Coercion in Nazi Germany* (Oxford: Oxford University Press, 2001).

6 Adam Tooze, *The Wages of Destruction: The Making and Breaking of the Nazi Economy* (New York: Penguin Books, 2006), p. 62; Tim Schanetzky, *Kanonen statt Butter: Wirtschaft und Konsum im Dritten Reich* (Munich: Beck, 2015), pp. 58–64; Dan P. Silverman, *Hitler's Economy: Nazi Work*

    Creation Programs, 1933–1936 (Cambridge, MA: Harvard University Press, 1998), p. 220.

7 Schanetzky, *Kanonen statt Butter*, p. 63.

8 Alfred C. Mierzejewski, *The Most Valuable Asset of the Reich: A History of the German National Railway*, 2 vols. (Chapel Hill: University of North Carolina Press, 2000), vol. 2, ch. 2.

9 Kiran Klaus Patel, *Soldiers of Labor: Labor Service in Nazi Germany and New Deal America, 1933–1945* (Cambridge: Cambridge University Press, 2005).

10 David Welch, *Propaganda and the German Cinema, 1933–1945*, rev. ed. (London: Tauris, 2001), pp. 132–33.

11 Matthew Stibbe, *Women in the Third Reich* (London: Arnold, 2003), pp. 85–86.

12 Silverman, *Hitler's Economy*, p. 245; Tooze, *Wages of Destruction*, p. 207.

13 Harold James, *The German Slump: Politics and Economics 1924–1936* (Oxford: Oxford University Press, 1986), pp. 373–77; Schanetzky, *Kanonen statt Butter*, pp. 75–76.

14 It was actually officially titled the Second Four Year Plan, in order to create the impression that the economic policies of the preceding four years had followed a coherent plan.

15 Tooze, *Wages of Destruction*, p. 220.

16 Stibbe, *Women in the Third Reich*, pp. 87–88.

17 Ibid., p. 91; Dörte Winkler, *Frauenarbeit im "Dritten Reich"* (Hamburg: Hoffmann und Campe, 1977), pp. 194–95.

18 Jonathan Wiesen, *Creating the Nazi Marketplace: Commerce and Consumption in the Third Reich* (Cambridge: Cambridge University Press, 2011).

19 Tooze, *Wages of Destruction*, ch. 5.

20 David Schoenbaum, *Hitler's Social Revolution: Class and Status in Nazi Germany 1933–1939* (Garden City, NY: Doubleday, 1966).

21 Shelley Baranowski, *Strength through Joy: Consumerism and Mass Tourism in the Third Reich* (Cambridge: Cambridge University Press, 2004); Julia Timpe, *Nazi-Organized Recreation and Entertainment in the Third Reich* (London: Palgrave Macmillan, 2017).

22 Timothy W. Mason, *Nazism, Fascism and the Working Class*, ed. Jane Caplan (Cambridge: Cambridge University Press, 1995), pp. 231–73.

23 Tim Mason, *Social Policy in the Third Reich: The Working Class and the "National Community"* (Providence, RI: Berg, 1993), pp. 104–5; Tooze, *Wages of Destruction*, p. 102.

24 Alfred C. Mierzejewski, *A History of the German Public Pension System: Continuity and Change* (Lanham: Lexington Books, 2016), ch. 5.

25 Mason, *Social Policy in the Third Reich*, p. 105.

26 Dietmar Süss, *"Ein Volk, Ein Reich, Ein Führer": Die deutsche Gesellschaft im Dritten Reich* (Munich: Beck, 2017), p. 85.

27 *Deutschland Berichte der Sozialdemokratischen Partei Deutschlands (SOPADE), 1934–1940*, 7 vols. (Salzhausen: P. Nettelbeck, 1980) (hereafter *SOPADE*), 1935, p. 811.

28 *SOPADE*, 1935, p. 655; Mason, *Nazism, Fascism and the Working Class*, p. 258.

29 Gustavo Corni, *Hitler and the Peasants: The Agrarian Policy of the Third Reich*, trans. David Kerr (New York: Berg, 1990).

30 Ibid., p. xvi.

31 Ibid., pp. 8–11, 19, 21–22.

32 Ibid., pp. 66, 74.

33 Ibid., pp. 87, 89, 91–93.

34 Ibid., pp. 105–8.

35 Ian Kershaw, *Popular Opinion and Political Dissent in the Third Reich, Bavaria 1933–1945* (Oxford: Oxford University Press, 1983), pp. 45–47, 49, 52.

36 Corni, *Hitler and the Peasants*, p. 144.

37 Ibid., ch. 7, p. 143; Friedrich Grundmann, *Agrarpolitik im "Dritten Reich": Anspruch und Wirklichkeit des Reichserbhofsgesetzes* (Hamburg: Hoffmann und Campe, 1979).

38 Kershaw, *Popular Opinion and Political Dissent*, p. 43.

39 Corni, *Hitler and the Peasants*, p. 145.

40 Ibid., p. 148.

41 Ibid., chs. 8–11.

42 Kershaw, *Popular Opinion and Political Dissent*, pp. 83, 93, 128.

43 Corni, *Hitler and the Peasants*, p. 164.

44 Michael Grüttner, *Brandstifter und Biedermänner: Deutschland 1933–1939* (Stuttgart: Klett-Cotta, 2015), pp. 267–75.

45 Ibid., p. 269.

46 Martin Broszat, *The Hitler State: The Foundation and Development of the Internal Structure of the Third Reich*, trans. John W. Hiden (London: Longman, 1981), pp. 156–63.

47 Grüttner, *Brandstifter und Biedermänner*, p. 270.

48 Benno Nietzel, "Nazi Economic Policies, Middle-Class Protection, and the Liquidation of Jewish Businesses, 1933–1939," in Christoph Kreutzmüller, Michael Wildt, and Moshe Zimmermann, eds., *National Economies: Volkswirtschaft, Racism and Economy in Europe between the Wars 1918–1939/45* (Newcastle upon Tyne: Cambridge Scholars Publishing, 2015), pp. 108–20.

49 Adelheid von Saldern, "The Old Mittelstand 1890–1939: How 'Backward' Were the Artisans?," *Central European History* 25, no. 1 (1992): 27–51.

50 Grüttner, *Brandstifter und Biedermänner*, pp. 272–73.

51 Michael H. Kater, *Doctors under Hitler* (Chapel Hill: University of North Carolina Press, 1989).

52 Ibid., p. 260.

53 Konrad H. Jarausch, *The Unfree Professions: German Lawyers, Teachers, and Engineers, 1900–1950* (Oxford: Oxford University Press, 1990), p. 159.

54 Ibid., p. 169.

55 Ibid., p. 128.

56 Kater, *Doctors under Hitler*, ch. 6; Judith Hahn and Rebecca Schwoch, *Anpassung und Ausschaltung: Die Berliner kassenärztliche Vereinigung im Nationalsozialismus* (Berlin: Hentrich & Hentrich, 2009), chs. 4 and 7.

57 Ulrich Herbert, "Good Times, Bad Times: Memories of the Third Reich," in Richard Bessel, ed., *Life in the Third Reich* (Oxford: Oxford University Press, 1987), pp. 97–110.

5 Nazi Society, 1933–1939

1 A good brief introduction to the subject remains Ute Frevert, *Women in German History: From Bourgeois Emancipation to Sexual Liberation* (Oxford: Berg, 1988), ch. 4.

2 This discussion is based on Elizabeth Harvey, "Gender," in Shelley Baranowski, Armin Nolzen, and Claus-Christian W. Szejnmann, eds., *A Companion to Nazi Germany* (Hoboken, NJ: Wiley, 2018), pp. 315–31.

3 Raewyn Connell, "Masculinity and Nazism," in Anette Dietrich and Ljiljana Heise, eds., *Männlichkeitskonstruktionen im Nationalsozialismus* (Frankfurt: Peter Lang, 2013), pp. 37–42.

4 Thomas Kühne, *Belonging and Genocide: Hitler's Community, 1918–1945* (New Haven: Yale University Press, 2010), pp. 32–54. See also: Thomas Kühne, *The Rise and Fall of Comradeship: Hitler's Soldiers, Male Bonding, and Mass Violence in the Twentieth Century* (Cambridge: Cambridge University Press, 2017).

5 Kühne, *Belonging and Genocide*, p. 32.

6 Peter H. Merkl, *Political Violence under the Swastika: 581 Early Nazis* (Princeton: Princeton University Press, 1975); Peter H. Merkl, *The Making of a Stormtrooper* (Princeton: Princeton University Press, 1980); Andrew Wackerfuss, *Stormtrooper Families: Homosexuality and Community in the Early Nazi Movement* (New York: Harrington Park Press, 2015).

7 Kühne, *Belonging and Genocide*, p. 47.

8 Ibid., pp. 32–54.

9 Irene Guenther, *Nazi Chic?: Fashioning Women in the Third Reich* (Oxford: Berg, 2004).

10 Burkhard Jellonnek, *Homosexuelle unter dem Hakenkreuz: Die Verfolgung von Homosexuellen im Dritten Reich* (Paderborn: Schöningh, 1990), pp. 140–75; Claudia Schoppmann, *Nationalsozialistische Sexualpolitik und weibliche Homosexualität* (Pfaffenweiler: Centaurus, 1997), pp. 125–62.

11 Günter Grau, *Hidden Holocaust? Gay and Lesbian Persecution in Germany 1933–45*, trans. Patrick Camiller (London: Cassell, 1995), pp. 26–33.

12 Nikolaus Wachsmann, *Hitler's Prisons: Legal Terror in Nazi Germany* (New Haven: Yale University Press, 2004), pp. 145–46.

13 Jason Crouthamel, "Homosexuality and Comradeship: Destabilizing the Hegemonic Masculine Ideal in Nazi Germany," *Central European History* 51 (2018): 419–39.

14 Grau, *Hidden Holocaust?*, pp. 64–67.

15 Hans Günter Hockerts, *Die Sittlichkeitsprozesse gegen katholische Ordensangehörige und Priester, 1936–37: Eine Studie zur nationalsozialistischen Herrschaftstechnik und zum Kirchenkampf* (Mainz: Matthias-Grünewald Verlag, 1971); Geoffrey J. Giles, "The Denial of Homosexuality: Same-Sex Incidents in Himmler's SS and Police," *Journal of the History of Sexuality* 11, no. 1/2 (January/April 2002): 256–90.

16 Stefan Micheler, "Homophobic Propaganda and the Denunciation of Same-Sex-Desiring Men under National Socialism," *Journal of the History of Sexuality* 11, no. 1/2 (January/April 2002): 105–30.

17 Wachsmann, *Hitler's Prisons*, pp. 145–46.

18 David R. Snyder, *Sex Crimes under the Wehrmacht* (Lincoln, NE: University of Nebraska Press, 2007).

19 Wachsmann, *Hitler's Prisons*, p. 146.

20 Jellonnek, *Homosexuelle unter dem Hakenkreuz*, pp. 23–31.

21 Ibid., pp. 135–39.

22 Nikolaus Wachsmann, *KL: A History of the Nazi Concentration Camps* (New York: Farrar, Straus, Giroux, 2015), pp. 127–28.

23 Rüdiger Lautmann, Winfried Grikschat, and Egbert Schmidt, "Der Rosa Winkel in den nationalsozialistischen Konzentrantionslagern," in Rüdiger Lautmann, ed., *Seminar: Gesellschaft und Homosexualität* (Frankfurt: Suhrkamp, 1977), pp. 325–65.

24 Claudia Schoppmann, "The Position of Lesbian Women in the Nazi Period," in Grau, *Hidden Holocaust*, pp. 8–15.

25 Claudia Schoppmann, "Lesbische Frauen und weibliche Homosexualität im Dritten Reich: Forschungsperspektiven," in Michael Schwartz, ed., *Homosexuelle im Nationalsozialismus* (Munich: Oldenbourg, 2014), pp. 85–91.

26 Matthew Stibbe, *Women in the Third Reich* (London: Arnold, 2003), p. 34; Harvey, "Gender," 321. There is no English-language biography of Scholtz-Klink. In German, see Christiane Berger, *"Reichsführerin" Gertrud Scholtz-Klink: Eine nationalsozialistische Frauenkarriere in Verlauf, Retrospektive und Gegenwart* (Saarbrücken: Müller, 2007); Massimiliano Livi, *Gertrud Scholtz-Klink: Die Reichsfrauenführerin: Politische Handlungsräume und Identitätsprobleme der Frauen im Nationalsozialismus am Beispiel der "Führerin aller deutschen Frauen"* (Münster: LIT-Verlag, 2005).

27 Stibbe, *Women in the Third Reich*, pp. 36–39.

28 Dagmar Herzog, *Sex after Fascism: Memory and Morality in Twentieth-Century Germany* (Princeton: Princeton University Press, 2005), ch. 1.

29 Stibbe, *Women in the Third Reich*, pp. 50–51.

30 Ibid., p. 53.

31 This discussion is based on Lisa Pine, *Nazi Family Policy, 1933–1945* (Oxford: Berg, 1977), pp. 19–20, and Atina Grossmann, *Reforming Sex: The German Movement for Birth Control and Abortion Reform, 1929–1950* (Oxford: Oxford University Press, 1995), pp. 149–53.

32 Claudia Koonz, *Mothers in the Fatherland: Women, the Family and Nazi Politics* (New York: St. Martin's, 1987), p. 187.

33 Grossmann, *Reforming Sex*, p. 153.

34 Much of the following is from Michael H. Kater, *Hitler Youth* (Cambridge, MA: Harvard University Press, 2004).

35 Ibid., pp. 77–78.

36 Ibid., p. 16.

37 Ibid., pp. 9–10.

38 Ibid., p. 19.

39 Ibid., p. 24.

40 Ibid., p. 23.

41 Ibid., p. 78.

42 Ibid., p. 27.

43 Ibid., pp. 1, 4.

44 Alan E. Steinweis, *Kristallnacht 1938* (Cambridge, MA: Harvard University Press, 2009), pp. 60, 80–82, 87, 92, 150, 160.

45 Kater, *Hitler Youth*, pp. 62–65.

46 Ibid., p. 67.

47 Thomas Gloy, *Im Dienst der Gemeinschaft: Zur Ordnung der Moral in der Hitler-Jugend* (Göttigen: Wallstein, 2018), pp. 259–317.

48 Kater, *Hitler Youth*, pp. 2–4.

49 Alfons Heck, *A Child of Hitler: Germany in the Days When God Wore a Swastika* (Frederick, CO: Renaissance House, 1988), p. 2.

50 Melita Maschmann, *Account Rendered: A Dossier on My Former Self* (Lexington, MA: Plunkett Lake Press, 2016), p. 77.

51 Kater, *Hitler Youth*, pp. 80–82.

52 Konrad H. Jarausch, *Broken Lives: How Ordinary Germans Experienced the Twentieth Century* (Princeton: Princeton University Press, 2018), ch. 3

53 Kater, *Hitler Youth*, p. 113.

54 Ibid., pp. 116–17.

55 Ibid., p. 139.

56 Detlev J. K. Peukert, *Inside Nazi Germany: Conformity, Opposition, and Racism in Everyday Life*, trans. Richard Deveson (New Haven: Yale University Press, 1982), pp. 154–66.

57 Ibid., pp. 166–69; Kater, *Hitler Youth*, pp. 140–48; Michael H. Kater, *Different Drummers: Jazz in the Culture of Nazi Germany* (Oxford: Oxford University Press, 1992).

58 Anne C. Nagel, *Hitlers Bildungsreformer: Das Reichsministerium für Wissenschaft, Erziehung und Volksbildung 1934–1945* (Frankfurt: Fischer Taschenbuch Verlag, 2012), pp. 152, 163.

59 Lisa Pine, *Education in Nazi Germany* (Oxford: Berg, 2010), pp. 13–15.

60 Charles B. Lansing, *From Nazism to Communism: German Schoolteachers under Two Dictatorships* (Cambridge, MA: Harvard University Press, 2010), pp. 25–26; Konrad H. Jarausch, *The Unfree Professions: German Lawyers, Teachers, and Engineers, 1900–1950* (Oxford: Oxford University Press, 1990), pp. 130–31.

61 Pine, *Education in Nazi Germany*, pp. 15–18.

62 Sabine Omland, *NS-Propaganda im Unterricht deutscher Schulen 1933–1943: Die nationalsozialistische Schülerzeitschrift "Hilf mit!" als Unterrichts- und Propagandainstrument: Längsschnittuntersuchungen im Erscheinungszeitraum 1933–1943, Herausgabebedingungen, Autorenbiografien und tabellarische Darstellung von Analyseergebnissen*, 2 vols. (Münster: LIT-Verlag, 2014).

63 Werner Bergmann and Rainer Erb, *Anti-Semitism in Germany: The Post-Nazi Epoch since 1945*, trans. Belinda Cooper and Allison Brown (New Brunswick, NJ: Transaction, 1997), pp. 55–57.

64 Michael Grüttner, "Wissenschaftspolitik unter dem Hakenkreuz," in Michele Barricelli, Michael Jung, and Detlef Schmiechen-Ackermann, eds., *Ideologie und Eigensinn: Die Technischen Hochschulen in der Zeit des Nationalsozialismus* (Göttingen: Wallstein, 2017), pp. 24–48.

65 Alan E. Steinweis, *Studying the Jew: Scholarly Antisemitism in Nazi Germany* (Cambridge, MA: Harvard University Press, 2006).

66 Alan Beyerchen, *Scientists under Hitler: Politics and the Physics Community in the Third Reich* (New Haven: Yale University Press, 1977).

67 Wolfgang Bialas and Anson Rabinbach, eds., *Nazi Germany and the Humanities* (Oxford: Oneworld, 2007); Bernard M. Levinson and Robert P. Ericksen, eds., *The Betrayal of the Humanities: The University during the Third Reich* (Bloomington: Indiana University Press, 2022).

68 Petra Umlauf, *Die Studentinnen an der Universität München 1926 bis 1945: Auslese, Beschränkung, Indienstnahme, Reaktionen* (Munich: DeGruyter Oldenbourg, 2015), p. 113.

69 Geoffrey Giles, *Students and National Socialism in Germany* (Princeton: Princeton University Press, 1985), p. 3.

70 Anselm Faust, "Überwindung des jüdischen Intellektualismus und der damit verbundenen Verfallserscheinungen im deutschen Geistesleben," in Joachim Scholtyseck and Christoph Studt, eds., *Universitäten und Studenten im Dritten Reich: Bejahung, Anpassung, Widerstand* (Münster: LIT-Verlag, 2008), pp. 107–14.

71 Michael Grüttner, *Studenten im Dritten Reich* (Paderborn: Schöningh, 1995), p. 504.

72 Konrad H. Jarausch, *Deutsche Studenten, 1800–1970* (Frankfurt: Suhrkamp, 1984), p. 168.

73 Faust, "Überwindung des jüdischen Intellektualismus."

74 Ibid., pp. 111–12.

75 Ibid., p. 112.

76 Ibid., p. 113.

77 Ibid.

78 Giles, *Students and National Socialism in Germany*, pp. 186–222.

79 Ibid., p. 252.

80 Ibid., pp. 254–58.

81 Grüttner, *Studenten im Dritten Reich*, pp. 117, 487, 492–93.

82 Umlauf, *Die Studentinnen an der Universität München*, pp. 351–52, 394–433, 444–45.

83 Grüttner, *Studenten im Dritten Reich*, pp. 212–27.

84 Ibid., pp. 213–216, 220.

85 Ulrich Herbert, "Good Times, Bad Times: Memories of the Third Reich," in Richard Bessel, ed., *Life in the Third Reich* (Oxford: Oxford University Press, 1987), pp. 97–110.

6   Policing the Boundaries of the People's Community

1 Detlev J. K. Peukert, *Inside Nazi Germany: Conformity, Opposition, and Racism in Everyday Life*, trans. Richard Deveson (New Haven: Yale University Press, 1982).

2 Neil Gregor, "Nazism – A Political Religion? Rethinking the Voluntarist Turn," in Neil Gregor, ed., *Nazism, War and Genocide* (Exeter: University of Exeter Press, 2005), pp. 1–21.

3 Nikolaus Wachsmann, *KL: A History of the Nazi Concentration Camps* (New York: Farrar, Straus, Giroux, 2015), pp. 23–78.

4 Ibid., p. 32.

5 Ibid., pp. 53–63.

6 Robert Gellately, *Backing Hitler: Consent and Coercion in Nazi Germany* (Oxford: Oxford University Press, 2001).

7 Wachsmann, *KL*, pp. 125–47.

8 Ibid., pp. 157–68.

9 George C. Browder, *Hitler's Enforcers: The Gestapo and the SS Security Service in the Nazi Revolution* (New York: Oxford University Press, 1996).

10 Robert Gellately, *The Gestapo and German Society: Enforcing Racial Policy, 1933–1945* (New York: Oxford University Press, 1990).

11 Andrew Stuart Bergerson, *Ordinary Germans in Extraordinary Times: The Nazi Revolution in Hildesheim* (Bloomington: Indiana University Press, 2004), pp. 146–59; Detlef Schmiechen-Ackermann, "Social Control and the Making of the Volksgemeinschaft," in Martina Steber and Bernhard Gotto, eds., *Visions of Community in Nazi Germany: Social Engineering and Private Lives* (Oxford: Oxford University Press, 2014), pp. 240–53.

12 Friedrich Kellner, *My Opposition: The Diary of Friedrich Kellner, a German against the Third Reich*, trans. and ed. Robert Scott Kellner (Cambridge: Cambridge University Press, 2018), pp. 152, 179.

13 Karl Christian Führer, "'Hoist the Flag!' Flags as a Sign of Political Consensus and Distance in the Nazi Period," in Elizabeth Harvey, Johannes Hürter, Maiken Umbach, and Andreas Wirsching, eds., *Private Life and Privacy in Nazi Germany* (Cambridge: Cambridge University Press, 2019), p. 157.

14 Bergerson, *Ordinary Germans*, pp. 140–41; ibid., pp. 156–81.

15 Rainer Auts, *Opferstock und Sammelbüchse: Die Spendenkampagnen der freien Wohlfahrtspflege vom Ersten Weltkrieg bis in die sechziger Jahre* (Paderborn: Schöningh, 2001), pp. 264–74.

16 Konrad Kwiet and Helmut Eschwege, *Selbstbehauptung und Widerstand: Deutsche Juden im Kampf um Existenz und Menschenwürde, 1933–1945* (Hamburg: Christians, 1986).

17 Mark Roseman, *Lives Reclaimed: A Story of Rescue and Resistance in Nazi Germany* (New York: Metropolitan Books, 2019).

18 Peter Steinbach, *Der 20. Juli 1944: Gesichter des Widerstands* (Munich: Siedler, 2004).

19 Wolfram Wette, *The Wehrmacht: History, Myth, Reality*, trans. Deborah Lucas Schneider (Cambridge, MA: Harvard University Press, 2006), pp. 1–89; Johannes Hürter, *Hitlers Heerführer: Die deutschen Oberbefehlshaber im Krieg gegen die Sowjetunion 1941/42*, 2nd ed. (Munich: Oldenbourg, 2007), ch. 3.

20 Robert P. Ericksen and Susannah Heschel, "Introduction," in Robert P. Ericksen and Susannah Heschel, eds., *Betrayal: German Churches and the Holocaust* (Minneapolis: Fortress, 1999), pp. 1–21.

21 Doris Bergen, *Twisted Cross: The German Christian Movement in the Third Reich* (Chapel Hill: University of North Carolina Press, 1996).

22 Wolfgang Gerlach, *And the Witnesses Were Silent: The Confessing Church and the Persecution of the Jews*, trans. Victoria J. Barnett (Lincoln, NE: University of Nebraska Press, 2000), pp. 230–36.

23 Kevin Spicer, *Resisting the Third Reich: The Catholic Clergy in Hitler's Berlin* (DeKalb: Northern Illinois University Press, 2004).

24 Gerlach, *And the Witnesses Were Silent*, pp. 144–45.

25 Detlef Garbe, *Between Resistance and Martyrdom: Jehovah's Witnesses in the Third Reich*, trans. Dagmar G. Grimm (Madison: University of Wisconsin Press, 2008); Wachsmann, *KL*, p. 126.

26 Much of the following presentation relies on Hans-Walter Schmuhl, "Zwangssterilisation," in Robert Jütte, ed., *Medizin und Nationalsozialismus: Bilanz und Perspektiven der Forschung* (Göttingen: Wallstein, 2011), pp. 201–10.

27 Adolf Hitler, *Mein Kampf*, trans. Ralph Mannheim (New York: Houghton Mifflin, 1943), p. 255.

28 Karl Dietrich Bracher, *The German Dictatorship: The Origins, Structure, and Effects of National Socialism*, trans. Jean Steinberg (New York: Praeger, 1970), p. 225.

29 Stefan Kuhl, *The Nazi Connection: Eugenics, American Racism, and German National Socialism* (New York: Oxford University Press, 1994), p. 39.

30 Henry Friedlander, *The Origins of Nazi Genocide: From Euthanasia to the Final Solution* (Chapel Hill: University of North Carolina Press, 1995), p. 26.

31 Sheila Faith Weiss, *The Nazi Symbiosis: Human Genetics and Politics in the Third Reich* (Chicago: University of Chicago Press, 2010).

32 Michael Kater, *Doctors under Hitler* (Chapel Hill: University of North Carolina Press, 1989), pp. 237–38.

33 Robert Proctor, *Racial Hygiene: Medicine under the Nazis* (Cambridge, MA: Harvard University Press, 1988), p. 109.

34 Ibid., p. 111; Friedlander, *Origins of Nazi Genocide*, pp. 31–32.

35 Udo Benzenhöfer and Hanns Ackermann, *Die Zahl der Verfahren und der Sterilisationen nach dem Gesetz zur Verhütung erbkranken Nachwuchses* (Münster: Kontur, 2015).

36 Percentage estimate from Proctor, *Racial Hygiene*, p. 109.

37 Reiner Pommerin, *"Sterilisierung der Rheinlandbastarde": Das Schicksal einer farbigen deutschen Minderheit 1918–1937* (Düsseldorf: Droste, 1979).

38 Daniel Kevles, *In the Name of Eugenics: Genetics and the Uses of Human Heredity* (New York: Knopf, 1985).

39 Weiss, *Nazi Symbiosis*, pp. 305–6.

40 Phrase in Erika Thurner, *National Socialism and Gypsies in Austria*, trans. Gilya Gerda Schmidt (Tuscaloosa: University of Alabama Press, 1998), p. 9.

41 Christian Faludi, *Die "Juni-Aktion" 1938: Eine Dokumentation zur Radikalisierung der Judenverfolgung* (Frankfurt: Campus, 2013).

42 Wachsmann, *KL*, p. 148.

43 Michael Zimmermann, *Rassenutopie und Genozid: Die nationalsozialistische "Lösung der Zigeunerfrage"* (Hamburg: Christians, 1996), pp. 79–162; Guenter Lewy, *The Nazi Persecution of the Gypsies* (Oxford: Oxford University Press, 2000), pp. 1–55.

44 This section is informed by the following synthetic studies of the Holocaust: Saul Friedländer, *Nazi Germany and the Jews, 1933–1939: The Years of Persecution* (New York: HarperCollins, 1997); Raul Hilberg, *The Destruction of the European Jews*, 3 vols. (New Haven: Yale University Press, 2003); Peter Longerich, *Holocaust: The Nazi Persecution and Murder of the Jews* (Oxford: Oxford University Press, 2010).

45 Alan E. Steinweis, *Studying the Jew: Scholarly Antisemitism in Nazi Germany* (Cambridge, MA: Harvard University Press, 2006).

46 Longerich, *Holocaust*, p. 38; Hans Mommsen, *Beamtentum im Dritten Reich* (Stuttgart: Deutsche Verlags-Anstalt, 1966), pp. 47–53.

47 On the purge of Jews from German professions, see Konrad H. Jarausch, *The Unfree Professions: German Lawyers, Teachers, and Engineers, 1900–1950* (Oxford: Oxford University Press, 1990); Alan E. Steinweis, *Art, Ideology, and Economics in Nazi Germany: The Reich Chambers of Music, Theater, and the Visual Arts* (Chapel Hill: University of North Carolina Press, 1993); Kater, *Doctors under Hitler*.

48 Martin Dean, *Robbing the Jews: The Confiscation of Jewish Property in the Holocaust* (Cambridge: Cambridge University Press, 2008); Christoph Kreutzmüller, *Final Sale in Berlin: The Destruction of Jewish Commercial Activity, 1930–1945*, trans. Jane Paulick and Jefferson Chase (New York: Berghahn, 2015).

49 Michael Wildt, *Volksgemeinschaft als Selbstermächtigung: Gewalt gegen Juden in der deutschen Provinz 1919 bis 1939* (Hamburg: Hamburger Edition, 2007).

50 Alan E. Steinweis, *Kristallnacht 1938* (Cambridge, MA: Harvard University Press, 2009).

51 Susanna Schrafstetter and Alan E. Steinweis, eds., *The Germans and the Holocaust: Popular Responses to the Persecution and Murder of the Jews* (New York: Berghahn, 2016).

52 David Jünger, *Jahre der Ungewissheit: Emigrationspläne deutscher Juden 1933–1938* (Göttingen: Vandenhoeck & Ruprecht, 2016); Katharina Bergmann, *Jüdische Emigration aus München: Entscheidungsfindung und Auswanderungswege (1933–1941)* (Munich: DeGruyter Oldenbourg, 2022).

53 Ian Kershaw, *Hitler, 1936–1945: Nemesis* (New York: Norton, 2000), p. 153.

54 Longerich, *Holocaust*, p. 124.

55 Saul Friedländer, *Nazi Germany and the Jews, 1939–1945: The Years of Extermination* (New York: HarperCollins, 2007), pp. 132, 136, 280.

7 A New Order in Europe

1 The literature on Nazi foreign policy and the road to war is enormous. My own analysis draws heavily on three works in particular: Gerhard L. Weinberg, *The Foreign Policy of Hitler's Germany*, 2 vols. (Chicago: University of Chicago Press, 1970/1980); Brendan Simms, *Hitler: A Global Biography* (New York: Basic Books, 2019); and Wilhelm Deist, Manfred Messerschmidt, Hans-Erich Volkmann, and Wolfram Wette, *Ursachen und Voraussetzungen der deutschen Kriegspolitik* (Stuttgart: Deutsche Verlags-Anstalt, 1979), vol. 1 of the series *Das Deutsche Reich und der zweite Weltkrieg*.

2 Ian Kershaw, *The Nazi Dictatorship*, 4th ed. (London: Arnold, 2000), pp. 134–60; Weinberg, *Foreign Policy*, vol. 1, p. 1.

3 Birgit Kletzin, *Europa als Rasse und Raum: Die nationalsozialistische Idee der Neuen Ordnung* (Münster: LIT-Verlag, 2000), p. 42.

4 Deist et al., *Ursachen und Voraussetzungen der deutschen Kriegspolitik*, pp. 177–207.

5 Adolf Hitler, *Mein Kampf*, trans. Ralph Manheim (New York: Houghton Mifflin, 1943), p. 139.

6 Adolf Hitler, *Hitler's Second Book, The Unpublished Sequel to Mein Kampf*, ed. Gerhard L. Weinberg, trans. Krista Smith (New York: Enigma Books, 2003), p. 113.

7 Deist et al., *Ursachen und Voraussetzungen der deutschen Kriegspolitik*, pp. 529–32.

8 Ibid., pp. 449–96.

9 Complete translated text in Jeremy Noakes and Geoffrey Pridham, *Nazism, 1919–1945*, 4 vols. (Exeter: University of Exeter Press, 1998–2008), vol. 3, document 503, pp. 72–79. Sources for this discussion of the Hossbach meeting: Weinberg, *Foreign Policy*, vol. 2, pp. 35–41; Deist et al., *Ursachen und Voraussetzungen der deutschen Kriegspolitik*, pp. 623–26.

10 Harold Deutsch, *Hitler and His Generals: The Hidden Crisis, January–June 1938* (Minneapolis: University of Minnesota Press, 1974).

11 Peter Hoffmann, *The History of the German Resistance, 1933–1945* (Cambridge, MA: MIT Press, 1977), pp. 69–96, 128–44; Johannes Hürter, *Hitlers Heerführer: Die deutschen Oberbefehlshaber im Krieg gegen die Sowjetunion 1941/42* (Munich: Oldenbourg 2007), pp. 151–52; Christian Hartmann, *Halder: Generalstabchef Hitlers 1938–1942* (Paderborn: Schöningh, 1991), pp. 99–116.

12 David L. Hoffmann, *The Stalinist Era* (Cambridge: Cambridge University Press, 2018), pp. 118–22.

13 Gerhard L. Weinberg, *A World at Arms: A Global History of World War II* (Cambridge: Cambridge University Press, 1994), pp. 215–24.

14 Peter Fritzsche, *Life and Death in the Third Reich* (Cambridge, MA: Harvard University Press, 2009), pp. 62–63.

15 Lore Walb, *Ich, die Alte – ich, die Junge: Konfrontationen mit meinen Tagebüchern 1933–1945* (Berlin: Aufbau, 1997), p. 73.

16 *Deutschland Berichte der Sozialdemokratischen Partei Deutschlands (SOPADE), 1934–1940* (Salzhausen: Nettelbeck, 1980) (hereafter *SOPADE*), 1938, p. 256.

17 Friedrich Kellner, *My Opposition: The Diary of Friedrich Kellner, a German against the Third Reich*, trans. and ed. Robert Scott Kellner (Cambridge: Cambridge University Press, 2018), p. 145.

18 Ian Kershaw, *Public Opinion and Political Dissent in the Third Reich: Bavaria 1933–1945* (Oxford: Oxford University Press, 1983), pp. 152, 383.

19 "Rede Hitlers vor der deutschen Presse (10 November 1938)," ed. Wilhelm Treue, *Vierteljahrhefte für Zeitgeschichte* 6 no. 2 (1958): 175–91.

20 *SOPADE*, 1939, p. 965.

21 Ibid., p. 977.

22 Walb, *Ich, die Alte – ich, die Junge*, p. 129.

23 *SOPADE*, 1939, p. 979.

24 Ibid., p. 978.

25 Ibid., pp. 980–83.

26 *Meldungen aus dem Reich 1938–1945: Die geheimen Lageberichte des Sicherheitsdienstes der SS*, ed. Heinz Boberach, 17 vols. (Herrsching: Pawlak, 1985), vol. 2, p. 339.

27 Peter Steinbach and Johannes Tuchel, *Georg Elser: Der Hitler-Attentäter* (Berlin: Be.Bra Verlag, 2010).

28 *SOPADE*, 1940, p. 221.

29 *Meldungen aus dem Reich*, vol. 4, pp. 1127, 1139, 1151, 1163, 1261, 1293, 1323; vol. 5, pp. 1362, 1388–89.
30 Ibid., vol. 5, pp. 1424, 1441, 1461, 1479.
31 Kellner, *My Opposition*, September 15, 1940, p. 84.
32 *Meldungen aus dem Reich*, vol. 5, pp. 1525, 1563, 1595, 1652.
33 Anna Haag, *Leben und gelebt werden: Erinnerungen und Betrachtungen*, ed. Rudolf Haag (Tübingen: Silberburg, 2003), p. 226.

8 The Nazi Empire

1 Jürgen Kilian, *Krieg auf Kosten anderer: Das Reichsministerium der Finanzen und die wirtschaftliche Mobilisierung Europas für Hitlers Krieg* (Berlin: De Gruyter Oldenbourg, 2017), p. 445.
2 Richard J. Overy, "The Economy of the German 'New Order'," in Richard J. Overy, ed., *Die "Neuordnung" Europas: NS-Wirtschaftspolitik in den besetzten Gebieten* (Berlin: Metropol, 1997), pp. 11–28.
3 Michael R. Marrus and Robert O. Paxton, *Vichy France and the Jews*, 2nd ed. (Stanford: Stanford University Press, 2019), pp. 1–17.
4 Alan E. Steinweis, "Eastern Europe and the Notion of the 'Frontier' in Germany to 1945," in Keith Bullivant and Geoffrey Giles, eds., *Germany and Eastern Europe* (Berlin: De Gruyter, 1999), pp. 56–69.
5 Thomas Kühne, "Colonialism and the Holocaust: Continuities, Causations, and Complexities," *Journal of Genocide Research* 15, no. 3 (2013): 339–62; Rachel O'Sullivan, "Integration and Division: Nazi Germany and the 'Colonial Other' in Annexed Poland," *Journal of Genocide Research* 22, no. 4 (2020): 437–58.
6 Ulrich Herbert, *Hitler's Foreign Workers: Enforced Foreign Labor in Germany under the Third Reich*, trans. William Templer (Cambridge: Cambridge University Press, 1997), p. 48.
7 Adam Tooze, *The Wages of Destruction: The Making and Breaking of the Nazi Economy* (New York: Penguin Books, 2006), p. 517.
8 Mark Spoerer, *Zwangsarbeit unter dem Hakenkreuz: Ausländische Zivilarbeiter, Kriegsgefangene und Häftlinge im Deutschen Reich und im besetzten Europa 1939–1945* (Stuttgart: Deutsche Verlags-Anstalt, 2001), pp. 219–29.
9 Charles Dick, *Builders of the Third Reich: The Organisation Todt and Nazi Forced Labor* (London: Bloomsbury, 2021).
10 Tooze, *Wages of Destruction*, p. 363.
11 Spoerer, *Zwangsarbeit unter dem Hakenkreuz*, p. 228.
12 Dietmar Süß, "'Herrenmenschen' und 'Arbeitsvölker': Zwangsarbeit und Gesellschaft," in Stefan Hördler, Volkhard Knigge, Gunnar Lüttgenau, and Jens Christian Wagner, eds., *Zwangsarbeit im Nationalsozialismus* (Göttingen: Wallstein, 2016), pp. 244–53.
13 Martin Broszat, *Nationalsozialistische Polenpolitik 1939–1945* (Stuttgart: Deutsche Verlags-Anstalt, 1961); Czesław Madajczyk, *Die Okkupationspolitik Nazideutschlands in Polen 1939–1945* (Cologne: Pahl Rugenstein, 1988).
14 Stephan Lehnstaedt and Jochen Böhler, *Die Berichte der Einsatzgruppen aus Polen 1939* (Berlin: Metropol, 2013).

15 Alexander B. Rossino, *Hitler Strikes Poland: Blitzkrieg, Ideology and Atrocity* (Lawrence: University Press of Kansas, 2003), pp. 14, 58–74.

16 Catherine Epstein, *Model Nazi: Arthur Greiser and the Occupation of Western Poland* (Oxford: Oxford University Press, 2010).

17 Jonathan Huener, *The Polish Catholic Church under German Occupation: The Reichsgau Wartheland, 1939–1945* (Bloomington: Indiana University Press, 2021).

18 Sybille Steinbacher, *"Musterstadt" Auschwitz: Germanisierungspolitik und Judenmord in Ostoberschlesien* (Munich: K. G. Saur, 2000); Robert Jan van Pelt and Deborah Dwork, *Auschwitz: 1270 to the Present* (New Haven: Yale University Press, 1996).

19 Broszat, *Nationalsozialistische Polenpolitik*, p. 101.

20 Alexa Stiller, "Gewalt und Alltag der Volkstumspolitik," in Jochen Böhler and Stephan Lehnstaedt, eds., *Gewalt und Alltag im besetzten Polen 1939–1945* (Osnabrück: Fibre, 2012), pp. 45–66.

21 Elizabeth Harvey, *Women and the Nazi East: Agents and Witnesses of Germanization* (New Haven: Yale University Press, 2003), pp. 83–84.

22 Rolf-Dieter Müller, *Hitler's Ostkrieg und die Deutsche Siedlungspolitik* (Frankfurt: Fischer, 1991).

23 Harvey, *Women and the Nazi East*.

24 Ibid., p. 79.

25 Jan Tomasz Gross, *Polish Society under German Occupation: The Generalgouvernement, 1939–1944* (Princeton: Princeton University Press, 1979), pp. 45–50.

26 Lothar Kettenacker, *Nationalsozialistische Volkstumspolitik im Elsaß* (Stuttgart: Deutsche Verlags-Anstalt, 1973), pp. 250–52; Johnpeter Horst Grill, *The Nazi Movement in Baden, 1920–1945* (Chapel Hill: University of North Carolina Press, 1983), pp. 502, 511.

27 Chad Bryant, *Prague in Black: Nazi Rule and Czech Nationalism* (Cambridge, MA: Harvard University Press, 2007), ch. 3.

28 In addition to the sources specifically cited in the notes, this section relies on Saul Friedländer, *Nazi Germany and the Jews*, vol. 2: *The Years of Extermination* (New York: Harper Collins, 2007), chs. 1–3.

29 *German Reich and Protectorate, September 1939–September 1941*, ed. Andrea Löw (Berlin: Degruyter Oldenbourg, 2020) (hereafter *PMJ* 3), vol. 3 of *The Persecution and Murder of the European Jews by Nazi Germany, 1933–1945*, p. 49.

30 Atina Grossmann, "Jewish Refugees in Soviet Central Asia, Iran, and India: Lost Memories of Displacement, Trauma, and Rescue," in Atina Grossmann, Mark Edele, and Sheila Fitzpatrick, eds., *Shelter from the Holocaust: Rethinking Jewish Survival in the Soviet Union* (Detroit, MI: Wayne State University Press, 2017), pp. 185–218.

31 *PMJ* 3, pp. 35–37; Beate Meyer, *Tödliche Gratwanderung: Die Reichsvereinigung der Juden in Deutschland zwischen Hoffnung, Zwang, Selbtsbehauptung und Verstrickung (1939–1945)* (Göttingen: Wallstein, 2011), pp. 61–69.

32 *PMJ* 3, pp. 37, 41–42, and documents 36, 42, 50, 96, 97.

33 *The Jews in the Secret Nazi Reports on Popular Opinion in Germany, 1933–1945*, ed. Otto Dov Kulka and Eberhard Jäckel, trans. William Templer (New Haven: Yale University Press, 2010), documents 482, 501, 504, 539.
34 *PMJ* 3, documents 6, 67.
35 Gerhard Botz, *Wohnungspolitik und Judendeportation in Wien 1938 bis 1945: Zur Funktion des Antisemitismus als Ersatz nationalsozialistischer Sozialpolitik* (Vienna: Geyer, 1975).
36 *PMJ* 3, pp. 38–41 and documents 39, 41.
37 Jeffrey Herf, *The Jewish Enemy: Nazi Propaganda during World War II and the Holocaust* (Cambridge, MA: Harvard University Press, 2006), pp. 50–91.
38 *The Jews in the Secret Nazi Reports*, documents 467, 468, 471, 483, 513, 517.
39 Ibid., documents 458, 465; *Deutschland Berichte der Sozialdemokratischen Partei Deutschlands (SOPADE), 1934–1940* (Salzhausen: P. Nettelbeck, 1980), 1940, pp. 256–60.
40 Konrad Kwiet, "Nach dem Pogrom: Stufen der Ausgrenzung," in Wolfgang Benz, ed., *Die Juden in Deutschland 1933:1945: Leben unter nationalsozialistischer Herrschaft* (Munich: Beck, 1988), pp. 545–659, section on Judenhäuser on pp. 631–36.
41 *PMJ* 3, documents 15, 215.
42 Victor Klemperer, *I Will Bear Witness: A Diary of the Nazi Years*, 2 vols., trans. Martin Chalmers (New York: Random House, 1999), vol. 1, entry for June 6, 1940, p. 417.
43 Wolf Gruner, *Jewish Forced Labor under the Nazis: Economic Needs and Racial Aims, 1938–1944*, trans. Kathleen M. Dell'Orto (Cambridge: Cambridge University Press, 2006), chs. 1 and 2; PMJ 3, pp. 43–44 and document 152.
44 Christopher R. Browning, *The Origins of the Final Solution* (Lincoln, NE: University of Nebraska Press, 2003), ch. 4; Dan Michman, *The Emergence of Jewish Ghettos during the Holocaust* (Cambridge: Cambridge University Press, 2011), ch. 7.
45 Gruner, *Jewish Forced Labor*, chs. 6–9.
46 Mario Wenzel, *Arbeitszwang und Judenmord: Die Arbeitslager für Juden im Distrikt Krakau des Generalgouvernements 1933–1944* (Berlin: Metropol, 2017), pp. 139–60.
47 Magnus Brechtken, *Madagascar für die Juden: Antisemitische Idee und politische Praxis 1885–1945* (Munich: Oldenbourg, 1998); Christopher R. Browning, *The Final Solution and the German Foreign Office: A Study of Referat DIII of Abteilung Deutschland 1940–1943* (New York: Holmes and Meier, 1978), pp. 35–43.
48 *PMJ* 3, documents 98, 125, 142.
49 Klemperer, *I Will Bear Witness*, vol. 1, entry for September 8, 1941, p. 432.
50 Friedländer, *Nazi Germany and the Jews*, vol. 2, pp. 251–55.
51 Sources used for this section: Ulf Schmidt, *Karl Brandt: The Nazi Doctor: Medicine and Power in the Third Reich* (London: Hambledon Continuum, 2007), ch. 5; Henry Friedlander, *The Origins of Nazi Genocide: From Euthanasia to the Final Solution* (Chapel Hill: University of North Carolina Press, 1995).

52 Karl Binding and Alfred Hoche, "Die Freigabe der Vernichtung lebensun-werten Lebens: Ihr Maß und ihre Form," full text reprinted in Anneliese Hochmuth, ed., *Spurensuche: Eugenik, Sterilisation, Patientenmorde und die v. Bodelschwinghschen Anstalten Bethel 1929–1945* (Bielefeld: Bethel, 1997), pp. 171–211.
53 Friedlander, *Origins of Nazi Genocide*, pp. 14–16.
54 Hans-Walter Schmuhl, "'Euthanasie' und Krankenmord," in Robert Jütte, ed., *Medizin und Nationalsozialismus: Bilanz und Perspektiven der Forschung* (Göttingen: Wallstein, 2011), p. 230.
55 Anna Haag, *Leben und gelebt werden: Erinnerungen und Betrachtungen*, ed. Rudolf Haag (Tübingen: Silberburg, 2003), p. 222.
56 Winfried Süß, *Der Volkskörper im Krieg: Gesundheitspolitik, Gesundheitsverhältnisse und Krankenmord im nationalsozialistischen Deutschland 1939–1945* (Munich: Oldenbourg, 2003), p. 314; Schmidt, Karl Brandt, p. 164.
57 Süß, *Volkskörper im Krieg*, ch. 6.

9   The War of Annihilation

1 This summary of military events relies on Gerhard L. Weinberg, *A World at Arms: A Global History of World War II* (Cambridge: Cambridge University Press, 1994), and *The Cambridge History of the Second World War, Vol. 1: Fighting the War*, ed. John Ferris and Evan Mawdsley (Cambridge: Cambridge University Press, 2015).
2 David Stahel, ed., *Joining Hitler's Crusade: European Nations and the Invasion of the Soviet Union, 1941* (Cambridge: Cambridge University Press, 2018).
3 Friedrich Kellner, *My Opposition: The Diary of Friedrich Kellner, a German against the Third Reich*, trans. and ed. Robert Scott Kellner (Cambridge: Cambridge University Press, 2018), pp. 124, 126, 128.
4 Gerhard L. Weinberg, *World in the Balance: Behind the Scenes of World War II* (Hanover, NH: University Press of New England, 1981), pp. 75–95.
5 Richard J. Overy, *The Bombers and the Bombed: Allied Air War over Europe, 1940–1945* (New York: Viking Penguin, 2013), p. 228.
6 Felix Römer, *Der Kommissarbefehl: Wehrmacht und NS-Verbrechen an der Ostfront 1941/1942* (Paderborn: Schöningh, 2008).
7 Ibid., pp. 75–81.
8 Ibid., p. 56.
9 Karl Dürkefälden, *"Schreiben, wie es wirklich war!": Aufzeichnungen Karl Dürkefäldens aus den Jahren 1933–1945*, ed. Herbert and Sybille Obenaus (Hanover: Fackelträger, 1985), p. 103.
10 Reinhard Otto, *Wehrmacht, Gestapo und sowjetische Kriegsgefangene im deutschen Reichsgebiet 1941/42* (Munich: Oldenbourg, 1998).
11 Dieter Pohl, *Die Herrschaft der Wehrmacht: Deutsche Militärbesatzung und einheimische Bevölkerung in der Sowjetunion, 1941–1944* (Munich: Oldenbourg, 2008), pp. 202–42.
12 Alex Kay, "'The Purpose of the Russian Campaign Is the Decimation of the Slavic Population by Thirty Million': The Radicalization of German Food Policy in Early 1941," in Alex Kay, Jeff Rutherford, and David Stahel, eds.,

Nazi Policy on the Eastern Front, 1941: Total War, Genocide, and Radicalization (Rochester: University of Rochester Press, 2012), pp. 101–29.

13 Swantje Greve, *Das "System Sauckel": Der Generalbevollmächtigte für den Arbeitseinsatz und die Arbeitskräftepolitik in der besetzten Ukraine 1942–1945* (Göttingen: Wallstein, 2019), pp. 365–400.

14 Wendy Lower, *Nazi Empire-Building and the Holocaust in Ukraine* (Chapel Hill: University of North Carolina Press, 2005), pp. 162–79.

15 Pohl, *Herrschaft der Wehrmacht*, pp. 282–97.

16 Norman Davies, *Rising '44: The Battle for Warsaw* (New York: Viking, 2003); Włodzimierz Borodziej, *The Warsaw Uprising of 1944*, trans. Barbara Harshav (Madison: University of Wisconsin Press, 2006).

17 Jozo Tomasevich, *War and Revolution in Yugoslavia, 1941–1945: Occupation and Collaboration* (Stanford: Stanford University Press, 2001), p. 218.

18 Ben Shepherd, *Terror in the Balkans: German Armies and Partisan Warfare* (Cambridge, MA: Harvard University Press, 2012).

19 Mark Mazower, *Inside Hitler's Greece: The Experience of Occupation, 1941–44* (New Haven: Yale University Press, 1993), pp. 153–79, 256.

20 Stefan Klemp, *Rücksichtlos ausgemerzt: Die Ordnungspolizei und das Massaker von Lidice* (Münster: Villa ten Hompel, 2012).

21 Gerhard Schreiber, *Deutsche Kriegsverbrechen in Italien: Täter, Opfer, Strafverfolgung* (Munich: Beck, 1996).

22 Ahlrich Meyer, *Die deutsche Besatzung in Frankreich 1940–1944: Widerstandsbekämpfung und Judenverfolgung* (Darmstadt: Wissenschaftliche Buchgesellschaft, 2000), pp. 61–64, 130–31.

23 Sarah Farmer, *Martyred Village: Commemorating the 1944 Massacre at Oradour-sur-Glane* (Berkeley: University of California Press, 1999), ch. 1.

24 Michael H. Kater, *Hitler Youth* (Cambridge, MA: Harvard University Press, 2004), ch. 5.

25 Omer Bartov, *Hitler's Army: Soldiers, Nazis, and War in the Third Reich* (Oxford: Oxford University Press, 1991).

26 Bernd Wegner, *Hitlers Politische Soldaten: Die Waffen-SS 1933–1945*, rev. ed. (Paderborn: Schöningh, 1997), pp. 135–49.

27 This section is informed by the following synthetic studies of the Holocaust: Saul Friedländer, *Nazi Germany and the Jews, 1939–1945: The Years of Extermination* (New York: HarperCollins, 2007); Raul Hilberg, *The Destruction of the European Jews*, 3 vols. (New Haven: Yale University Press, 2003); Peter Longerich, *Holocaust: The Nazi Persecution and Murder of the Jews* (Oxford: Oxford University Press, 2010).

28 Andrej Angrick, *Besatzungspolitik und Massenmord: Die Einsatzgruppe D in der südlichen Sowjetunion 1941–1943* (Hamburg: Hamburger Edition, 2003), pp. 104–13.

29 Alan E. Steinweis, "Hitler and Himmler," in Peter Hayes and John Roth, eds., *The Oxford Handbook of Holocaust Studies* (Oxford: Oxford University Press, 2010), pp. 113–27.

30 Christopher R. Browning, *Ordinary Men: Reserve Police Battalion 101 and the Final Solution in Poland* (New York: HarperCollins, 1992).

31 Pohl, *Herrschaft der Wehrmacht*, pp. 258–68.

32 Waitman Wade Beorn, *Marching into Darkness: The Wehrmacht and the Holocaust in Belarus* (Cambridge: Cambridge University Press, 2014).

33 Hamburger Institut für Sozialforschung, ed., *The German Army and Genocide: Crimes against War Prisoners, Jews, and Other Civilians in the East, 1939–1944*, trans. Scott Abbott (New York: New Press, 1999); Hannes Heer, ed., *The Discursive Construction of History: Remembering the Wehrmacht's War of Annihilation*, trans. Steven Fligelstone (New York: Palgrave Macmillan, 2008).

34 Walter Manoschek, ed., *"Es gibt nur eines für das Judentum: Vernichtung": Das Judenbild in deutschen Soldatenbriefen 1939–1944* (Hamburg: Hamburger Edition, 1995), pp. 16, 65. Similar material in Ortwin Buchbender and Reinhold Sterz, *Das andere Gesicht des Krieges: Deutsche Feldpostbriefe 1939–1945* (Munich: Beck, 1982), pp. 168–73.

35 Klaus Latzel, *Deutsche Soldaten – nationalsozialistischer Krieg? Kriegserlebnis – Kriegserfahrung 1939–1945* (Paderborn: Schöningh, 1998), pp. 201–5.

36 Steinweis, "Hitler and Himmler," pp. 113–27.

37 Klaus-Michael Mallmann and Martin Cuppers, *Nazi Palestine: The Plans for the Extermination of the Jews in Palestine*, trans. Krista Smith (New York: Enigma, 2010).

38 Karin Orth, "Camps," in Hayes and Roth, eds., *Oxford Handbook of Holocaust Studies*, pp. 364–77.

39 See Hilberg's breakdown of "Deaths by Cause" in Hilberg, *Destruction*, vol. 3, pp. 1, 320.

40 Michael Wildt, *An Uncompromising Generation: The Nazi Leadership of the Reich Security Main Office*, trans. Tom Lampert (Madison: University of Wisconsin Press, 2009); Isabel Heinemann *"Rasse, Siedlung, deutsches Blut": Das Rasse- und Siedlungshauptamt der SS und die rassenpolitische Neuordnung Europas* (Göttingen: Wallstein, 2003).

41 Hannah Arendt, *Eichmann in Jerusalem: A Report on the Banality of Evil* (New York: Viking, 1963).

42 David Cesarani, *Eichmann: His Life and Crimes* (London: Heinemann, 2004).

43 Kellner, *My Opposition*, p. 145.

44 Anna Haag, *Leben und gelebt warden: Erinnerungen und Betrachtungen*, ed. Rudolf Haag (Tübingen: Silberburg, 2003), p. 204.

45 Dürkefälden, *"Schreiben, wie es wirklich war!"*, p. 126.

46 Peter Fritzsche, "Babi Yar, but not Auschwitz: What Did Germans Know about the Final Solution?," in Susanna Schrafstetter and Alan E. Steinweis, eds., *The Germans and the Holocaust: Popular Responses to the Persecution and Murder of the Jews* (New York: Berghahn, 2016), pp. 85–104.

47 Victor Klemperer, *I Will Bear Witness: A Diary of the Nazi Years*, 2 vols., trans. Martin Chalmers (New York: Random House, 1999), vol. 2, entry for March 16, 1942, p. 47.

48 Jeffrey Herf, *The Jewish Enemy: Nazi Propaganda during World War II and the Holocaust* (Cambridge, MA: Harvard University Press, 2006).

10 The Destruction of Nazi Germany

1 Friedrich Kellner, *My Opposition: The Diary of Friedrich Kellner, a German against the Third Reich*, trans. and ed. Robert Scott Kellner (Cambridge: Cambridge University Press, 2018), p. 234.

2 Peter Longerich, *Goebbels: Biographie* (Munich: Siedler, 2010), pp. 543–53.

3 Jutta Sywottek, *Mobilmachung für den totalen Krieg: Die propagandistische Vorbereitung der deutschen Bevölkerung auf den Zweiten Weltkrieg* (Opladen: Westdeutscher-Verlag, 1976).

4 Magnus Brechtken, *Albert Speer: Eine deutsche Karriere* (Munich: Siedler, 2017), pp. 157, 176–77, 179–83, 213.

5 Adam Tooze, *The Wages of Destruction: The Making and Breaking of the Nazi Economy* (New York: Penguin Books, 2006), pp. 358–59, 515; Leila J. Rupp, *Mobilizing Women for War: German and American Propaganda, 1933–1945* (Princeton: Princeton University Press, 1978).

6 Nicole Kramer, "Mobilisierung für die 'Heimatfront': Frauen im zivilen Luftschutz," in Sybille Steinbacher, ed., *Volksgenossinnen: Frauen in der NS-Volksgemeinschaft* (Göttingen: Wallstein, 2007), pp. 69–92.

7 Franka Maubach, "'Expansionen weiblicher Hilfe': Zur Erfahrungsgeschichte von Frauen im Kriegsdienst," in Steinbacher, ed., *Volksgenossinnen*, pp. 93–111.

8 Elizabeth Harvey, "'Ich war überall': Die NS-Propagandaphotographin Liselotte Purper," in Steinbacher, ed., *Volksgenossinnen*, pp. 138–53.

9 Geoffrey J. Giles, *Students and National Socialism in Germany* (Princeton: Princeton University Press, 1985), pp. 272–75.

10 Michael Grüttner, *Studenten im Dritten Reich* (Paderborn: Schöningh, 1995), pp. 361–68, 387–97, 487–93.

11 Michael Buddrus, *Totale Erziehung für den totalen Krieg: Hitlerjugend und nationalsozialistische Jugendpolitik*, 2 vols. (Munich: Saur, 2003), vol. 1, pp. 1–3; vol. 2, pp. 764–70, 807–9, 832; Jakob Benecke, ed., *Die Hitler-Jugend 1933–1945: Programmatik, Alltag, Erinnerungen: Eine Dokumentation* (Weinheim: Beltz Juventa, 2013), pp. 247–55.

12 Gert Geißler, *Schulgeschichte in Deutschland: Von den Anfängen bis in die Gegenwart* (Frankfurt: Peter Lang, 2011), pp. 576, 605–8.

13 Key sources for this section: Ralf Blank, "Kriegsalltag und Luftkrieg an der 'Heimatfront'," in Jörg Echternkamp, ed., *Die deutsche Kriegsgesellschaft 1939 bis 1945* (Munich: Deutsche Verlags-Anstalt, 2004), vol. 9, part 1, of the series *Das Deutsche Reich und der Zweite Weltkrieg*, pp. 357–468; Dietmar Süß, *Tod aus der Luft: Kriegsgesellschaft und Luftkrieg in Deutschland und England* (Munich: Siedler, 2011).

14 Ingo Müller, *Hitler's Justice: The Courts of the Third Reich*, trans. Deborah Lucas Schneider (Cambridge, MA: Harvard University Press, 1991), p. 196.

15 Wolfgang Form, Theo Schiller, and Lothar Seitz, eds., *NS-Justiz in Hessen: Verfolgung – Kontinuitäten – Erbe* (Marburg: Historische Kommission für Hessen, 2015), pp. 99–101.

16 *The Jews in the Secret Nazi Reports on Popular Opinion in Germany, 1933–1945*, ed. Otto Dov Kulka and Eberhard Jäckel, trans. William Templer (New Haven: Yale University Press, 2010), documents 694, 699, 706, 707, 733.

17 F. L. Carsten, *The German Workers and the Nazis* (Aldershot, UK: Scolar Press, 1995), pp. 138–61.

18 Beatrix Herlemann, *Auf verlorenem Posten: Kommunistischer Widerstand im zweiten Weltkrieg: Die Knöchel-Organisation* (Bonn: Neue Gesellschaft, 1986);

Detlev J. K. Peukert, *Die KPD im Widerstand: Verfolgung und Untergrundarbeit an Rhein und Ruhr 1933 bis 1945* (Wuppertal: Peter Hammer, 1980).

19 Hans Mommsen, *Die Rote Kapelle und der Widerstand gegen Hitler* (Bochum: Stiftung Bibliothek des Ruhrgebiets, 2011).

20 Sönke Zankel, *Mit Flugblättern gegen Hitler: Der Widerstandskreis um Hans Scholl und Alexander Schmorell* (Cologne: Böhlau, 2008); Michael C. Schneider and Winfried Süß, *Keine Volksgenossen: Studentischer Widerstand der Weissen Rose* (Munich: LMU, 1993).

21 Peter Hoffmann, *The History of the German Resistance, 1933–1945* (Cambridge, MA: MIT Press, 1977); Winfried Heineman, *Unternehmen "Walküre": Eine Militärgeschichte des 20. Juli 1944* (Berlin: De Gruyter-Oldenbourg, 2019).

22 Kellner, *My Opposition*, p. 351.

23 Gerhard L. Weinberg, *A World at Arms: A Global History of World War II* (Cambridge: Cambridge University Press, 1994), pp. 438–39.

24 Mary Kathryn Barbier, "The War in the West, 1943–1945," in John Ferris and Evan Mawdsley, eds., *The Cambridge History of the Second World War, vol. 1: Fighting the War* (Cambridge: Cambridge University Press, 2015), pp. 389–419.

25 Ian Kershaw, *The End: Germany 1944–45* (New York: Penguin, 2011), p. 236.

26 Alfred C. Mierzejewski, *The Collapse of the German War Economy, 1944–45: Allied Air Power and the German National Railway* (Chapel Hill: University of North Carolina Press, 1988), pp. 183–85.

27 Horst Boog, "Strategischer Luftkrieg in Europa und Reichsluftverteidigung 1943–1944," in Horst Boog, Gerhard Krebs, and Detlef Vogel, eds., *Das Deutsche Reich in der Defensive* (Stuttgart: Deutsche Verlags-Anstalt, 2001), pp. 380–415. The book is vol. 7 of the series *Das Deutsche Reich und der Zweite Weltkrieg*.

28 Kellner, *My Opposition*, p. 348.

29 David R. Stone, "Operations on the Eastern Front," in Ferris and Mawdsley, eds., *The Cambridge History of the Second World War*, vol. 1, pp. 331–57.

30 Peter Fritzsche, *Life and Death in the Third Reich* (Cambridge, MA: Harvard University Press, 2009), p. 291.

31 David K. Yelton, *Hitler's Volkssturm: The Nazi Militia and the Fall of Germany, 1944–1945* (Lawrence: University Press of Kansas, 2002).

32 Perry Biddiscombe, *Werwolf! The History of the National Socialist Guerrilla Movement, 1944–1946* (Toronto: University of Toronto Press, 1998).

33 Sven Keller, *Volksgemeinschaft am Ende: Gesellschaft und Gewalt 1944/45* (Munich: Oldenbourg, 2013).

34 Ibid., pp. 225–27.

35 Ibid., pp. 345–53.

36 Kershaw, *The End*, pp. 289–92.

37 Daniel Blatman, *The Death Marches: The Final Phase of Nazi Genocide*, trans. Chaya Galai (Cambridge, MA: Harvard University Press, 2011), pp. 117–25; Kershaw, *The End*, pp. 184–86.

38 Jeffrey Herf, *The Jewish Enemy: Nazi Propaganda during World War II and the Holocaust* (Cambridge, MA: Harvard University Press, 2006), pp. 254–55.

39 Atina Grossmann, *Jews, Germans, and Allies: Close Encounters in Occupied Germany* (Princeton: Princeton University Press, 2007), pp. 48–52; Miriam Gebhardt, *Crimes Unspoken: The Rape of German Women at the End of the Second World War*, trans. Nick Somers (Cambridge: Polity, 2017); Norman Naimark, *The Russians in Germany: A History of the Soviet Zone of Occupation* (Cambridge, MA: Harvard University Press, 1995), pp. 106–7; Manfred Zeidler, *Kriegsende im Osten: Die Rote Armee und die Besetzung Deutschlands östlich von Oder und Neiße 1944/45* (Munich: Oldenbourg, 1996), pp. 135–42.

40 Regina Mühlhäuser, *Eroberungen: Sexuelle Gewalttaten und intime Beziehungen deutscher Soldaten in der Sowjetunion, 1941–1945* (Hamburg: Hamburger Edition, 2010).

41 Christian Goeschel, "Suicide at the End of the Third Reich," *Journal of Contemporary History* 41, no. 1 (2006): 153–73.

42 Text of Hitler's testament in Jeremy Noakes and Geoffrey Pridham, *Nazism, 1919–1945*, 4 vols. (Exeter: University of Exeter Press, 1998–2008), vol. 4, pp. 668–71.

Conclusion

1 War-related death figures taken from the rear flap of Rolf-Dieter Müller, ed., *Der Zusammenbruch des Deutschen Reiches 1945* (Munich: Deutscher Verlags-Anstalt, 2008). The book is vol. 10/2 in the series *Das Deutsche Reich und der Zweite Weltkrieg*.

Index